She
Memes
Well

She Memes Well

Quinta Brunson

Houghton Mifflin Harcourt
Boston   New York
2021

For information about permission to reproduce selections
from this book, write to trade.permissions@hmhco.com or to Permissions,
Houghton Mifflin Harcourt Publishing Company, 3 Park Avenue,
19th Floor, New York, New York 10016.

hmhbooks.com

Library of Congress Cataloging-in-Publication Data
Names: Brunson, Quinta, author.
Title: She memes well : essays / Quinta Brunson.
Description: Boston : Houghton Mifflin Harcourt, 2021.
Identifiers: LCCN 2020057705 (print) | LCCN 2020057706 (ebook) |
    ISBN 9781328638984 (hardcover) | ISBN 9781328637079 (ebook)
Subjects: LCSH: Brunson, Quinta. | American wit and humor. |
    LCGFT: Essays.
Classification: LCC PS3602.R8626 S54 2021 (print) |
    LCC PS3602.R8626 (ebook) | DDC 814/.6 [B]—dc23
LC record available at https://lccn.loc.gov/2020057705
LC ebook record available at https://lccn.loc.gov/2020057706

Book design by Chloe Foster

Printed in the United States of America
1 2021
4500825210

To my family, and to all of the kids of the internet. Keep going!

Contents

Hey, Reader

Being someone that people recognize from the internet is quite the experience. The first time I was meme'd, strangers all over the world saw me making this face:

It's the face of a girl whose jaw hit the floor upon hearing that her date paid for BOTH movie tickets. A girl who could not *believe* she was just treated to a large popcorn from the concessions stand. A girl who was not used to the finer things in a life. A girl who was a character made up and played by me.

Was this how I expected to first get noticed as an entertainer? No. Was it hilarious? Yes, very much so. Not only was the video funny, but I still laugh at the fact that the role that pushed me into "fame" was a character that became known as the "He Got Money" girl. When I shot that video, I had no idea it'd be my start in the industry; I was just fooling around with a camera phone, hoping I could get some of my Instagram followers to laugh. But even though I didn't have a solid plan for how to launch my career, I knew I wasn't *just* going to be the girl who's never been on a nice date—I had so much more to prove to the world.

I've always liked making people laugh. I think it was because comedy was the thing that connected me to my four much older siblings. That's right: my parents were *active*. Together, they produced Kalid, Njia, Kiyana, Kwei, and me, the appropriately named Quinta (which means "fifth" in Spanish).

Being the youngest and the smallest of the Brunson crew, I learned the importance of attention and how to get it quickly early on in life. Perhaps that's why I fell in love with the internet the first time I laid on eyes on it. Here was a place with endless opportunities to not only grab attention, but grab it on a global level. What's not to love? Turns out, oh so much, but we'll get to that and more (including but not limited to my thoughts

on Philly, models, boys, protests, Apple, and Black education).
Welcome to my head, reader.

The truth is, it's intimidating to go from the rapid-fire humor of the internet to pouring all of my thoughts onto physical paper. This shit is scary! It feels weightier, more significant, more permanent. I can't just delete a book like I can with a tweet that doesn't land. But still, I wanted to write this because I have a lot to say, and a lot that I want to share. I'm hoping that my words bring you some of the happiness that I'm always trying to put into my work—now just in a have-it-on-your-shelf, forever kind of format.

Although I'm relatively new to the game, I came up during a crazy period in media and technology. There's been a lot of evolution packed into my career as an entertainer. Creating stuff for the internet forced me to become my own writer, producer, director, actor, editor, you name it. All of this helped me make the seemingly impossible leap from messing around on the internet, to getting paid to mess around on the internet, to working in the traditional entertainment media space (and still messing around on the internet).

Watching the stuff I've posted over the years evolve as more people share it with their own jokes and comments has been an incredibly joyful experience. People online—strangers, really—helped me multiply, expand, and become coded into the DNA of the internet. All this has taught me how to embrace the unknown, let go of full control, and finally open up to sharing more of myself with the world. After all, I believe recording our lives is recording history.

I owe a lot of my evolution to the people who have followed me since the early days of my internet-ing, back when I was uploading weird videos of me unenthusiastically singing the theme song to *Space Jam* and whatnot. Through your likes, comments, and shares, I've grown more confident in my words, stories, and experiences. I've learned that I *do* have something to say beyond a caption's length. You're the ones who shifted my perspective in a major way and motivated me to take up a little more space in the creative world. Thank you for that.

In return, I'd like to utilize my experiences to teach you some of the valuable lessons I've learned as a meme, as a woman, as a Black person, as a shorty, as a performer, as a Will Ferrell lover, as a whatever other label I've been given over the years. The most important takeaway I hope this book will give you is how to embrace the act of evolution. Memes would not exist without their ability to morph and carry new meanings as they pass from person to person, and neither would I.

Speaking of evolution, I'm a completely different person than when I first sat down to write to you. When I started working on this book, I was just leaving a stable job of four years. I peeled off my security blanket (BuzzFeed) and was naked in the dawn of change. (This is both a metaphorical and literal analogy. I actually do sleep naked. People say, "But Quinta, what if there's a fire?" And I'm just like, the streets will be blessed to see my gifts.) I had no clue what the future would hold for me, but I was excited to push myself even further and see what resulted. Since then, I've moved in with my boyfriend (who then became a fiancé). Got a cat. Transitioned from my twenties and into my thirties. Earned some money and then spent too much of that money. Deleted Twitter from my phone, redownloaded it, and then got rid of it again. Lost friends to demons and gained followers through jokes. Went to Costa Rica. Celebrated my parents' fortieth wedding anniversary. Got angry, got sad, got excited, and got motivated. Successfully gave myself passion twists. Uploaded, downloaded, cropped, and deleted. I sold a few shows and got a series regular job on HBO's *A Black Lady Sketch Show*. It's been a whirlwind, and I'm excited to share all of these experiences and more with you.

So . . . looks like we're going to be hanging out together for a bit, and since you're about to invite me into your life, let me invite you into mine: I'm currently sitting on my Crate and Barrel couch with my computer resting on my lap. There's a lone Nike sneaker in the middle of my living room floor and my orange tabby cat, Jack, is eyeing me like I owe him rent. The sun is shining through my living room window because here in LA the sun is always doing shit like shining through windows. My jaw hurts for no specific reason, and I can't wait to play *Mario Party*—but first—this. Let's get into it.

She
Memes
Well

1

V Is for Victory

···

I got a taste for the stage at the ripe age of five, dancing in one of those little-kid recitals nobody wants to go to. As soon as the theater began cheering and clapping for me (and, sure, for the other kids who were dancing up there with me, too), I knew I liked that feeling and would be chasing it forever.

To say I was an energetic kid would be an understatement. My mother, who is a dedicated and brilliant kindergarten teacher, always believed in solving problems with education. Seeing that I needed an outlet for my hyperactive tendencies, she signed me up for acrobatics and ballet as a way to get all of my restless energy out. It was a genius move: if you have a child who is literally spinning circles around you all day, flipping and knocking over the vase you just bought from Kmart, sign her up for dance class so at least those circles can look more like pirouettes.

When I first got to L and L Dance Productions, a modest three-floor rowhome turned dance studio, I immediately fell in love. First of all, the building itself was cool. The two studio spaces on the first floor had floor-to-ceiling mirrors up front, with a ballet barre attached to the back wall. The second floor was one big studio space with a locker room and another room for changing. The third floor served as creepy storage space you ventured to when you got older to be rebellious because no one was allowed up there. The lobby was filled with little girls who were giggling, gossiping, and jumping while waiting for their class to start. There were three women who ran the desk, affectionately known as Aunt Lynne, Aunt Linda, and Aunt Stacy. They somehow always seemed totally fine with all the wild energy.

On my first day, the main thing I noticed was that I was the smallest one in my class. Seeing myself next to all the other girls my age, I was immediately like, "I know I was the shortest one in kindergarten, but dang—ya'll taller than me too?" Before this, I didn't realize that I'd have that reaction every time I entered a group setting for the rest of my life.

Consistently being the smallest person in the room does either one of two things: it can help you be noticed, or it can help you be ignored. To be straight with you, when I was a little girl, my height made people fawn over me . . . a lot. I was fucking *cute*. I looked like a little bobblehead baby doll.

When it came to dance, though, the teachers were smarter than to let themselves be charmed by my adorableness. They had been there and seen cute. The question was: Could I perform? It was the exact challenge I needed.

The teachers were my favorite part of dance—they were all so cool and stern, so you had to work hard to impress them. You had to get good at your craft; you had to pay attention, hit your marks, and be technically proficient. When they said "Positions!" you got in those positions or else you delayed the whole class. When they said "Point your foot!" you pointed your foot, or else your perfect arabesque was worthless. They demanded excellence.

Two teachers stood out to me from my time at L and L. The first was Miss Hollie. Miss Hollie, who could've been anywhere from twenty-two to forty-seven (my age radar hadn't developed yet), was the coolest person to me. She was a dancer for Philadanco, one of the best companies in America. At a quick glance, she looked like my sister Kiyana, pretty and soulful, and I liked that about her immediately. Most importantly, she once threw ballet shoes at the wall when a girl in the class wasn't paying attention. That was badass, and earned my six-year-old respect.

Miss Hollie had a warm presence until the classroom door shut and it was time to learn some routines. Obviously, our early moves weren't too complicated, because we were tiny, kid idiots, but like I said, there was still an expectation of excellence. Being held to such a high standard, we were made to feel like we were real dancers—even though we were basically playing a drawn-out game of Simon Says.

Early on in the lessons, Miss Hollie told us that something exciting was upcoming.

"Okay, ladies, we're going to start practicing a routine for the recital," she informed us, extending the pronunciation of the word "recital." That's how you know something is important —when someone really takes their time to enunciate the word.

She said we'd be performing on stage, doing both ballet and acrobatics routines, in front of our parents and friends.

While most of the class was practicing a move I like to call "picking a leotard wedgie out of the butt," I perked up. Recital. It sounded like something I'd be into, especially after the way Miss Hollie set it up. Doing routines on a stage with the lights on us and our families in the audience sounded so glamorous and special.

"You're going to need to work extra hard to show your families how much you've learned," Miss Hollie told us.

I solemnly nodded. A chance to show off in front of everyone? I was going to take this *seriously*.

The next time Miss Hollie yelled, "Get in positions!" I sprinted to my spot like my life depended on it. Having four older siblings in the house, I was rarely granted the opportunity to lead things, so in dance class, I took advantage of every chance that I got to run shit. We arabesqued and pliéd, being sure to point our feet perfectly to the classical music. I pointed as hard as I could in order to seem better than I was — ballet is all about presenting perfection, even when you're in pain.

That pressure for perfection may have motivated me, but at the same time, it was good to have an outlet in my other L and L class: acrobatics. Acrobatics was really where my chaotic talents would shine. I loved tumbling and flipping and wanted to learn all that I could about how to defy gravity. My acrobatics teacher, Miss Denise, was cool and I immediately liked her. She was short like me and a bit less rigid than Miss Hollie. Rigid in that we were still doing flips and tricks that could literally break our necks, so you had to pay attention, but the mood of the class was fun. In ballet, we were firmly bouncing to Bach to prepare for the recital, while in acrobatics, there was a more laid-back vibe as we cartwheeled in prep for our big routine.

"Okay, girls," Miss Denise hollered one day as we prepped. "Now we're gonna put this all to music. You ready?" She popped a CD into the boom box and hit play.

"Everybody get up, it's time to slam now," Jelanna LaFleur's voice rang out. "We've got the real jam going down . . . Welcome to the Space Jam . . ."

Yes, that's right, we were going to be dancing to the Quad City DJ's breakout hit from the Michael Jordan/Bugs Bunny vehicle *Space Jam,* aka one of the greatest basketball stories ever told. The movie had just come out and was all the rage in animation, music, and all-around hilarity. First graders like me gave it five stars. My personal favorite line? "Let's all laugh at the duck!" The delivery from Daffy takes me out. What a comic genius. Anyway, young Quinta was ECSTATIC that we'd be performing to this song, and so was everyone else in the class.

Have you ever seen a group of five- and six-year-old aspiring ballerinas go HAMMER to bass music? It's magnificent. As soon as the beat dropped, everyone started doing roundoffs and back handsprings, creating absolute chaos in the classroom. The CD would skip and Miss Denise would holler at us to get back to positions, until that chaos became more coordinated. This play-pause-groan process repeated itself for the next month or so as we learned our routines for the recital. Little by little, Miss Hollie and Miss Denise drilled the moves into our developing brains.

As the summer recital approached, Miss Hollie and Miss

Denise started to page though the costume catalogs that were released every year from companies like Costume Gallery, Dansco, and Bloch. These magazines would be filled with frilly, fun, and glitzy outfits that could add some necessary dramatic effect to whatever song you were dancing to. Us kids would crowd around, trying to look over their shoulders and see what cute costumes we might be getting. I always tried to give my input, but they left me out of the important decision-making.

The day our costumes arrived, Miss Hollie and Miss Denise skipped warm-ups for the day, combined their classes, and had all the girls try on their ensembles instead. We were giddy and coming down off our sugar highs from lunch. I was so excited, I couldn't stop hopping up and down.

Miss Hollie helped me into my ballet costume, a bluish leotard with sequins and a sheer skirt that made me feel like a fairy. I twirled and looked into the mirror. But the best was yet to come: my acrobatics costume, a cheerleader ensemble to match the *Space Jam* theme. The leotard was bright white with a satiny shine to it, with sleeves down to my wrists and gold sequin bands sewn on around the edges. It also had a turtleneck, you know, because nothing says breathable dancewear like long sleeves, gold handcuffs, and a turtleneck. The jazziness was highlighted by red sequin stripes down the skirt and a gold sequin belt. With new matching white acrobatic shoes, the look was complete. I felt like a Christmas ornament and looked like a disco ball. The red sequin *V* proudly displayed on the front of the leotard was everything. *V,* if you are wondering,

See? Cute.

stood for "victory." What was it a victory over? I'm gonna say the Monstars!

Then, from nowhere, Miss Denise pulled out the game changer: pom-poms. They were made of gold, well, at least to six-year-old me, it looked like gold. In reality (and after some googling) I'm pretty sure they were made of gold-colored Mylar. Regardless, they were the most luxurious and fun things I'd ever set eyes on. They were cute, they made noise, and doggone it . . . they meant I could be a real cheerleader if I wanted. If I close my eyes tight enough, I can still see the slinky metallic strands glimmering in my Dunkaroo-icing-covered hands.

At home that night, still in costume, I couldn't put my pom-poms down. I sprinted around the house shaking them in my siblings' faces, shrieking the lyrics to "Space Jam."

"These are pretty, huh?" my exhausted, but entertained, mother said, affirming that they were indeed the epitome of childhood opulence.

Even though I wanted to live in the costume forever, my mother, who saw the pristine white shimmer as a challenge (and had four kids' worth of experience when it came to keeping things clean), knew better than to let me wear my outfit beyond the initial fitting. Back into the bag it went, along with the gold pom-poms. It was almost painful to wait until the recital to wear my costume again, but somehow, I made it through the experience.

On the day of the recital, my mom took my face into her hands and looked me squarely in the eye and said, "You know what?"

"What?!" I yelled in extreme and unnecessarily loud little-kid volume.

"You're gonna be so good!" she responded. I was feeling empowered and extremely antsy to show off my costume to my siblings. "Hold on." My mom pulled out some makeup to add that finishing touch. It was my first time wearing makeup, and I can't say that I loved it. I squirmed the whole time as my mom applied the foundation and rouge. It felt like I'd put on a second layer of skin, a restrictive skin that kind of itched.* I looked like a small Donna Summer.

I ran downstairs to show off my costume and gaudy makeup job. When I hit the living room, where the rest of my family was waiting to leave for the show, they had me do a little spin and show off some dance moves before they enveloped me in their versions of support.

My dad, who is the direct, no-nonsense type, looked me up and down. "Look at you." Which is my dad's language for "You look so pretty and cute! You're going to be so good, and I'm so happy I had you, even though you were a surprise!" He's the best. My brothers called me cute, but only to get the show on the road, their eyes fixed on the video game they were playing. My sisters fixed my hair and judged my mom's makeup job. It was the beginning of a Brunson family recital-day tradition.

My family is close-knit, despite being big. Not TLC-Baptist-family big, but whenever I tell people in Los Angeles that I have four siblings, they go, "Whoa, big family," so I guess it's not that common. This is probably because it's expensive as hell —I'm sure my parents could've been millionaires without all

---

* In the years to follow, there'd be a lot of makeup in my life due to dance. When I was in high school, I usually went for the kind you could get from Rite Aid that costs five dollars or less, because makeup culture for high schoolers wasn't what it is now. I eventually graduated to better makeup . . . like the kind you get from CVS . . . but the coloring was always horrible, so I had to settle for foundation that was two shades either lighter or darker. It would take years for me to figure out the right color to buy (thank you, Rihanna, for Fenty), but at the time, all I knew was that I wasn't "sand."

of us. They never thought about that, though — our home was filled with love, the kind money can't buy.

My parents were searchers, both individually and together. They came from sometimes unstable homes and had parents that were present yet imperfect. Both entered adulthood deeply craving to be part of something better than what they had growing up. They wanted something that would prove to them that they'd be okay. Their search for a community eventually led them to each other, after which they were quickly married. They've been glued together ever since.

Both of my parents came up in the seventies, right after the decades-long civil rights movement came to an end. Hippies and Black Panthers were exploding onto the cultural scene across the United States. Philly in the seventies was a revolutionary playground filled with all sorts of clubs: poetry, jazz, disco, you name it. Everything was about nonconformity, standing out, and breaking boundaries. At their wedding, my parents vowed not to walk the path of their parents, but to do something different, something radical in their own right: they were going to stay together and create their own community, aka have a lot of kids.

At the time, Black Power movements were encouraging Black Americans to embrace their culture fearlessly. One of the ways my parents did this was by giving their children names with a direct African influence. Because of this, all of my siblings have powerful names that carry a lot of meaning. I've always loved the names my parents chose because they're a sign of their pride and their resistance to the norms society had been pushing on them.

Their first child, Kalid, who is fifteen years older than me, is the oldest, tallest, and the most serious of us all. It's my theory that he took the entirety of my family's height genes for himself, leaving the rest of us to carry on the teeny frame of my mother. My parents chose the Arabic name Kalid because it means "eternal." That's very much how I see Kalid. He is an ever-present figure in my life who survives no matter what. Although I spent the least amount of time with Kalid because of our age difference, I always appreciated his spirit. Growing up with a brother who is that much older basically gave me free rein to be as fearless as I wanted to be. It wasn't scary to mouth off or confront my childhood enemies because I knew I had a secret weapon: a very tall, very big, very protective older brother, who also happened to (maybe) have a gun.

Njia, who we call "Jia," came three years later. Njia means "the way" in Swahili. Jia was very much the one who forged the way for us Brunson girls. She was always ahead of the curve when it came to fashion, looking immaculately put together at every event. Jia was the one who would straighten and style my hair from the time I was very young, so it wasn't a surprise when she went on to open her own beauty salon. Every school dance or performance was pregamed with Jia hovering around me, making sure I looked perfect.

My other sister, Kiyana, was born two years after Jia. Kiyana is a very spiritual name, meaning "light and deity." This fits Kiyana, as she's the earthiest and most Erykah Badu–ish one in my family. She pours love and spiritual guidance into every person she meets and has a very calming, yet chaotic presence. While Jia was the one who would straighten and style my hair, it was Kiyana who spent endless hours braiding it. "Sit still," she'd say, while positioning my head with one hand and lighting a candle with the other hand. Kiyana went into childcare, like my mom. It made sense, because she was so good with me. She was never mean, even when I took something from her room without permission.

Kwei, the closest sibling in age to me, is two years younger than Kiyana. My parents named him Kwei because of the name's Ghanian roots. (When I called my mom to ask the exact meaning behind Kwei's name, she said, "It's tied to royalty. And I liked the way it sounded. Why are you asking me this at four p.m. on a Friday?") Kwei is the sibling I spent the most time at home with, so influenced me a lot. Because of him, I loved *Zelda*, "Stone Cold" Steve Austin, brontosauruses, and Jim Carrey. Even though I drove him crazy when I was little, he's one of my loudest and biggest supporters. In fact, he's a hype man for all of us siblings; if you have an accomplishment, he'll shout it from the rooftops until his voice grows hoarse and eventually disappears. It's so sweet.

As for me, Quinta, well, my name means "fifth" in Spanish. As in, "this is our 'quinta' child and we are tired." I am eight years younger than Kwei, so it's not hard to figure out that my parents were not expecting me. According to Brunson family lore, my mom had assumed she couldn't get pregnant, so I was kind of a . . . treat. Apparently, my arrival pulled the seams of their marriage—which had become a bit strained over the years—a little tighter. Ever since my mother told me that in the car one day unsolicited on the way to a dance practice, I've felt it was my responsibility to keep the family close.

That's why I was so excited to have them come to my first

dance recital. These were the people I loved most in the world, and I wanted to make them proud. To this day, it's never been about the performance for me, it's always been about the audience.

That day, we all squeezed into my parents' green Plymouth minivan and headed down to Swarthmore College's Lang Performing Arts Center, where every one of my summer recitals was hosted until I turned seventeen. Swarthmore is a beautiful college in suburban Pennsylvania, with a green and lovely campus. The Lang Center was a little better than your average college theater hookup, but at the time, it might as well have been the Disney Concert Hall. It was big and beautiful, seated about three hundred people, and had a balcony. Lang is where I first experienced the joy and magic of a theater, with its big echoes and dim lights. I can still feel the too-cold air-conditioning on my skin and clearly see the seats that were just comfy enough until an intermission. When we got there, I practically ran inside, dragging my mom faster than she liked to move, leaving the rest of my family behind to go find their section.

Backstage at the recital, I stretched along with my classmates. IMHO five-year-olds don't really need to stretch before athletic activity, because they're basically Gumby dolls, but still, it felt professional. Miss Hollie, who was running back and forth and making sure everything was ready for the show, was sporting an all-black outfit with the name of the dance school printed on the back, while Miss Denise sat with us, focused on making sure every kid was prepared for our acrobatics performance right after ballet.

First up was the ballet performance. "Keep your spacing!"

Miss Hollie whispered as we pattered across the stage to hit our marks. "Smile and have fun," Miss Denise said. They knew that the night was no longer in their hands.

My class's ballet performance was beautiful, but boring. Not sure if anyone's ever told you, but ballet is ba-boring. That being said, I found the joy in it because it was an opportunity to show just how technical of a dancer I could be. The delicate and slow-moving routine required my tiny buzzing body to calm the hell down and *croisé effacé* for a bit.

As soon as the curtain went up, I realized it was the first time I was on stage in front of people—I was being seen! Well, I knew my parents could see me; I couldn't see them, but I had to trust that they could see me and know that I was doing my best. I think that was my first experience in having a "relationship from the stage." I had to trust that the people who loved me could see me. I ballet-ed my ass off. Miss Hollie didn't throw any shoes. Not because parents were watching, but because she was proud. When we finished our routine, we stood in place as the lights dimmed and the curtain closed. As soon as that last slither of light faded between the red curtains, I rushed backstage to change into my beloved cheerleader costume. I was buzzing with the excitement that came from being on stage, and couldn't wait to do it again.

Before I knew it, it was time for our closer: the acrobatics performance. The lights came up, the song came on, and it was time to kill it. From the first "Everybody get up," the crowd lost their minds.

With my hands grasped tightly around the golden pom-poms, I felt unstoppable. The energy from the audience bounced directly off the walls and into me. As the music picked up, I could feel it reverberating inside of my rib cage. I was drowning in the beat, hitting every move and tumble, nailing every landing.

During our dance, Miss Denise crouched in the shadows up front, doing the moves with us for guidance. I didn't look at her once. Instead I was enveloped by the energy of the moment. Then, just like that, "Space Jam" was over and the lights went out. I stood frozen in my final position, breathing heavily and wishing that the song would start over and we could do it all again as the crowd clapped.

The lights came up to highlight the audience, and from the stage I could see my entire family leap from their chairs in a standing ovation. The feeling of looking out in the crowd and seeing your whole family screaming your name is nearly indescribable. I fully attribute this moment as being the thing that drove me to pursue a life of performance. It flipped some sort of switch in my brain, a switch that could no longer be turned off: I wanted to entertain.

All six of my immediate family members would come to my every recital from then on. Even when Kalid, Jia, and eventually, Kiyana, moved out of the house, they still came to performances. My recitals became kind of an institution, one of the few times throughout the year my nuclear family would all gather together around one nucleus. It gave dance an importance beyond just a way for me to get my extra energy out.

I honestly don't think I'd be where I am today if I hadn't started dance so early on in life. Working on perfecting the right moves used to take hours, if not weeks, of repetitive motion. Repetitive motion is an annoying but unavoidable experience in any field. So, learning how to do it and do it well was a huge asset to me once I started branching out in my creative pursuits. Dance not only taught me the art of discipline and persistence, but it also demanded confidence and self-respect, something that I bring with me to any stage I stand upon.

Once I began setting my sights on comedy, my dance career slowly faded into the background; there just wasn't room for it in my life anymore. Of course, I still miss the days of rigorous physical training, and definitely miss my strong and bendable dance body. But no matter how much time passes, and how far away I get from those days in Miss Hollie's and Miss Denise's classes, I always remember to hit the stage with my eyes on the prize so I don't get hit with a shoe, literally or metaphorically.

2

Meme, Myself, and I

....

Growing up, the only peeks I got of the world outside of Philly came to me through books and movies. I was always getting lost in stories that transported me to different dimensions. Even though I loved my home base and all the people in it, I was curious about what happened outside of my own bubble. And then, sometime during my childhood, that curiosity was rewarded. The unknown got a dial-up connection, leading the world to feel like it quadrupled in size.

In 1997, as I was quickly developing into the opinionated person that you know and love today, my dad got our very first family computer. He hauled home an enormous box and inside was a hulking block of plastic. At the time, computers weren't that important to me; I was focused on making improvements to my Barbie dream house. But my brother was obsessed with it, so I guessed it had to be cool. It was sitting at this giant gray CPU a few years later, in 2001, that I saw my first meme.

"Check it out," Kwei told me, booting up the internet on

my dad's computer, which took approximately ten minutes, and meant that no one in the house could use the phone.*

He typed "peanut butter jelly" and "banana" into the Netscape search bar. Approximately thirty seconds later, a pixelated image of a banana dancing to "Peanut Butter Jelly Time," by the Buckwheat Boyz, appeared on screen. I had heard the song, and danced to it myself, but by God, I was no smiling and bopping banana! This video was comedy gold.

Kwei clicked refresh and the video played over again, the eight-bit banana dancing away.

I couldn't get enough of it. I pushed Kwei aside and kept refreshing the page, dancing along with the song. Eight-bit banana was brilliant! Something about the simplicity of the cyclical movement and repetitive song captivated me. I couldn't get enough.

And I wasn't the only one. The banana lit up the young internet like a bonfire. Parents were emailing it to their coworkers. It got a story on the local news. *Family Guy* parodied it. I'm pretty sure that banana was considered for mayor somewhere. Even though everyone was talking about it, no one had an exact name for the phenomenon that banana created, because that banana became a meme before "internet memes" were really even a thing.

In a weird way, stumbling upon the dancing banana changed my life. Most people saw a banana dancing to a Miami-bass track as silly, but I saw an inside joke spreading across the inter-

---

* Because of dial-up internet. Go look it up, young people.

net, jumping from medium to medium, transforming in front of my very eyes.

I wanted to see more of that banana, more of the internet, more of the codes and processes that made everyone pay attention to the same thing.

That day, I asked my parents if I could have a computer of my own. Seeing my newly formed interest in the internet, they said "Yes, let's give her direct access to that!" Kidding. They immediately said no, as they should have. While it was premature to ask for my own dial-up monstrosity, it didn't change the fact that from that day forward, I would become a child of the internet.

In the meantime, I settled for the family-room computer, claiming I was doing my homework, but heading off to the more playful corners of the internet the second my mom left the room. It was there that I discovered "Chocolate Rain," Keyboard Cat, "What What (In the Butt)," and more. I was watching videos go viral before there was a real word for it, and I loved it.

By the time my mom brought home a Mac laptop a few years later, I was already aware that a technological revolution was on the horizon. During the four years that I was in high school, Facebook, YouTube, the iPhone, and Twitter all came out. Messaging options were growing at lightning speed and so was I. (Not height-wise, clearly.)

I began to use the laptop for more sophisticated reasons beyond what I had done on the old Dell computer, like shooting and editing comedy sketches that only a few people would see. I'd later learn that this is called "making content," but at the time, I was just doing it to entertain myself. I would record a "talk show" with my friends, or a music video to a new song I liked, and then edit it in iMovie. The videos didn't go anywhere; they just lived in the Rolodex of the Photo Booth, becoming more and more embarrassing as the years went on.

The more time I spent on the internet, the more I saw people posting videos that looked a lot like the ones I was shooting at home for no one. But unlike me, they had people watching, people they didn't even know. I began to realize that even though the internet felt like a small, niche place for nerds and weirdos, there were people who were breaking through the noise to become something else. Notoriety on the internet was becoming accessible for the average person. No acting school, rich parents, or plastic surgery needed. If you had a laptop or a camera, you too could gain the attentions of hundreds . . . maybe even *thousands*. It was clear from the start of chat rooms and Myspace pages: the internet was providing space for marginalized voices, and that space was one I couldn't get enough of.

Like I mentioned earlier, I've always been attracted to the unknown. Since I was the youngest of five kids, everything, from clothing to customs, was passed down to me. Things were always familiar. Explored. But the internet felt different. *I* was the one showing self-made GeoCities pages to my family. *I* was explaining what Neopets were. *I* was taking advantage of the newly founded frontier.

In those early years of social media and the internet, I noticed there were two groups of people: those who got it, and those who didn't. The people who got it, the ones posting to Facebook, Insta, Twitter, while slowly becoming addicted to their algorithms, were largely Millennials and Gen Xers. The people who didn't get it were largely Baby Boomers.

It quickly became trendy for anyone who was born before 1960 to shit on those born after — a trend that, I think, is dying? At least I hope it is, because 1) it's tacky, 2) you guys are on the same apps now . . . so maybe you're the ones spending a little too much time lost in your screens. A lot of the finger-wagging and criticism came from people who were simply rejecting change. We've seen it time and time again.

Take the classic example of the printing press. When the printing press hit the scene in the fourteenth century, it revolutionized communication.* For the first time, words were being mass reproduced at a rapid pace. It made books cheaper to print and ideas easier to share. And you know what? That freaked some people the fuck out. They were worried that this sudden flood of knowledge would bring about disastrous consequences. There was even this scientist, Conrad Gessner, who said the average human was not equipped to handle so much information, as if our brains had a finite amount of space and this flood of knowledge would cause them to explode like an overstuffed burrito. Stuff that burrito, Conrad. More rice has never hurt anyone!

Every time technology causes a big societal shift, it comes

---

* We all know that Gutenberg's printing press was not the first, right? It was created in China, like four hundred years before Gutenberg lifted it.

with an underlying hum of fear. The same distrust occurred when trains, phones, and TVs were invented. I'll never forget the family story about my grandmother's own technological superstitions. "That's the work of the devil, right here," my grandma used to say, pointing to the microwave. Growing up, my mom heard a constant refrain from my grandmother about how she wouldn't allow one in her home, and that anyone who had a microwave was "playing with God's good." Naturally, when my mom got her own home, one of the first things she bought was a microwave, because feeding five kids required reheating and Kid Cuisine sometimes.

Even though it seems like we've evolved past the "not trusting microwaves" point in history, I still see insta-distrust of new technology patterns and means of expression today. Nobody likes feeling like culture is passing them by, but some people stubbornly stay put, sticking their head in the sand when it comes to advancements. A threat to the way they've done things for years is too much for them to handle, even if that "threat" will actually make life easier. Different often feels like wrong to this type of person, and so they get stuck in the same patterns of behavior, looking at anything new with a "get off my lawn" type mentality.

Generally speaking, I welcome change. While not all change is good, I approach everything from the point of view that this is all a part of evolution. It's natural. I never want to resist new frontiers just because I'm afraid of what those frontiers might bring. For example, I don't think TikTokers are weird; I think they are the next generation of digital innovators as it pertains to humor, editing, and communication. And so I refuse to hate on it. After all, memes are what got me into the career path that I have today.

While they may look simple, memes and gifs are nuanced forms of language. Yet most people do not respect the capabilities of the meme. Why? Because they require us to change how we see language and communication and (say it with me now) *people hate change.*

I can't tell you how many times I've heard versions of:

> *Kids are forgetting the written word and replacing it with bullshit images like idiots!*

> *These new generations won't learn to write cursive . . . or write at all!*

> *We are so much better, because we liked a little systemic racism in our communication!*

I bet when the ancient Egyptians started using hieroglyphs the even ancienter Egyptians were like, "What are these doodles? Stop wasting your time and go take the Sphynx out for a walk!" But those doodles eventually became letters, which became words, which became the written language, which eventually went back to images, or as we know them: memes.

If you look back through history, you'll see that the way

---

* Don't worry about this one, old-timers. It's still around.

we interact changes constantly: the text message used to be a phone call, the phone call used to be the letter, which is an updated version of a smoke signal. (I can make these connections all day, people.) Decade by decade, year by year, day by day, communication has evolved. It's never smart to spit in the face of evolution. Ignoring memes and gifs, or "internet speak," is ignoring a huge part of what's happening during our time on earth.

Memes themselves can't ignore evolution. Memes have grown to gifs, and gifs to moments in viral videos. Thanks to Twitter, it's grown to being video reactions on top of a retweet. And hey, I'll throw you a bone: I'm an old person in that I hate calling a video a meme, and I hate when people do. However, if that's where memes are evolving to, I can't ignore the flow. I'm not a grandma yet.*

People are having deep conversations through memes, too: they're organizing, they're keeping in touch, they're starting movements. It's happening every day. If you think about it, memes are a super-smart way to further difficult or complex conversations. Do you need an example? Thought you would. Here's a meme of my own making, from the popular "Spider-Man on a fan" moment on Twitter.

I shared this meme in 2017, when racial tensions were high in the country. Cops were (still are at the time of this writing) killing innocent Black men and weren't being charged, and nat-

---

* Can't wait to be one, though. I won't yell at young people about what I won't do. I'll just have my own garden I'll tend to and support the youths with pie or signs. Whatever they need.

The floor is "liberty and justice for all"

6/16/17, 7:23 PM

36.8K Retweets **66K** Likes

'Merica

urally, Trump was ignoring it all and only using this pain to instigate further divisiveness.*

Around the same time of these increasing racial tensions, the "Spider-Man Floor Is Lava" meme became the hit of the week.

---

* As I write this, there have been protests against police brutality erupting across the globe. This chapter has become a sad and exhausting time capsule of the unchanging times.

Most of the "floor is" memes were jovial and fun, but some got below the surface level and added a political perspective to them.

Here's a more recent meme, from the year of our reckoning 2020:

quinta brunson ✔ @quintabrunson · May 30

Get in Loser, we're going PROTESTING

💬 17   🔁 3.7K   ♡ 19.9K   ⬆

Notice the evolution of the political meme from '17 to '20. The photo on this screenshot is from the hit movie *Mean Girls,* wherein none of these characters would've said anything about protesting. But guess what? It doesn't matter. The deeper meaning here is that going to protest against police brutality *is* the "cool" girl thing to do. It *is* the "Get in, Loser, we're going shopping" (which is the actual line from this movie) of our era. You wanna be a hot girl? Speak up for those who need it. And that's a meme for ya, baby.

Ultimately, the ever-happening change in communication shows that we're all always working on new ways to connect.

As humanity evolves, so does our way of relating to each other. That's nothing to be afraid of. Memes are just another way to further the necessary conversations we're having, online and off.

The internet and I have been kicking it for a long time, and to be honest with you, a lot of that early amazement has worn off for me. The honeymoon period is long gone and now we're just sitting here staring at each other, scrolling away. But still, I have a lot of respect for what it's given us, and I have even more hope that it can help humanity reach new frontiers.

My generation will be the last to grow up with *and* without the internet as a main tool for . . . well . . . everything. Gen Z and beyond will never know what life was like without a computer, social networking, cell phones, or Amazon Prime.* But luckily, Gen Z and beyond will be the ones to take our creation of social media and elevate its use. And for that, I'm glad. This is just a statement of fact. Change is here. Change is inevitable —and memes are now part of language moving forward. And you know what? The Egyptians are stanning.

---

* Unless we all get rid of all this stuff because it's ruining the earth, but most likely we can find an eco-friendly fix for that. Or . . . idk . . . we really have to start taking better care of the earth, man, or it's gonna spit us off of the planet. I mean, the earth keeps spinning, but it got rid of the dinosaurs. Just saying. For real, I don't care if you believe in climate change or not, but like let's take care of our home a little better. Also, be nice to your neighbors. We really gotta get this human thing down. I believe in us? We can do pretty cool things when we put our minds to it.

3

Ahali

···

Do you remember the first time you realized that the earth was not necessarily a kind, nurturing place? Because I sure do. I was still rocking OshKosh B'gosh and ballies when I began to understand the harsh realities of what it meant to be a human on this planet. It wasn't a lesson I learned in a fun, John Hughesian way, where my parents' divorce taught me that love is fleeting, or my parents' neglect made me realize we're all alone on this earth, or my parents' unhappy marriage forced me to fall victim to peer pressure — jeez, now that I list this all out, Molly Ringwald's characters' parents were going through it. Anyway, my experience didn't fit into a fun teenage movie script. My introduction to the World of Hard Knocks came much earlier in life, thanks to Ahali, a first-to-fifth-grade learning program on the top floor of Harrity Elementary School.

Most people, if they think back on elementary school, remember eating paste, memorizing multiplication tables, and having super-fun playtimes. That wasn't the full case for me. That's because Ahali was an unconventional and progressive school where the curriculum centered Black history in all aspects of education. From first grade to fifth, the names Medgar

Evers, Phillis Wheatley, Shirley Chisholm, and Malcolm X were just as familiar as Abraham Lincoln, George Washington, Ben Franklin, and John F. Kennedy.

During movie days, we didn't get Disney classics; we watched movies like *Amistad* or *Roots*. (I actually didn't even see *Snow White* until I was eighteen and by then I was just like, "This girl is making a lot of bad decisions. She doesn't know these dwarfs.") After the school's principal had everyone recite the pledge of allegiance from the loudspeaker every morning, my teachers had us recite the Nguzo Saba before sitting down for class. From the get, we were always taught that Black education was just as vital as white American education.

I went to Ahali because of my mom's focus on schooling as an educator herself. When I left her kindergarten class, she wanted to make sure I was passed on to the best hands possible. Those hands belonged to my new teachers, Umi and Mwongozi, who were committed to educating their students beyond what a traditional syllabus could offer. Umi and Mwongozi weren't just teachers — they were mentors. They took it upon themselves to help guide us into the real world from day one.

Another thing that set Ahali apart from other elementary schools was that Umi and Mwongozi used a teaching method called "village learning." This meant that all the grades would often be in one class together. Occasionally, we'd break off for grade-specific lessons, but mostly we all hung out in a group, getting educated at the same time: first graders looking at fourth graders, thinking, "I'm gonna be you in a few years"; fifth graders looking at second graders, thinking, "I remember when I used to be you."

Coming up through a village learning program gave all the students an innate respect for who they were and who they would grow into. It taught us to take care of each other in a way that I don't think traditional education would have, what with its focus on individualism and competition. Ahali demonstrated the importance of building a strong community around yourself and nourishing that community with good energy and education. Even today, I'm always nurturing my village, whether it's in my work, social, or family.

Incredibly, Umi and Mwongozi were the only two teachers for all 150-plus students at Ahali. Somehow, they made each and every one of us feel heard and seen. These two women took so much time and care to instill important lessons into all of us, their voices still occasionally run through my brain when I'm going about my day.

Umi was petite, kind, and soft-spoken. She had this maternal energy that always made me feel like everything would be all right. "That's okay, try again," she'd encourage when I couldn't figure out a math problem. I liked her because she was close to my size, had the most beautiful locs—truly aspirational—and was constantly floating around in loose-fitting African-print clothing. She was like Tinkerbell, if Tinkerbell came from West Africa. She even smelled amazing, like freshly lit sage. Her whole vibe exuded a warmth that welcomed everyone into her orbit.

Mwongozi was a different story. She wore a different hair wrap for every day and billowy African-print dresses—but that was just about the only thing that was flowy about her. She had a big, boisterous voice that rattled in your chest when she used it to get the class's attention, and she could quiet down the most rambunctious kids with just a stare. Mwongozi was a serious person who could be very strict when she needed to be—which was quite often, since she was one of only two adults managing over a hundred kids.

As an adult, I now understand that Mwongozi's harshness came from a deep passion and love for her students, but at the time, I was terrified of her. Not only was she one of those teachers who could destroy you with one look, but Mwongozi also happened to be the mother of my aunt through marriage on my dad's side. In other words, she had a direct line to my parents; one wrong move and my mom would hear all about it at our next family cookout. Because of this, I never misbehaved in school. I constantly made sure to be on point, crossed my t's and dotted my i's with form so good it'd make a calligrapher jealous. My good student–ness followed me throughout my academic years, but Ahali was the place that first taught me that I needed to take my education seriously.

Umi and Mwongozi took turns teaching us all the classic subjects, including English, social studies, geography, French, science, and financial planning, always finding a way to keep a focus on Black history.

"Today we will be learning our multiplication tables," Umi would tell us, "and about Mary Jackson, NASA's first Black female engineer, whose math skills helped put Neil Armstrong on the moon." I used to sigh, wondering why we had to have to a history lesson just to learn some bum-ass math, but our teachers' ability to tie everything back to the experiences of our ancestors was not only incredibly eye-opening, but it also helped connect us to the subject matter in a deeper way. It made me really feel like I was learning about my own history, which was in and of itself American history.

While having that type of education gave me an understanding of reading, writing, and math that I'm pretty positive you couldn't get anywhere else, the lessons that always stuck with me most were the out-of-the-classroom experiences.

One such lesson that I think about often involved the process of building a boat with our own bare hands. When I was in fourth grade, Umi and Mwongozi told us they were taking us to a boat shop while handing out permission slips for us to take home to our parents. I had never been on a boat before, and after seeing *Titanic* I wasn't too keen on it. However, a field trip is a field trip, and I, like all kids, was excited to go on one.

This lesson took us out to Manayunk, a charming little neighborhood in the outskirts of Philly. Manayunk is filled with ancient rowhomes, river views, and a mix of hardworking older Philadelphians and hipsters who think the area is kitschy. It also has hills like San Francisco, which was always exciting to me as a kid. Philly is pretty flat, so our bus going up huge hills felt like going to Six Flags without having to take the two Coke cans to get in on a discount.

When we got on the bus, I sprinted to the first open seat to ensure there was room for my friend CC and me. It was imperative that we shared a seat on the way to Manayunk, because we were best friends, and everyone knows that if best friends don't sit together on the bus, then there's a very real chance that they are, in fact, not best friends. They're acquaintances at best, and in a fight at worst.

When CC got on the bus, she wordlessly plopped down next to me, knowing that the open space was hers. CC and I met my first day at Ahali. She had these big, inquisitive eyes and a bright presence that enveloped everyone she met. It was clear from day one that we would be overachieving competitors for the rest of our Ahali lives and beyond, but the kind that only wants to see the other doing well.

Our friendship forced us to push each other and make each other great, but it also drove me crazy, because CC was consistently a hair better than me at everything. If I got an A, she got an A+. If I got an A+ on an assignment, the plus on her work was always bigger. Even Mwongozi, who always treated every kid equally, was charmed by CC's excellence. It was clear that CC was Mwongozi's favorite because of how smart and mature she was. AND! Mwongozi was technically like . . . my aunt? So the rules state that she was supposed to like me more, no? But CC had that effect on people. Everyone loved her, including me.

On the bus, CC rattled off information about math while I quietly stared out the window.

"Do you know that two times anything will never be an odd number?" she said, poking me in the side.

"Uh-huh," I responded while watching trees zip by.

"And so it's easy, everything will end in either zero, two, four, six, or eight?'" she followed.

"Everyone knows that," I said, even though I did not know that and hated math.

When we arrived at our location, I was underwhelmed after

CC and her best friend, Two-front-teeth Brunson,
kicking it on the playground.

the initial hype from Mwongozi. It was just a big lot, with a nondescript building and a wooden sign that said "Manayunk Timber." It didn't look like a place that would teach me one of the biggest lessons of my life, but you never know which people, places, and experiences are going to shift your perspective until after you've left them behind and had some time to look back.

My class filed into the lot, where we were met by a skinny white man. I don't remember his name or much about him, all I remember is that his hair seemed to be made of sawdust and his enormous hands sported leathery calluses. This was one of those dudes who you see, and you're like, "Ohhh, you're a *real* manly man. Got it. Got it."

This guy, Joe, I'll call him, worked at "Philadelphia's #1 sawmill" (according to the website) and would be our boat-building guide for the next five days. CC and I used our toes to draw hearts in the gravel while the rest of the class bumbled about, shoving and jumping, in the way that little students do when they're out in the real world. CC and I knew better than to be wylin' out while Mwongozi was in charge.

"Everybody!" Mwongozi yelled, causing the childhood shenanigans to abruptly stop. "Gather around, NOW!" We obediently did as we were told and Mwongozi went on to explain to us that they brought us to Manayunk Timber as part of a lesson about slavery in the early 1800s.

"Slaves were not only brought over to America on ships, but they also used boats to escape captivity," Mwongozi told us. "It was both a tool for imprisonment and freedom." We quietly listened along, understanding that now was not the time for our excited chatter. "You will build a boat. You'll learn about carpentry and history. And then, you'll ride in it," she continued.

CC and I exchanged looks. *Build a boat? And ride in it?* I mean, it sounded fun, but we were just kids! My Lego boats couldn't survive the bathtub—what made Mwongozi think this was possible?

When Mwongozi was finished with our history lesson, Joe took over to explain the safety rules and precautions. He passed out goggles and shared some horror stories about missing fingers. It was a very strange juxtaposition: our stoic African teacher standing next to this weathered white dude who made his living selling wood.

I remembered being confused by why our very pro-Black teachers, who taught us how horrible white people had been every chance they got, were taking us to learn anything at all from a white man. But as I watched Mwongozi and Umi shake his hand and talk with him, it seemed like he was not only receptive to their history lesson, but was excited to help. I guess that this was my first experience in what the kids called allyship. He listened, helped, and shut up.

Every morning for the next four days, we dutifully made our way back to Manayunk Timber to continue our history class on slavery, which also braided in lessons about math, engineering, science, and artistry. My whole class worked together to use our child hands to cut wood, bind the pieces together, and construct the frame, little by little. We were creating five small boats to ride in, and one large one that would be symbolic of what our entire class could do together.

I can still picture the sawmills, kind of like the one my dad had in our basement, but way larger. While I was initially scared to use it, the adults guided our hands in cutting the wood so none of us would lose a finger. After sawing, we then would carry the cut pieces of wood to the carpentry table and lay them down for bending. The work was hard, and the fun wore off quickly.

Spending a week sweating in this sawdust-covered shop, my knees buckling under the weight of impossibly heavy pieces of wood, I began to understand my past in a way a book never could've taught me. My people were doing this while living in damning conditions and, in many cases, their freedom depended on it. At the end of each day, we were reminded what a privilege it was to go home to families, food, and a warm bed.

At the end of the five days, each student got a chance to physically feel the importance of their work, by using their boat to take a ride down the Schuylkill River. When it was my turn to go, I was giddy with anticipation. The guide clipped me into my two-sizes-too-big life vest and handed me a bright orange oar. He gently lowered me into my boat, and then got in himself, using his oar to push off the riverbank. As we glided into the center of the Schuylkill, I squealed with excitement and, to be honest, a little bit of fear. I had never been out in the open water before like that, and definitely not on a boat that I had built with my own two hands. Good time as any to learn, I guess.

A huge wave of accomplishment washed over me as this thing that I had worked so hard to build bobbed along delicately in the current. I never thought I'd ever even ride in a boat, let alone build one. My parents had driven by Boathouse Row in Philadelphia so many times when I was a kid, but it seemed so otherworldly to me, like boats were only for the rich white college kids. But it turns out the river was for everyone.

"Whoaaaa!" the guide exclaimed as we floated down the river. "Check it out!" I followed his gaze to see the Philadelphia

I'm on a boat. Everybody, look at me.

skyline unfolding in front of me. Even though we were technically *in* Philly, it still felt so far away.

"Wow," I whispered. As I took in the city and everything it
had to offer, I felt a little bit sad. *This is what my people had to
do? For freedom? And without all of the tools we had at the lumber-
yard?* As the waves of the Schuylkill River rocked my little body
up and down, I could feel a deep connection to my history and
also my future. I'd learned many horrific details about my past
that week, but I also learned about the resilience of my ancestors. That resilience felt like mine to claim now, too.

On the bus back to school that day, CC and I sat quietly in our seats. Even though she was silent, I could tell the trip had a profound impact on CC, as well. We left the curves of Manayunk and made our way back to the less-motion-sickness-inducing West Philly, but that lesson stayed fresh for years.

CC and I are still friends to this day, and even though our lives are different — she's a cool-ass biochemist and molecular biologist, and I'm someone who tries to make a living getting people to laugh — we often discuss how Ahali made us the people we are today. We've both admitted that our experiences in elementary school were so rare that sometimes it almost feels like maybe they never really happened. But they did, and I am so glad for it. Without Mwongozi and Umi and their commitment to our education, I don't know if I ever would've succeeded the way I have.

The Philadelphia school district, a school district that ranked as one of the worst in America a few years ago, does not have a lot of stories of positivity swirling around it. Ahali is one of the few. Even though there was no money, no real support from the city, and community hardships made it difficult to get anything productive done within the school system, Umi and Mwongozi figured out a way to persevere. Instead of letting disadvantages define their students' futures, they went out of their way to make sure their students had the richest experience possible. They gave us music class with actual musicians, who of course incorporated our Black history into every note and lyric. They gave us our first bank accounts, because they knew it was important for us to know how having one works. They gave us

French lessons, because they knew it was important for us to be bilingual. As new words left our tongues, broadening our scope for expression, we understood that there were tangible ways, through language, to expand our understanding of culture. Our minds grew exponentially under the guidance of Umi and Mwongozi.

Even when it was time to part ways, those two women gave us graduation ceremonies that felt spiritual and royal, because they wanted us to understand that tomorrow is a gift, and that we accomplished something big today. Within those classroom walls, rich with lessons about our past, they gave us the world.

Ahali was shut down about three years after I graduated. In hindsight, I think what Umi and Mwongozi were doing may have been . . . illegal? But regardless, it's a tragic and unfathomable loss to the educational community in my hometown. Having a school program that operated outside of the system may have been risky business, but there was an undoubtable benefit to the type of education they gave us. And for those who can't believe that the city would shut down a school that ultimately benefited African American students, I urge you to read up on how slave masters kept slaves from reading and writing, because they were worried their slaves might educate their way out of captivity. That American cycle, baby.

Ahali taught me who I was and where I came from. Learning our Black history—both triumphant and tragic—at such a young age gave us a base level of understanding about our futures. It grounded us and helped us prepare for the world and its racism to come. Even though an enormous weight was dropped on my back at a young age, I felt like I could take on the world because I was also given a keen awareness of how society worked and treated Black people.

I want that difficult and necessary understanding to be available for more of this country's children. I wish there were more Ahalis to help make Black children proud and aware before the world can teach them otherwise.* I want everyone to know as much about Black history as I've been able to learn. I want them to teach their friends about who and what Black people are, about how strong, resilient, beautiful, game-changing, and magnificent Black people are. Make Black history an anchor in everyone else's lives, too—it deserves the space. Do it village learning style, because after all, we're family—or as it's said in Swahili, we're ahali.

---

* Plus, now I know how to build a boat, which is a good skill to have because, you know, when the apocalypse does finally come, I'll be able to row, row, row my boat the fuck out of here.

4

On Friendship

....

If there are any lessons I can teach you in this book, this one I cannot emphasize enough: do not enter a fight without a razor. I repeat: do not enter a fight without a razor. Don't do it. It's like traveling without headphones—you wanna sit there looking stupid when someone runs up on you, disrupting your comfort to talk about the weather? No?! Then carry a razor (and headphones)! Take it from me, a person who has been in exactly 1.5 fights in her entire life.

The incredibly important "razor fight" lesson was learned during my sophomore year of high school, a seminal time in any teenage girl's life. A time when every young woman learns how to drive, kiss, and beat somebody's ass.

Sophomore year of high school was particularly tricky for me because I had transferred schools in the middle of the year. A midyear transfer usually implies some sort of family move or kicked-out-of-school controversy, but that wasn't the case for me. I was always a good student, but I was struggling in school, just in a different kind of way.

I started my high school career at the North Philadelphia hidden gem George Washington Carver High School of Engi-

neering and Science. My freshman year was wonderful; I fell in
with the popular crowd, made the cheerleading team, and even
got a boyfriend who was the tenth cutest in the class according
to a chart I made. But then, the next year, all of that stuff was
stripped away from me in a very dramatic, teen-movie-worthy
fashion. Was it deserved? Not really. But, you be the judge.

So, I had a friend named Cassandra who I used to ride the
train to school with. She was my commuter buddy, which,
when you go to school in a city, is a very important buddy to
have. We mostly rode together because we lived in the same
neighborhood and got along well enough, but we also protected
each other from creeps and pervs and whatever other nastiness
was lurking in the corners of public transit.

One day, during sophomore year, Cassandra told me she
had sex with this boy in our grade. No judgment here. A lot
of kids were sexually active in my school, and if they weren't,
they wanted to be, so Cassandra was killing it. Right on track.
I asked her how it was ("Decent.") and then kind of forgot
about it.

I have always been a very open and frank person, even in
high school. My mantra is that you shouldn't be ashamed of
anything, and therefore should feel free to discuss everything
that's going on with you. I often forget that this is not the case
for everyone around me. A few weeks later, I ended up carelessly
mentioning Cassandra's hookup to some friends. We were having a conversation about the guy she had "done" and I blurted
out something like "Oh, yeah! Cassandra and him had sex. Bet
it was cool."

I'd assumed this was common knowledge because of the casual way Cassandra had mentioned it to me, but what I didn't know was that Cassandra hadn't told anyone but me, her train buddy. In not paying attention to the context of the information I had received, I'd inadvertently let out a secret. And I was about to pay for it.

Secrets, in the teenage girl world, are social currency tainted with poison — they make you feel rich, but can strip you of everything. This accidental secret-slip resulted in a massive smear campaign against me, led by, of course, Cassandra. She launched an attack so vicious and so widespread, I didn't know where to turn. I was called disloyal, a traitor, a hoe (not sure how that one got thrown in there, but it's really easy to be called a hoe if you're a girl), and a number of other terms that labeled me persona non grata.

One by one, my friends began to turn on me. I didn't have it in me to fight, partially because I thought the whole thing was stupid, and partially because, deep down, I knew that I shouldn't have talked about who Cassandra was sleeping with in the first place, regardless of whether or not it was a secret. It wasn't my business to share.

To make matters worse, my boyfriend at the time left me . . . as in, he wound up going to juvie for selling weed on school property. It's incredibly hard to lose a boyfriend, even harder when he gets picked up by cops and locked up. We all do stupid things when we're young, but some of us don't have the privilege of growing out of it. Between that and the fact that everyone in school seemed to be staring daggers into my back, I was hitting an all-time low.

Instead of confronting my growing loneliness or the social war in the hallways, I simply stopped going to school. I'd show up to first period, turn in my homework, get my assignments for the next day, then promptly sneak out afterward to either walk around the city, or come home to watch *Spider-Man* and/ or *Drumline*. I liked being home during the weekday because I was able to enjoy the peace of an empty house that was usually buzzing with at least three family members.

There's something extremely comforting about spending hours watching TV during the day, too. It soothes the soul— like walking into an empty Target. Things felt easier when I numbed my brain with repetitive story lines. I felt safe while watching those movies because I'd memorized exactly what the characters would say, and it was never "You a dumbass hoe, Quinta."*

As you can imagine, my daily adventures outside the classroom did not last very long. A month or so into my ditching, the guidance counselor called my parents and threatened to label me a truant. My mom was not having it—she was so angry that she skipped getting mad at me and took action right away.

---

* This is an avoidance technique that I still use today. When there seems to be nothing I can do about a shitty situation, I go home and watch whatever is going to make me laugh. Escaping to the fantasy of TV comedies is a lot easier than dealing with whatever is causing me grief. And look, I handle things, eventually, because running away isn't the answer. But in the event that you can't do something immediately, be like me and use laughter as a safe space until change is made. I recommend *New Girl*.

She yanked me out of school that day, before I could even be kicked out.

Unfortunately, my mom and I had different ideas of what I should do from there. I wanted to pursue a professional career in writing *Spiderline,* a *Spider-Man / Drumline* mash-up, while she wanted me to go to a school that would better fit my unorthodox learning needs.

Unsurprisingly, my mom won the argument and promptly enrolled me in Philly's brand-new Charter High School for Art and Design (CHAD), where she thought my "unique" energy could be put into a curriculum that celebrated and encouraged creativity.

CHAD had the objective of bringing creativity to the forefront of the learning experience for Black kids in Philly. The individuals who founded the school did so after seeing that there was a very low percentage of licensed Black architects in America. To quote the school's website, "CHAD is the national model for integrated design education, where students discover the power within their hands and minds to meet the world's challenges and design their future."* Design my own future? Okay, CHAD. I see you.

---

* Cool, right? Important, right? Well, I guess, then, it's too bad that the Philly school board VOTED TO CLOSE CHAD in 2020, twenty-one years after those classroom doors first opened. For those of you counting at home, that is now the closure of two schools specifically designed to enrich Black children's lives that had a great impact on my life and directly contributed to my current success. These two extremely important schools do not exist anymore. Hm.

I stepped into those art-covered halls and loved the vibe of the school immediately. It was located right at the meeting of Old City and Center City, literally down the street from the Liberty Bell. We were surrounded by culture and history, and we were encouraged to soak it all in. I didn't even have to cut class to explore the city, because the teachers actually took us outside to sketch drawings of the historical buildings once a week.

As you can imagine, transferring during your sophomore year of high school could be a pretty socially disorienting experience, but doing it when you were basically ejected from every friend group at your other school is even worse. I started my first day of CHAD with defenses raised, unsure of what to expect. I'd never had trouble making friends before, but the experience with Cassandra really threw me off my game. For the first time in my life, I was nervous walking into a new situation.

The nervousness didn't last long, though, because almost immediately a group of three girls approached me in the hall. The semi-leader of the crew, Tiara, got to me first. "You should hang with us," she suggestively demanded. She was pretty and assertive, so I listened.

One benefit of attending a new school in the middle of the year, I learned, is that you bring with you the allure of novelty. Everyone's curious about you, everyone is watching you, everyone wants to know what's up with you. The boys are naturally into you because you're "fresh meat." They think you look cuter in your uniform (blue shirt, khaki pants) than the rest of the girls. Knowing stuff about the new girl becomes a popularity chip—and luckily for these three girls, I was an open book. Within a few days Tiara and company deemed me worthy of their crew and took me under their teen-girl wings—where I stayed for the remainder of high school.

The full group consisted of Tiara, Tanae, and Brittny:

Tiara's name matched her personality in that she was a freaking princess. She looked like Keisha from the spectacular hood film *Belly* and was armed with a slick mouth, which was only eclipsed by her sweetness. She was well liked by everyone in high school, and having her by your side meant you were good to go.

Brittny was quick to laugh, extremely loyal, and always wore cool socks. (When you wear a uniform, you find ways to show your individuality. Mine was cute earrings.) We went to an art school, so everyone was a good artist, but Brit was exceptionally good. She had mastered the bubble-style Powerpuff Girl–esque characters; I loved her work. She also exuded the kind of warmth that drew people into her world. I immediately felt comfortable around her.

Tanae had the demeanor of a sixty-year-old woman. She was extremely level-headed and always had a game plan. I feel like every group of friends has a Tanae, the responsible one who always keeps their cool, makes sure the rest of the group stays grounded, and is wise enough to chuckle at what's funny and ignore what's not.

These three girls became my ride-or-dies. They showed me the ropes of CHAD and told me what the cool after-school hangouts were. Mainly, it was the Gallery—an underground mall with a sick food court (Chick-fil-A and Taco Bell, aka high

Tiara and Brit on the right, Tanae on the left. The girl in the middle hung with us sometimes, hated us others. I forgive her. It was high school.

school Quinta heaven) and fast-fashion stores we could browse before hopping on the train. I had been to the Gallery with my mom, but going with a group of girlfriends was different. Now, it was my after-school temple. Every day, we would spend about an hour there, gossiping, goofing off, and inevitably getting caught up in the sticky high school who's-who web. The store owners probably hated us because no one had enough money to buy anything besides an eight-piece nugget or a Mexican pizza to share, but at least we were consistent customers.

One day, while gathered around one of those plastic food

court tables, Tiara looked me up and down and declared, "You need a boyfriend." I had broken up with the boyfriend who had gotten taken to juvie—our young love could not handle all of the drama. So, I considered Tiara's proposition. *Did I need a boyfriend?* Probably. I needed to show the school that I was a desirable it-girl. (Yeah, yeah, I know . . . I don't need a man to make me feel worthy, but I was fifteen at the time, remember? I didn't learn that lesson until later in life, and my high school operated like most high schools still do. Hindsight is easier than the moment, don't forget!)

"Oh, you know who's cute?" Brittny asked, and then answered herself without waiting for my reply. "Julian."

"Julian is definitely cute, you should go with him. No one's dated him yet," Tanae followed.

Julian was a kid from our school who was (can confirm) adorable. He was a tall, lighter-skinned guy—like, if you combined all of the main players on the 2016 Golden State Warriors into one person—and he seemed like a bad boy, probably because he carried a gun in his backpack. That was cool in Philly. Everyone liked him, and I guess I did, too, because we began dating within a week of Tiara picking him out for me.

Soon, my dramatic fallout with George Washington Carver felt like it was years in the past. I had a new group of friends, a new boyfriend, and a newfound interest in going to classes. My high school life split into two: Before Excommunication and After Excommunication. After Excommunication Quinta was even cooler than before. In this new environment, I felt fresh. I felt good. I felt like I had a do-over, and this time, there was no way I was going to allow other people to banish me to a fate of watching *Spider-Man / Drumline* on loop (even though I loved it and *will* write that crossover one day).

Now, I don't mean to shock you, but Julian and I didn't last. This breakup wasn't as dramatic as my previous one, and it was mostly my decision. You see, shortly after we began dating, Julian ran from a fight that he and some boys got into with kids from a rival charter school in the area. That was enough for me to call things off. You. Don't. Run. Away. From. A. Fight. Philadelphia High School Laws* state that you must leave your boyfriend if this happens, so I did. But still, the short-lived relationship really helped me sink into my new life at CHAD and get to know a lot of different people. Rebuilding my social network helped me leave the past behind and got me excited about the present again.

About three months into my friendship with Tiara, she asked me for a favor. Well, she didn't really ask me—it was understood that she needed my help. I was walking from design class to design class (yes, I had two design classes—remember, art school kids) when Tiara sidled up to me.

"So, some girls are messing with my little cousin at Uni," she said in a matter-of-fact tone. Uni was short for University High School, a public high school in West Philly. I knew Tiara's statement was not-so-sly code for "This is a friendship test. I might

---

* Philadelphia High School Laws also say that you must be loud on the train and that TastyKakes count as breakfast.

have to get into a fight for my family. Are you going to back me up in my time of need?"

I had to go to the fight because it was Philadelphia High School Law, and I already knew the harsh effects of the system. I mean, I lost a boyfriend to it! No way I was backing down.

"I got you," I told Tiara. The heartache from going through a friendship breakup still pulsed within me, and I wasn't about to mess another one up. I was keeping this group of friends by any means necessary. Shout-out to Malcolm X.

Tiara explained to me that her little cousin was having a disagreement with a girl at her high school and the two of them were planning on "exchanging words" at the end of the day. Tiara was one of those people who had a ton of family members who made up her life outside of school. She loved her little cousins so much and talked about them all the damn time, so I felt like I knew them and that they were my cousins, too. In short, everyone who met Tiara knew you don't mess with her family. You just don't.

I can't lie—I was a little nervous about going to throw hands. At that point in my life, my main experience with physical fighting was a scuffle I got into with my classmate Chels in the seventh grade.

Chels was one of those girls who was tall, statuesque, cute, and yet still awkward. By the time we were in the seventh grade, Chels had developed a shape that any grown woman would die for, but she carried it like she was still learning about tampons. She had a crush on our math teacher, Mr. Riscavage. Mr. Riscavage was young, with floppy hair and a chill-older-brother, cool-dude vibe. You know those teachers who had inside jokes with the students and sat on top of his desk? Mr. Riscavage was one of those. Chels looovvveeeddd his *Blue's Clues*–looking ass. Even though Mr. Riscavage wasn't my type, I still enjoyed his laid-back approach to teaching us the order of operations.

The next details are a bit fuzzy because I did a lot of molly after college, but I must've done something that annoyed Chels. Something like pointing out that liking a teacher was weird. What I do remember is her not liking it too much.

Moments later we were in each other's faces, chests puffed, nostrils flared. It was your typical middle school brawl between two girls who are ultimately Goody Two-shoes: there was a lot of shoving and winding up, but little else, mostly because 1) Mr. Riscavage split us up (I'm sure Chels didn't hate that) and 2) neither of us actually knew how to fight.

Would I say that my experience with Chels prepared me for what was going down with Tiara's cousin's bullies? No. But would I say that I was ready to cut a bitch to prove my friendship to Tiara? Hell yeah.

By the end of the school day, Tiara "recruited" Brittny and Tanae to come too. Both Brittny and Tanae are good to have on your side for a fight. Brittny, despite all her sweetness, was always quick to let people know she wasn't to be played with. Tanae, the mature one, could talk circles around anyone — make them feel bad with words, bound to drop some lines like "Maybe if you weren't so ugly, you would care about getting your face messed up." I'm not too bad to have around either; I'm small, but I have direct access to ankles and knees. The four of us shaped up to be a fairly decent crew: The High School Fight Avengers. Four Black Widows.

At the end of that school day, we made our way to the Gallery, but we skipped Chick-fil-A and got on the train headed toward Uni instead. When we neared the stop, Tiara pulled out a single-edge razor blade and slipped it into her hair.

"Shit," I immediately let out.

"What is it?" Tiara asked.

"I don't have a razor."

"Maybe we can find one at a corner store," Tanae offered.

The four of us got off the train and walked to the first corner store we saw. We casually entered, trying to exude the chill attitude of a group of teenage girls who weren't about to physically assault another group of teenage girls.

I browsed the aisles, looking for sharp objects. Pens, too messy. A wooden kebab stick, too useless. Ah, a baby blue eyebrow razor, perfect! I made my purchase and slipped the razor into the waistband of my uniform.* Tan khakis and a blue polo were not my ideal street-fight outfit, but I didn't have time to change into something more aggressive.

During the walk over, we didn't even really talk about the fight; we exchanged stories from our day, pointed out cute outfits in store windows, and tried to make each other laugh. The energy was relaxed and light, almost as if we were running errands. I've said it before and I'll say it again: there's nothing tougher than a bunch of teenage girls from Philly.

When we showed up to the parking lot, Tiara's cousin in-

---

* To this day, I still have literal nightmares about that school uniform, usually that I can't find it before an important event.

formed us that the other girls were already there. Sure enough, there was a group of approximately five girls, standing under the severe architecture of their high school.

Endorphins coursed through my veins as I prepared to tear those girls apart. I gave them my best mean mug—which, at that age with my face, probably looked more cartoonish than intimidating. Before my wrath could build any further, a girl popped Brittny in the chest. Landed a juicy one square on Brittny's boob. It was *on* . . . and all of a sudden, it wasn't. The "fight" had barely begun but quickly broke up when Tiara yelled at the girls to just leave her cousin alone. That was it. Somehow, the words were enough. We were done. We were out.

Even with razors on our person, when it came down to it, Tiara, Brittny, Tanae, and I were not fighters. We were just a group of pipsqueaks studying Frida Kahlo trying to look tough in front of another group of pipsqueaks. I take back my previous statement: there are probably lots of things tougher than a bunch of teenage girls from Philly. For example, a bunch of teenage girls from Philly who don't go to art school.

If you were hoping to hear a story of the time I cut a bitch with an eyebrow razor, I'm sorry to disappoint. I didn't even have time to reach into my waistband to pull out the "weapon." Yet, this day has latched itself onto my memory because it was the moment that permanently bound the four of us as friends. From that day on, I knew nothing would penetrate our friendship. Fake-razor fighting is the type of shit that sticks with you forever.

As I float further into my career and an increasing number of strangers recognize my face, the friends I made fifteen years ago have become more important to me than ever before. Learning at a young age what can happen when friendship is suddenly stripped away made me realize what a privilege it is to have good friends in your corner, especially ones that have known you for a long time and who have seen you both struggle and succeed. These are the girls that will always have my back, through thick and thin. Though we may not talk all of the time, it is an absolute fucking privilege to have friends who have known me for over half my life. Most of my friendships are old enough to drive.

I can't lie. It sometimes bothers me when I see people spending more time with the friends they've never met before in their screens than with their friends they know from real life. Social media, more specifically Facebook, has changed the value of the word "friend." It's now assigned to people left and right, to anyone who types your name into a search box and makes a request to you. There's no effort in that, no nuance. And it's made us lazier in our real-life friendships, which deserve that nuance.

I get why it's easier to pick up a phone and stare at it, instead of picking up a phone and calling an old friend. I get why it's easier to feel closer to someone over Twitter who has shared interests than your old friend who now has a baby while you're still trying to figure out how to take care of the fungus on your big toe. We're buried under alerts and updates, and it's somewhat soothing to have minutes and hours melt away inside a screen. Even our strongest friendships can start to devolve to only comments and likes. I'm guilty of leaving a heart emoji under a picture, instead of calling my friend to tell her, "I loved that pic of your nails, boo. How are you, how's your family?" But I'm trying to be more conscious of that.

I probably sound like a cranky old person right now, but I just care about genuine connection, because it has given me so much. How often do you physically engage with what your friends are going through? Does a comment fill the same space as a call? Does a like replace a lunch? If you're lucky enough to have multiple close friends, even if they aren't lifelong ones, what are you doing to show that you value those people? That you want to maintain the relationship? What more can you do besides sending a meme, or an emoji reaction? Sure, social media can bring us together, but it will not always foster those connections that can get us to grow together.

I often see people invest more energy into their jobs, or partners, or hair, than the friends who were with them before those jobs, partners, and hair. My fifteen- and twenty-year friendships have taken *work*. They take heart-to-hearts, wine, and time. It's worth it, though, because these friendships have been critical to my success. I've learned that it's necessary to cherish and respect the people who choose to stand by my side. These are the same friends who will keep me grounded when my head gets stuck in the clouds. It's a lesson that I hold dear: make sure to honor your chosen family. You'll be surprised how much you'll need them later in life.

It's been about fifteen years since I met Tiara, Tanae, and Brittny. My friendship with each of them has evolved and changed shape over time, but I try to keep in touch. Even though our lives have grown in different directions, I still reach out to Tiara when I'm home. It's gotten harder. She's religious now, and a mom. I'm not either of those things. She's settled down in a way I have yet to do. But, don't get it twisted: I'd still show up to a parking lot if she told me she was going to a fight —razor in slacks. Without a doubt.

5

Understanding Mom

A s of writing this, I just got engaged two days ago. My boyfriend waited until I was wearing my favorite dress — my gray T-shirt for washing dishes — and took me to my favorite place in the world: our couch. Then he dropped down to one knee and pulled a little black box out of nowhere. Inside the box was our sparkling future together. Even though I knew it was coming, I still yelped and screamed like people in the movies. The rest is a blur of emotions and smiles. There was champagne?

Excited beyond all measure, I knew I had to tell my mom immediately. She had been wondering when we'd get engaged since she first heard me gush about him three years earlier. I wiped my happy tears away and decided to FaceTime so she could gawk.

"Hey," my mom answered, clearly in the middle of watching the local news in her homey living room. The camera only showed her face from the nose up, as it usually does until she readjusts the frame. I held up my hand to reveal the ring and squealed "I'm engaged!"

My mom yelped twice while smiling, before leaning closer to the camera and exclaiming, "My ring didn't look like that!" I laughed and reminded her that she and my dad were in a very different place financially when they got engaged. She followed with "He did a great job! But where are your eyebrows? Did you cry them off? This is a big day, put some eyebrows on." I mean, she wasn't wrong. I had no makeup on, but it was so true to form that my lack of makeup became my mom's main focus. That's my mom. I wouldn't have Norma Jean Brunson any other way.

My mom and I chat on the phone almost every day. Our conversations range from reasons why the president (at the time) is an idiot to whether or not she thinks my period is normal to what rerun of *The King of Queens* she just watched. We're all over the place, but most importantly: we talk. This wasn't always the case. When I was in college, my mom and I used to fight . . . a lot. The worst one of which all started because of a pair of earrings.

The hoops were $2.99. Big. Fake gold (obviously). Flashy as hell. And for the cost of two and a half Snickers bars, they were my new prized possession. I had been on the hunt for a new pair after my old reliable pair broke, and, being a broke college student myself, my replacement hunt was limited to the corner stores/beauty shops scattered throughout Philly.

I used to love wandering into those stores after class because they had everything you could ever want: fake eyelashes, scratchers, Herr's, magazines, mouthwash, airplane-sized bottles of Captain Morgan, candy, sandwiches. These stores are dubbed "poppy stores" when owned by Hispanics or Asians and selling food in the back, and "the beauty supply" when owned by Blacks or Asians and selling mainly hair and jewelry. Before taking the hoops to the cashier, I examined them for any scratches or paint chips—always a possibility when your jewelry costs less than a hoagie.

They passed the test, so I headed to check out. "Cutetwoninetynine," the cashier said like it was all one word. It felt pricey for my bank account at the time, but worth it in the grand scheme of looking good. I had been wearing my hair super straight those days, and thought the hoops would be a nice addition to my face. I didn't love wearing makeup outside of eyeliner and lip gloss, and I tended to dress in oversize clothes and hats, so hoops seemed like an easy way to assert my femininity.

The thing I love about hoops is that no matter how I dressed or what new nerd thing I was into, they always asserted my hood girl status. They said, "I'm from West Philly, and I'm cute and I'm proud." Hoops became even more of a trait of being a hood girl after Lauren London donned them as New New in *ATL*. Everyone wanted to be New New, even me. Hoops are and always will be a hood girl staple, no matter what kind of hood girl you are. And being a hood girl will always be the most stylish.

Before I even paid for my earrings, I already knew they were going to be a problem at home. My mom would definitely have something to say about them—"too big, too flashy, too hoochie." I threw my gold-colored silver into my messenger bag (I was committing to 2008 hard) and headed back to campus for my advertising and public relations class.

Since starting classes at Temple University, my relationship with my mom had grown super rocky. We were constantly getting into it in a way that we hadn't when I was in high school. It felt like every move I made was the wrong one in my mom's eyes, which felt even more absurd because I was a parent-pleasing Goody Two-shoes; I was excelling at school, spent my free time teaching dance to little kids, and didn't mess with anything that'd get me into trouble. I was a good kid. I hadn't even started with weed yet, and wouldn't try molly for another two years! Yet my mom seemed to always find a way to cut me down.

I even chose Temple as a way to please my parents. I wanted to look at schools out of state, but my parents wanted me to stay closer to home (read: live under the same roof). Attending Temple meant they could keep an eye on me.

Even though I was a little disappointed I wasn't going away for college like some friends, Temple's School of Communications felt like a good fit because it could provide stability and a creative outlet. Even though I really wanted to study acting, I knew my mom wouldn't go for it. I figured communications was close enough to entertainment and was a degree my parents could get behind.

As senior year of high school was coming to an end, and all the conversations shifted to the future, I decided to tell my parents my plans for school.

"So, I decided what I'll major in," I said one night during dinner.

"Oh yeah?" my mom responded.

"Yeah, communications."

"Quinta, why not education . . . or even nursing?" Her tone bludgeoned me.

"This is what I want to do. I think it would be good. There are different studies within the school. Like advertising!"

"Okay, well. You can always switch to education later. That's more stable. I don't even know what communications means."

"It's like TV, and everything behind media and stuff," I said, playing in my greens.

"Ugh," my mom groaned.

My mom has always been a no-nonsense person, so this wasn't entirely unexpected. But still, it knocked my confidence when she didn't support the things I wanted to do. I admired my parents and wanted them to be proud of me, so seeing disapproval wash over my mom's face as I discussed my future plans was tough to get out of my head.

"You'd make such a good teacher," she continued. "And it's a great way to give back to the community . . . be a good servant to God!" She loves bringing God into work.

My entire life, my mom would drop little comments like these, constantly trying to inch me toward a career in education —and every time, it would only make me recoil harder. Even though I was a good student and enjoyed being a dance teacher, I wasn't interested in becoming an educator.

"Well, I don't want to be a teacher," I told my mom, as I reached for seconds, "so I'm not going to be one." Even though I always attempted to be on my best behavior around my mom, I never really did a good job of holding my tongue. It drove her mad. "Communications will diversify my job opportunities, and allow me to make cool things and entertain people. Don't you want me making money off my interests?"

"The country needs more teachers, especially Black ones," my mom responded, clearly unimpressed with my goals.

"Well, it's too late. I already decided," I told her as I finished my meal.

"Okay, fine," my mom sighed, crossing her arms. "Well, you can always change it. Remember, we're paying for this."

Her constant suggestions to dedicate my life to educating the youth of America made me even more nervous to admit my secret goal, which was becoming a writer/actress/comedian. So, I didn't. Instead, I just pushed that goal into the recesses of my brain—a "wouldn't that be nice" kind of thing.

I could understand why my mom wanted me to be a teacher. Teaching is a good job. My mother could personally attest to its stability and benefits. Plus, the path to teaching is level, attainable, tidy. Comedy's path is notoriously uneven, filled with potholes and all sorts of other opportunities to slip and fall. A full-time comedy job felt farfetched for me, so I knew it was better not to even bring it up. But still, I was determined to at least head in that direction. Ever since getting my whole family to crack up at my Martin impressions at four years old, I kept searching for ways to make people laugh. From learning all the lines of *The Fresh Prince of Bel-Air* episodes to shooting fake news reports on my mom's laptop, I knew I had something that could be explored, some type of yearning to engage in comedic storytelling.

I didn't want to tell her in that moment, but it was also *kind of* her fault that I wanted to pursue a creative career instead of a more practical one. After all, she was the one who enrolled me in CHAD, as a means to awaken the artistic impulses within me. And I was even being sensible about it. I didn't know anyone who had actually made a successful career out of being an artist alone, hence why I centered my sights on communications, and more specifically: advertising.*

It was a career path that was fresh in my brain after finishing an enormous project my senior year at CHAD, where I designed a multifaceted ad campaign for the school. I shot and edited my own commercials, came up with a slogan, designed a print campaign — the works. I centered my campaign around a little wooden mannequin artist guy and gave him a sign that said "Imagine That." Seeing the words "Imagine That" flash in front of my face every day for months made me do just that: imagine a life where I could get paid for my creativity.

After seeing my mom's lackluster reaction to my enormous life decision, I began to mentally prepare for four years of passive-aggressive (straight-up aggressive) commentary from her.

Through the years, my mom was never shy to state her opinion: "You should not wear that spaghetti-strap tank top out in public! It's showing far too much skin." But when I was younger, I was able to ignore it. "Okay, got it! Bye, Mom!" I'd yell back at her. She'd inevitably respond, "Don't get smart!" which would get me to shut up. "Don't get smart" in Norma Jean Brunson language means if you say one more word, you could get smacked.

---

* I have this theory that there are a lot of aspiring writers and comedians who settle for jobs in the advertising industry. No shade toward advertisers, y'all probably make a lot more money and have better health insurance than comedians. But it's just my theory.

But our years of disagreements went from a grumble to a scream my freshman year of college. What started off with the quiet disapproval of my major escalated into picking apart every little thing about me. One morning, I came down wearing black leggings and a tight black T-shirt.

"Why are you dressed like that?" my mom asked, sensing that I was up to something.

"Oh, I'm gonna audition for the step team today," I explained.

"Quinta, no, come on, that's not . . . that's not a good use of your time. And you shouldn't be walking around in tights."

What. The. Fuck. I couldn't believe it. This is the same

That's my mom to the right. Yes, I know. Crazy, right?
Even I did a double take.

woman who found refuge in the world of dance, who enrolled me in dance before I was even old enough to start school, who drove me to and from lessons and recitals and events. The same woman who demanded I keep up with all sorts of extracurriculars because staying busy and staying educated meant I could make it out of the trenches of Philly. The same woman who made sure that I was never part of the status quo, that I was always reaching beyond my peers. The same woman who bought me my first pair of leggings! All of a sudden she didn't want me doing dance anymore? It made zero earthly sense.

"Well, I think it is." I grabbed my bag and walked out the door knowing I had just started a war. Defying my mom *openly* was new territory.

When I was in high school, it was easy for my mom to oversee most, if not all, of my activities. No school dances. No hanging out with people who weren't Jehovah's Witnesses (the religion I was raised in). No staying out late. All I heard was no. No. No. It was hard to push against her restrictions because I still felt like a child. But like most children, as soon as I turned eighteen, I began to question the boundaries placed upon me.

The more I branched out in my extracurriculars, the more I liked what I saw. When I got to Temple, I auditioned for the step team to preserve my passion for dance and teamwork. I saw step as an opportunity to expand my boundaries in a constructive and healthy way—just like my mom had always taught me.

I made the team, by the way. I joined the Ladies of Excellence and then never talked about step with my mom ever again. That was the beginning of me whittling away at the details I shared with my parents. Slowly but surely, I began to lead a sort of double life: at-home Quinta and at-school Quinta. It was clear that the only way I could seek fulfillment was to split in half. It was a matter of preserving myself while also preserving the peace in my family. When I had practice for my dance squad, I'd just tell my parents I'd be staying on campus late to study. They never questioned it. Eventually, I started staying at friends' dorms overnight, telling my parents it was easier to just stay on campus to be on time for my 8 a.m. classes. Really, I was just staying up late and hanging with my friend Lauren watching *Tim and Eric*.

When I joined the school's improv team, Fowl Play,* I didn't even tell my mom. But she began to notice that I'd be gone for hours at a time during the weekends, and I couldn't use class as a cover for my absences.

"Excuse me. Where are you off to?" she asked me one Saturday when I was heading out the door to improv practice at my friend Scott's house. I was wearing a green jersey I got from the thrift store, some black skinny shorts, Converse, and a weird cloth round-brim hat (horrible outfit today, cute for college back then). On this specific day, I decided to add some shimmer to the shine: my new, big, flashy $2.99 gold hoops.

"I'm going to a friend's spot," I told her. I could tell my mom's suspicions were instantly raised. Scott lived in a house on Temple's campus with some other white nerd roommates.

---

* Our school mascot was an owl, so we were contractually obligated to name the team using a bad bird pun.

They listened to Ray Lamontagne, their definition of "raging" on Saturday night was doing karaoke with other theater kids, and they were friends with the first genderqueer person I'd ever met. Big at the time. They were harmless.

"At this hour?"

"Yup."

"For what?"

"To hang out."

"Hm." Sometimes judgment made through silence is even worse than getting chewed out. A quiet disappointment is hard to push up against, but at this point I'd learned how to let it roll off my back.

"Okay, bye, Mom." I headed toward the door.

"Well, let me drive you. I don't want you taking the train at night."

"He's right off the El," I told her. Oops. *He.* I immediately realized my mistake and so did my mom.

"He? You're hanging out with a boy? At night?"

"It's not like that. And it's not night, it's five o'clock." I stepped closer to the door. My mom, knowing that I was ultimately going to do what I wanted, reached for her car keys.

"I'll drive you," she insisted again. I sighed and relented.

In the car, my mom's disapproval began to get a little more intense. "I can't believe I'm taking you to a boy's house. You shouldn't be spending time with him at night without reason."

Scott was a cute little muffin who was not only hilarious and trustworthy, but also a gay man. I mean, I didn't know it yet and he wasn't out, but he surely gave off that "just a good friend because anything more would be gross" energy. So, it wasn't like I'd accidentally get pregnant . . . let alone at improv practice, arguably the least sexy environment on earth.

I ignored my mom and set my sights out the window instead, appreciating the view of all the people heading out to restaurants, bars, and movie theaters. People living their life, without their mom literally in the driver's seat.

"Quinta, are you paying attention?"

"Yup."

As the last child, I definitely gave my mom a run for her money when it came to my constant need for defiance. I know my sisters didn't give my mom as much grief as I did. Kiyana and Jia both got respectable, stable jobs that kept both sisters close to home. My brothers, well, they could do no wrong in my mom's eyes, even though they did do a lot of wrong. My mom never seemed that bothered by their complete disregard for rules. That's just how it goes sometimes with boy-versus-girl upbringings; the boys get dismissed for "just being boys," and the girls, well, they get put on the stand over and over again. And man, did I grate against that. My poor mom, she probably thought she'd gotten a handle on the whole "raising a kid" thing, and then here I come, unexpectedly, growing into her most outright difficult daughter. What a treat.

My mom pulled up to Scott's apartment and stared at the side of my face. I could feel her eyes searching for something to criticize. My eyeliner? Or maybe she didn't like the freshly dyed red streaks in my hair? Whatever it was, I didn't want to wait to find out.

"Thanks for the ride, Mom." I put my hand on the door handle.

"You should take off those earrings. They're too big. It's really unladylike, Quinta."

I let go of the handle and refocused my glare on my mom. As always, her face was perfectly done up in Mary Kay. Her hair looked the same way it did every single day of my life . . . pretty and in a ponytail. She pursed her lips together and gave me a stern look that I was all too used to. My mom was a woman of order and routine. Of course she was criticizing my innocent, cheap-ass earrings; the exact same earrings that cashier said were "Cutetwoninetynine." Why was a stranger giving me more compliments than my own mother? I was fed up with all of it: my mom monitoring my femininity, questioning my hobbies, and attempting to control every aspect of my life. I snapped.

"Are you seriously talking about my earrings right now? Mom, you know me. You know I'm a good kid. You have to trust the person you made. Just because I don't dress in the way you want doesn't mean I'm a whore . . . or whatever you think of me. You have been criticizing every single thing about me lately. Picking apart my hair, my clothes, my interests . . ."

Once I got going, I couldn't stop. "Why did you always make me do so much as a kid if you didn't want me doing anything as an adult? I just don't get it. Why did you instill in me all of these tools if you don't want me to use them?" I was fuming. Yes, my mom and I would snap at each other, but I'd never unleashed on her the way I was doing just then.

My mom absorbed my words for a moment before saying, "It's because I don't want you to get lost to the world, Quinta!"

"I don't even know what that means!" I spat. I'd heard versions of this my whole life, and it always made zero sense to me.

We sat there in silence for a second. It was like all the air had been taken out of the car and replaced with fuel. One wrong breath and we would both blow.

"It means that I don't want to lose you to worldly people!"

"Worldly people, give me a break!" I groaned. "Worldly people" is a Jehovah's Witness term for people who were not of the faith. I had heard it a lot as a kid, and honestly? Worldly people sounded fucking cool to me. They got to do stuff!

Right as I was winding up a clapback, I saw something in my mother's eyes that I hadn't seen before . . . tears. She blinked and they escaped her eyelashes, falling to her cheeks before she quickly wiped them away. It was too late. I saw them.

I sat in the discomfort, not really knowing what to do. I wasn't sure if I should hug my mom, fight more, or pretend not to notice that she was crying. I don't think I had ever really seen her cry. Maybe at a funeral once, but even those were controlled tears, reserved for a specific event where crying was acceptable. This was the first time I saw her cry from frustration. And the frustration . . . was me.

"Just go, Quinta," my mom said, giving up and taking the car out of park.

And so, I left. I heard the car pull away, but I didn't look back, maybe because I didn't want to see whether or not my mom began to cry harder. But still. All those tears over earrings?

I was confused . . . and then annoyed. It all felt unnecessary. I was doing well and working hard. Why couldn't my mom see that?

At Scott's door, I took a deep breath and shook off the fight. I got ready to be funny. I became an expert at leaving whatever I was going through personally at the door. With my double life, I learned to leave the "shit" me at home. I only brought the fun me to school, step, improv practice. I wanted to be like the other kids, seemingly carefree.

Most people who knew me then (and honestly, many who know me now) don't know that my family is very religious or that my parents were super strict with me. That's because I got very good at turning off any energy that I needed to in order to exist more freely in the world. In my desire to relate to everyone around me at all times, I had to learn how to compartmentalize the things that made me different.

That day at practice, no one knew about the scene that unfolded minutes before. They got the same Quinta they were used to, one that was full of energy, goofy, and 100 percent present. Spending a couple of hours laughing lifted my spirits.

When I came home from improv practice that night, my mom was watching TV in the living room. Exhausted from "Yes, and-ing" all evening, I wordlessly headed toward the stairs.

"Good night, Quinta," my mom said.

"Good night, Mom."

This simple exchange was our way of saying "I love you and I always love you even when you're pissing me off." The fight ended as quickly as it had started.

From that day on, my mom thought twice before commenting on my appearance and bringing up her concerns with my behavior. There was no way she was going to stop — she's still Norma Jean — but I could tell something happened during that blowout fight, so she'd tread carefully before diving in. I continued making decisions for myself, widening those boundaries. Eventually, I widened them so much that I eventually fell all the way across the country into Los Angeles when I was twenty-three.

As years went by, the world that used to feel so expansive, exciting, and desirable began to get smaller, more hectic, and, at times, heartbreaking. I found myself seeking out comfort in people and things I knew before the world became too hard, and as a result, my connection with my family started to grow. As I got closer to my mother's age when she had already had two kids — twenty-four — my perception of everything changed.

A lot of young people, myself included, have a view of themselves as indestructible. They think that they can't be touched and that they'll live forever. In a way, it's good to have this kind of thinking when you're just starting out in the real world so that you can fearlessly try everything and figure out your life. But then, as you start to lose more people in your life, you begin to realize that you're not impenetrable — you're simply human. This realization forces your center to shift from inside yourself to outside yourself.

Living so far away from my family, and having weekly, if not daily, conversations with my parents and siblings, made me cherish them in ways I hadn't before. It also made me think about things from my mom's perspective more often. I always knew my mom had a lot of hardships in her life, but I never really thought of them in relation to her parenting decisions. When I was still living at home, I could only see things from my point of view, and at the time, those decisions seemed stifling. But once I was out in the world, I began to see them the way my mom might have.

When my mom was young, she lost two of her siblings to drugs and alcohol. Her one brother was a good man—he did his best, but he got depressed and turned to the easiest way to manage that depression. He self-medicated to death. She lost her other sibling to the same thing, just a different drug. They were both younger than her, leaving just her and her older brother.

As her child, I only heard my mom bring up her siblings once, maybe twice. My mom is a woman who deals with her emotions on her own, so she never told me too many details aside from "They were worldly." That's about all I knew then and all I know now. I didn't really think about how the loss of her siblings affected her as a person and as a mother, because she kept it so close to her chest. I'm assuming she didn't want to indulge in the trauma of her past. Even writing about it now puts a shiver down my spine. Two siblings gone. I don't know how she survived.

Actually, I do know how she survived: she joined a strong religion with many rules. She built her life around these rules, and figured that as long as she was following them and making her kids follow them, too, she wouldn't lose any more family members to the dangers of society at large. Then I came along and began pushing back against those rules, getting farther and farther from her reach. It must've scared her.

Years later, I was out for drinks with the man who would eventually be my fiancé. We were having your typical first-date conversation: favorite color, best cookie, hopes, dreams, fears.

"You have any siblings?" he asked.

"Yup, two brothers and two sisters," I told him after taking a sip of red wine.

"You guys close?" he followed.

"Beyond close. They're everything. I don't know what I'd do if anything happened to them." Just like that, a phantom memory popped into my head. *Losing siblings.* My mom lost two of her siblings. It just hit me smack-dab in the forehead. *I don't want you to get lost to the world, Quinta.*

The thing is, my mom and I are alike in many ways. She herself was a dancer, and a dreamer who wanted to push back against the constraints life had assigned her. My mom channeled her energy into creativity and art, constantly looking for ways to improve herself and the world around her. From her, I learned resilience and patience. She sought to fight for her people, joining various political groups and societies, and she knew that education was key to that. I am a lot of who my mom was when she was younger, and that's why we were always fighting. When my mom saw that I was no longer following the path she'd paved for me, she felt like she was losing me. She could no longer enforce the very rules that she thought would protect me from the threats of the world. All this time I thought she was trying to smother me with her intentions, but in reality, she was just trying to hold me to her chest, where I'd be safest.

Thinking about everything the world had taken from my mom and how she didn't want it to take me too made my heart break for her. She didn't cry in the car because I was disobeying her—she cried because she was scared I was going to follow in the footsteps of her siblings.

The morning after my date, I woke up early to call my mom.

"Hi, Mom," I greeted her.

"Hey, Quinta. What's going on with you?"

"Oh, nothing, I just wanted to call and say I love you."

"Aw, well, I love you too. How's work going?"

Although my mom spent years trying to get me to walk a different path than comedy, she eventually came around to the fact that I'd dedicated myself to performing. I was happy to tell her that the new job was stable—I'd have a decent biweekly paycheck for doing something I liked. "Well, that's good! And what's it called again? FeedBuzz?" She made me smile.

That day in the car before improv practice, my mom showed me that she was human—I just hadn't realized it at the time. But the important thing is that I did eventually realize it. Empathizing with my mom allows me to look back and see the why behind a lot of her actions. Even though the disconnect was an odd and painful reality to grow up with, I eventually learned her intentions were all love. It was never about the hoop earrings—it was about protecting her baby. And you can't fault a mother for that.

At some point in every young adult's life, it's crucial to have this breakthrough, to finally see your parents as people instead of robots put on this earth to tell you what to do. They had a life before you, and they've learned things from it. They're healing from things, too. Seeing that your parents are human beings who don't always know the right answers and who can make mistakes may be difficult, but it will also explain a lot of confusion and unlock resentment that may be floating around in your soul. Once that resentment is unlocked, you'll be able to move forward in this world with increasing amounts of strength, grace, and empathy for those who came before you. Imagine that.

6

Three Great Loves

....

According to the movie *A Bronx Tale*, you get three great loves in your life. Granted, Sunny said, "you're only allowed three great women in your lifetime," but I turned that into what I needed to hear—three great loves. And, well, I've already had all three of mine.

The impact these loves had on me is incomparable. I've grown because of them. I've gained perspective because of them. I even discovered Bob Marley thanks to (one of) them. They weren't perfect, my great loves. In fact, one was quite terrible. But they were all defining.

My first great love was Malik Colder. A fake name he'd find very funny if he were to read this.

Malik and I met in tenth grade. I had just transferred to CHAD and I was the hot new girl. Like I've mentioned, when you transfer to a new high school and you're any type of cute at all, you instantly become a ten to the overly hormonal boys at school. Malik had his eye on me from day one, but decided to date other short girls until I was available (remember, I had that punk boyfriend first). Once I was single, he made it a point to tell me he liked me, but I wasn't really into him. Malik was popular, and that wasn't my type. My type was always the third off the bench. Like, with the Backstreet Boys, it was never Nick Carter, it was Brian. With B2K, it wasn't Omarion or even Lil' Fizz, it was J-Boog.

All the girls in school were into Malik because he was charming, attractive, and imaginative. He was an aspiring rapper— like most creative boys in Philly—and he was annoyingly extra. He even started his own power drink line in high school called CORE Drink, an offshoot of his record label, CORE Entertainment, or CORE ENT. for short. Yup. The "secret ingredients" in the drinks were "fruits and vegetables." He was so ambitious, and it was so corny to me.

Malik used to come to the lunch table and try to sell his "power drink" as a way to promote his "music label."

"CORE Drink, y'all! It's the future. You gotta drink like a winner to be one!"

Barf. He tried to sell it everywhere. One time, we were reading *To Kill a Mockingbird* in English class and I felt a tap on my shoulder. It was Malik, silently demonstrating the benefits of his drink—taking a big gulp, flexing his muscles, and pointing to the drink with eyebrows raised. I told you: corny. But at this point, I at least found him funny.

Despite his corniness and popularity, I became friends with Malik. We were both extremely silly people, and our mutual ridiculousness helped nurture the other's humor. We were about the only two people at the whole school who were obsessed with goofy comedy movies like *Napoleon Dynamite, Anchorman,* and *Dodgeball.*

As we grew closer, Malik vied hard for my love. I wasn't interested. I had my own priorities.

Fifteen-Year-Old Quinta's Priorities

1. Watching *Degrassi*
2. Discussing *Degrassi* in TheN.com chat rooms
3. Dance and cheer
4. Flirting with boys at camp
5. Flirting with boys at Kingdom Hall (where Jehovah's Witnesses worship)
6. Figuring out how to make anyone who wasn't Malik my boyfriend, especially Craig from *Degrassi*

None of my many distractions stopped Malik from pursuing me. After a year of talking big game, Malik began to get creative with how he professed his love. For example, this one time, he posted a photo of me giving him an irritated stare to Facebook and captioned it with "My future wife." I was annoyed by his persistence, but I cut him some slack because he had become one of my closest friends.

I still had Malik in the "close friend" pocket when prom time rolled around. Like most girls, I really wanted to go, but with parents as strict as mine, I knew I had to be strategic about it. Most other Jehovah's Witnesses didn't go to prom — it was considered unnecessary recreation. But once I found out I was nominated for prom queen, I decided I was going to go if it was the last thing I did on this earth. How can you be nominated for the

Oscars of high school and not go?! At first, I thought I should go alone, but I didn't want to be the outcast without a date to prom. Plus, I was cute, so I felt I should have a date just by default. I knew Malik would go with me in a heartbeat, but not only did I still find him a little wack, I knew my parents would never approve because he wasn't part of the faith. I needed to find a perfect date so that my parents couldn't say no . . . enter Afan.

All the girls loved Afan because he was attractive, sexually active, and had a handsome dad. There's something about a guy with a good-looking dad that just . . . does something to a girl. Anywho, Afan and all his sexually active energy was not my type at all, but his hot father was a Jehovah's Witness, so I knew I had better odds of my parents allowing me to go, even though Afan was very much not a Jehovah's Witness. Quite the opposite. This was the kid who taught the rest of us the names of sex positions.

Once I landed on my genius plan, I immediately went to Afan to ask him if he was going with anyone yet. He said no, and so I laid out my case for why he should go with me. I told him 1) I was popular, 2) he was popular, 3) I needed him as my JW angel, and 4) that it all made sense, so he should just do it. He was convinced, and was excited; he didn't want to go through the trouble of asking anyone anyway. What a prince.

When it came time to broach the subject with my parents, I made sure they were in a good mood first. I picked Sunday night after we came back from the Hall, when they were feeling refreshed and relaxed.

"So, I got asked to prom the other day." I framed it like I was asked to create the illusion of demand.

"Oh, you did?" my dad responded, immediately smelling my eagerness.

"Yeah, this nice Christian boy asked me, but I said I'd have to make sure it was okay with you. He's a Jehovah's Witness." Whole lie.

"Bad things happen at prom," my mother said sternly.

"Well, that's why I wanted to go with Afan, since he is as good a Christian as they come." Whole-ass lie. I once heard Afan say, "I'll get any STD as long as I can take a pill for it" in health class.

"Please, can I go? This is my last chance to go to a high school dance. I promise I'll be home early." My dad gave my mom a look, one of those "Let the girl have her fun / I'm not getting involved in this" looks that I so rarely got to see. Soon enough, I had my parents' approval. I couldn't believe I pulled that lie off! I was going to prom!

Next on my list was the exciting part—getting a dress. I knew *exactly* what I wanted. Beyoncé wore a beautiful baby blue dress in *Dreamgirls* that made her look like a glam mermaid. It was tight up and down her figure until right under the knee, where it billowed out like an upside-down flower. The dress was perfect. I wanted the exact same thing, but in mint green, my favorite color at the time. And I knew exactly who to go to: my uncle Brunsi.

My uncle Brunsi made all of the dresses for all of the girls' proms in our family. A fabulous gay man and retired seamstress, he happily made them for a low price (he didn't believe in doing anything for free, not even for family). I didn't care about having to pay for it; I was just happy that I would be part of

the family prom dress club! I brought him a photo of Beyoncé's blue dress from *Dreamgirls,* and a few months later I had a sparkly mint-green dress hanging in my closet. It looked nothing like the *Dreamgirls* dress, but I loved it all the same. He even made a matching jacket for Afan!

On prom night, my friends came to my house to see me off. Natasia, Phylicia, Cyerra, Najah, Rita, and Leslie were all older than me and had graduated. All of them were Jehovah's Witnesses, some of whom had finessed their way into prom and some of whom hadn't, but any one of us going was a win for the others. I was living the dream, and they had come to support me. They approved of my handsome date, Afan, when he arrived, giving me "oh, he's cute!" faces. Afan was checking them out until I had to nudge him to remind him to keep the act up of being a "nice boy" in front of my parents. He snapped back into upright good-guy shape.

My sister Jia had given me the best hair — a finger wave into a bun style that was as elegant as it was a hood classic. I loved it. I looked like I was in *B.A.P.S.* She checked my hair once more before I walked out of the door to Beanie Siegel's "Don't Stop." You see, in Philly, it is proper etiquette to have your friends and family send you off to a "walk out" song. You pick something that represents the mood of the night you want. "Don't Stop" may have meant a night full of fights and extreme gloating to some, but to me, it was elegance and prom night fanfare! Afan and I drove off to prom, confident we were about to have the night of our lives, just not with each other. The mission was complete!

I strutted into prom with a whole vibe, wearing my handmade *Dreamgirls* mint-green dress next to an attractive guy who probably had at least one STD. It was the perfect way to go out on my high school career. That night is a blur of dancing, reminiscing, and celebrating the definitive end of the teen experience.

Then, in the middle of us losing our minds to T Pain's "Buy U a Drank," the music cut out so that they could announce prom queen and king. I was standing in a group with my closest friends, sweaty from dancing, as one of our favorite teachers, Ms. Casanas, got on the mic with two small envelopes in hand.

"Your Charter High School of Architecture and Design prom king is . . ." She ripped open the envelope and smirked. "Malik Colder!"

Malik, who was standing nearby, laughed as we all pushed him toward the middle of the floor. He knew he had it in the bag. His whole high school career had basically been a campaign for prom king. Ms. Casanas placed a crown upon his head.

"And your prom queen is . . ." She opened the second envelope. "Quinta Brunson!!!"*

I couldn't believe it! Okay, actually, I could—I mean, I knew had a pretty good shot, but I would've been just as happy if Tiara or any of the other girls had gotten it. Still, I was excited. I went to the middle of the floor to get my crown, a cute accessory that looked pretty perfect with my dress. As we stood there smiling like dummies, Ms. Casanas nodded to the DJ. "Time for the king and queen dance!"

This part, I hadn't thought about: I was going to have to dance with Malik—my pal. In the years of our friendship, I definitely shoved him more often than hugged him. Dancing together would be a whole new (possibly awkward?) level.

---

* Can I just remind you that I won prom queen at an ART SCHOOL nick-named "CHAD." That's like being the coolest of the weirdos. I wouldn't have even gotten voted prom jester at a normal high school. Besides, it means nothing, young people reading this! I was once a queen and now I'm picking eye boogers and scooping up cat poop.

I went out to the middle of the dance floor with Malik, who quickly wrapped his arms around my waist.

"You've been waiting for this forever, haven't you?" I joked.

"Yup," he responded with a nod.

The next thing I knew, "Lost Without U" began playing on the speakers, and just like that, we were swaying back and forth in front of everyone. Despite the proximity of our bodies, we avoided looking in each other's eyes. And that's the moment it all shifted for me.

Something about the feeling of the night, being crowned queen, and the smooth pipes of predivorced Robin Thicke made me think, "This guy might not be so bad . . . and shit, he can dance." I could feel myself softening to him, playing back all the moments we had shared over our high school career together.

After prom was over, Malik texted me saying that he wanted to see me. I was curious, and still feeling a little something from that dance, so I told him he could stop by my house after Afan dropped me off. We'd have about fifteen minutes to talk before my parents would realize I was outside and yank me in, ending the prom night once and for all.

Malik got to my house about five minutes after Afan drove off. He hopped out of his car and stepped onto my porch, but before he could say anything, I said it first. "After giving it much thought," I told him, flirting with him officially for the first time, "I've decided that I like you back."

Malik busted out into a huge grin, and then he kissed me. It was a good kiss, filled with the innocence of young affection. When he left, I closed the door, pressed my back against it, took in a deep sigh, and slid down to the ground, just like in the movies. I was on cloud nine, produced by CORE ENT.

Our relationship began with an expiration date looming over our adolescent heads. Malik was going off to Columbia College in Chicago, while I was staying in Philly for Temple. We knew our time together was limited, but we didn't care. We were falling in love as if it was never going to end, because when you're seventeen, you don't think it will.

It was easy jumping into a whirlwind romance with Malik. We'd been close for so long that we had a head start on the kind of intimate knowledge that comes with being in love. While what we had felt epic, at the same time, our friendship made it effortless, too.

Our first date was a graduation movie night with friends. We went to see *Transformers,* which was the new summer blockbuster and blossoming franchise from Michael Bay. We. Loved. It. It quickly became one of our favorite movies, solidifying our shared interest in sci-fi action films and the fact that we both wanted Camaros when we were older. It was so fun to hang out and simply enjoy things I liked with a boy I loved. There was no need to front, or feel pressure to act a certain way.

Malik let me be silly in a way that no one ever had before. We loved cracking each other up with silly voices, jokes, and faces. We'd sit by the Schuylkill River for hours, and I'd double over in laughter as he gave stupid voices to the geese. He'd always name one of the geese Rodney and make it say things as if it were an old Black grandfather. "Ay, Cletus, where the hell did you get that bread! Share with a brotha." Rodney would waddle off and we'd yell, "Where ya going, Rodney? You know we don't

have any plans tonight. Come back to the Delawares, Rodney!"
It was so dumb and I fuckin' loved it. A goose named Rodney.
COMEDY!

Malik was also someone I could be hopeful with. He believed
that he was going to have a successful career in the music industry since the day I met him. The unapologetic ambition I previously found corny now allowed me to be unapologetic in my
own ambitions. He was the only person I could tell how much
I secretly wanted to do comedy for a living. It was a farfetched
dream for a little girl from West Philly, especially when most of
my friends were planning on becoming nurses or teachers. (My
mother's dreaaammmm!) Comedy felt like such an astronom-
ically different career to consider seriously, but I still nurtured
that hope. Even though all of my comedy heroes were white
guys at the time, I still wanted to be exactly like them. Which
was literally impossible. But whether or not it was realistic didn't
matter to Malik, because he believed in the impossible, too.

When our summer together finally came to an end, our love
for each other didn't. Malik left for Chicago, but we talked all
the time. We worked our class schedules out so that we always
had the same free time, and stayed up late Skyping so that we
both got in trouble for sleeping in class the next day. Though
we both had active social lives, it didn't stop us from keeping
in constant communication. S/O to text messaging, Facebook,
Twitter, and the final days of Myspace.

What mostly kept things moving, though, was the fact that I
snuck out to Chicago to visit Malik every chance I could. Now,
this was no easy feat: not only was I a broke college student, but
I was also living with my parents. I used to tell them I was stay-

ing over at a friend's dorm on campus and then would get on a plane without them knowing I was going to fly halfway across the country. I did this seven times, but my mom only knows about one, so keep this between us, reader.

When Malik came back to Philly for summer break after freshman year, our adventures grew in size. One day, when all of Philly was dealing with 102-degree devil's bootyhole heat, Malik and I heard that *Transformers 2* was filming in the city. *Transformers* had brought us together initially, and now that there was a part two, filming in our very city, we knew it was fate and that we had to go see if we could find the set.

We drove around for five hours, hunting around like we were Shane and Ryan on *BuzzFeed Unsolved* trying to find a ghost. It felt thrilling. He and I followed random tips from people claiming to have seen an Optimus Prime truck or a Megan Fox look-alike, and scoured all sorts of backdrop-worthy locations around Philly, hoping to stumble into filming. Nothing. We even followed people who looked like they might be Hollywood producers that actually turned out to be dentists on their casual day off.

Right when all hope seemed lost, we saw a few Paramount Pictures trucks ride past us on the street. Soon, we were in our very own action sequence. We chased them through yellow lights and busy streets to end up in the Laurel Hill Cemetery.

As Malik and I drove past buried generals and abolitionists, a proud calm washed over us. We actually did it. We found the shoot. Sure enough, in the distance was a huge Optimus Prime truck sitting atop a hill. We were like a couple of excited kids, squealing and sprinting to a nearby bridge to get a better view.

From our new vantage point, we could see one bright-yellow Bumblebee, one sweaty Shia LaBeouf, and one extremely frustrated Michael Bay (passersby kept messing up the shot, and might I remind you, it was like 110 degrees outside).

Seeing a real movie unfold before our very eyes was a dream come true, and one that neither of us would've gotten to experience without the other. When Malik and I were together, it felt like we could make the impossible happen. But that day, standing on a bridge in the cemetery, watching a sweat-soaked crew hustle to get shots, was the last time we'd feel extraordinary together. Summer was over, and it was time to return back to our hush-hush cross-country romance.

Malik went back to Chicago to start his sophomore year and I went back to being Philly Quinta, shifting between my on-campus life and my at-home life where my parents didn't even know I had a boyfriend. Things began to unravel a few weeks after the semester started, when Malik started to answer my calls less and call back even lesser.

"Um, what's going on?" I pleaded into the phone, on the way to step rehearsal.

"Nothing . . . I gotta go," he'd curtly respond.

It went on and on like this for a while. When I would start to question him about what was happening with us, he would tell me that I was tripping or overreacting. He made me feel like a crazy person for insisting that his behavior was changing. Later on in my life, I learned that this was called "gaslighting." At the time I called it "making me feel fucking crazy because I know I'm not crazy, I'm smart, but you're telling me what I'm feeling is wrong." It was infuriating.

Finally, after three months of me pushing to get pull in the relationship, he told me that he wanted to end things. Hearing that broke me. I couldn't believe it. He told me that he didn't want to be in a relationship anymore, that he wanted to be on his own.

His need to branch out on his own shocked me—a girl who had lied to her parents to be with him, who rearranged her entire class schedule for visits, who spent every cent she had to fly to Chicago. I genuinely did not understand how he could decide that he didn't want to be with me anymore. This was the same guy who spent two years patiently and meticulously pursuing me, the same guy who confidently told people that I'd be his wife someday. I couldn't comprehend where all of that affection went, and as I mentioned before—I'm pretty smart . . . so my inability to understand made it hurt even more.

I begrudgingly told myself I'd move on, and tried my best to distract myself with friends, school, and dance. But still, I couldn't comprehend the idea that my best friend didn't want to be with me anymore. It made me visibly sad. My friends would try to cheer me up, and my family would check in to see what was wrong, but I couldn't really tell any of them the truth —that I was heartbroken and couldn't get over it. I felt like a loser because of that.

One month after we broke up, I started noticing a girl popping up on his Facebook. Malik being in pictures with girls was not unusual—he was a (wannabe) rapper after all, and hot girls are kind of the rapper accessory—but my concern grew when I started to see this same one girl over and over. She was pretty. She was artsy. She was short. I was livid.

Now, mind you, he and I continued to talk. Even though he had broken up with me, he kept calling and talking to me as if we were still together, which made me feel like there was actually some hope. Malik wouldn't let me be free, and I couldn't free myself. It was miserable getting calls from the love of my life. These calls would last three hours, but then at the end of them, he still didn't want me.

Because we were in such constant communication, I had no problem questioning my ex-slash-phone-a-friend about this new, short, pretty girl in his life. Malik promised it was nothing, but I knew he was lying. The knife went in further; any deeper, and it'd probably come out the other side.

Finally, after days of me pushing him, Malik confessed that he was seeing that short artsy girl. One month after we broke up, one month after he said he wanted to be on his own, he had gotten a new girlfriend. And worst of all, she was like the Chicago version of me.

After that, I fell into a deep depression. At the time, I didn't really have "depression" in my vocabulary, so I didn't know what I was dealing with. Nowadays, there are healthier dialogues around mental health, but in 2009, there hadn't been a discussion in my family, in my community, online, or in school about it at all. I had no words to describe what I was going through; I was just paralyzed with sadness. At the time, I honestly thought depression was only something that could happen after someone died or if you were sick, not from heartbreak.

I began to deteriorate. I stopped going to my classes. I stopped eating. I stopped getting out of bed. I would smoke out of a homemade bong made from a Coke bottle and tinfoil and watch the same DVD of *Bruce Almighty* over and over again, not because I loved the movie (though I did), but because I couldn't pick myself up out of the bed to change the disc to a different one. I dropped to eighty pounds and lost my academic good standing at Temple. It was all bad.

I didn't tell my family what I was going through, because they didn't even know I had a serious boyfriend. I just couldn't admit to my very Christian parents that my heart was so broken because a relationship I secretly kept from them had ended. They'd be disappointed in me for even starting it, and the idea of their disappointment made me even sadder. I gotta give them credit though—they knew something was wrong, so they did their best to just be there for me. Their version of "being there" was watching *The King of Queens* with me and laughing together. That was something; any bit of serotonin helped.

It took me a year to pull through my bout of depression, two years to stop talking to Malik daily, and four years to fully get over him. I didn't get handed closure; I earned it—second by second, hour by hour, until I was finally able to shut the door on Malik, forgive him for hurting me, and move on.

At twenty-two years old, I was just about fully recovered from Malik. By fully recovered, I mean I'd stopped going to school, became skin-and-bones thin, and had quit dancing, but at least I wasn't dead inside anymore. Zest for life and a hope for the future returned to my spirit.

When I told my parents I was taking a break from Temple midway through my junior year, I paired it with the news that

I was going to get a part-time job to help offset tuition costs. I would just reenroll next semester, so there was *noootthinggggg* to worry about, I told them. Part of me *was* convinced I'd go back to school as soon as I made some extra cash. But there was another part of me that was fantasizing about a move to Los Angeles. Either way, I knew I couldn't make a decision until I made some money.

To look for work, I took the bus an hour north to the Philly mecca of job opportunities: the King of Prussia Mall. I'd worked at the mall once before, at an overpriced mother-child clothing store called Oilily. Their mantra was "A thing of beauty is a joy forever," a slogan that meant absolutely nothing but allowed them to sell hundred-dollar white T-shirts. There was no way I was going back there. I was all about forward motion. In with the new!

I had my sights set on a specific store: one that was sleek, modern, and filled with state-of-the-art technology. A store that represented the future. A store where I'd gladly use my employee discount, negating the whole point of trying to make money. It was: the Apple Store. I distinctly remember walking through the mall, my heart beating out of my chest as I arrived to the glowing storefront. I wanted this job—needed it, really—and put on my best face to try and land it.

After a vigorous monthlong screening process (the rumors are true—it's harder to get an Apple job than it is to get into college), I was hired as a Family Room Specialist, which is what Apple calls their mobile technicians. The gig paid a whopping thirteen dollars an hour. When I heard this, my eyes nearly popped out of my head: I was going to be fucking *rich*. My dream of moving to LA to make it as a comedic actress was becoming less farfetched.

Getting hired at Apple was a dream come true. Everyone who worked there looked so happy and healthy and carefree; I wanted to befriend them all and be as happy as they were. I could tell they were living the life I wanted to live, and if I was there long enough, maybe I'd have that life too.

As a Family Room Specialist, it was my job to help people with their technology, to "repair" relationships, as the onboarding manual instructed. Before I could start repairing relationships, though, I was assigned a mentor to show me the ropes. My mentor was Joshua, a guy who I had been scoping out before he was even assigned to work with me.

I'll get to the juicy stuff in a sec, but let me just say first that Joshua was a spectacular mentor. He was passionate about Apple and very patient with me as I learned the responsibilities of the job. Not that he needed a lot of patience—I was a pretty fast learner, and naturally good with Apple tech—but still, he created a friendly work environment that I was excited to go to every day.

Joshua had this geeky young-Drake-meets-Justin-Long thing going on, like a nerd with swag. He also had a witty remark for anything thrown his way, which somehow never came off as offensive. His quips made you like him even more, kind of like Iron Man.

Even though I had an instant crush on him, I didn't show it because I was taking my job seriously and knew I needed to learn from him. Besides, Joshua was six years older than me, and so it seemed a little out of my reach, even though we immediately clicked.

Joshua trained me for two months, after which I was set free to interact with customers. Guess what? I was really good at my job. Duh, I love people and I love fixing problems. As I moved further and further away from the breakup with Malik, I began gaining some of my old spark back. I even cut my hair off, because I felt that hair was symbolic of who I used to be, and not who I wanted to become.

My makeover and newfound confidence clearly did something for Joshua, because the week after my training ended, I got a text from him.

Joshua: Hey! I really like spending time with you. Would you maybe want to hang outside of work?

I was elated. I had a hunch that he liked me, even though he had never overstepped the boundary of being a "superior" to flirt with me. Now that all of that was over, he was able to make a move. And I was fucking *with it.* This Apple job was giving me way more than a paycheck, it was giving me a potential boyfriend! We love(d) to see it.

That weekend Joshua took me out on a real "this is a date right now" date to a bar near his house in Manayunk, the hilly hipster alt-living side of Philly where you may remember I once learned how to build a boat as part of a unit on slavery. I went with him after work, wearing a brand-new shirt from the Row, which was a clothing line by Mary-Kate and Ashley Olsen. I loved them when I was younger, and they had since turned into

couture fashion moguls. I used the little money I made to buy
one of their thirty-dollar shirts because it made me feel closer to
greatness, and it worked. I was going on a date!

Even though I'd been in a two-year long relationship previously, I had never been on an actual date. Most of my romantic
life involved vague titles, sneaking around, casual hangs, and
awkwardly laughing through an R-rated movie. This, though?
This felt grown-up. This felt official.

We walked into the bar, where there was a trivia night happening, something I'd also never experienced. It seemed like the
kind of thing white people in movies do . . . but now I got why!
It was the perfect conversation starter! We half played and half
giggled to each other from a small booth in the back, pointing
out what facts we knew and what facts were potentially racist.
The night was incredible, magical even, so when he invited me
back to his place, I was not only game, I was practically running
to the bedroom. We had some more beers, which led to making
out, which led to sex. And right smack-dab in the middle of the
sex, Joshua pulled the ultimate surprise move . . . by saying "I
love you."

Now, yes, this was too soon and WILD. But I was a recently
heartbroken twenty-two-year-old. When you're that young and
your crush blurts out "I love you" in the middle of your first
sexual encounter, you run in the direction of love. So, I laughed
and said, "I love you too." When I think back to how utterly
ridiculous it is that he said "I love you" on our first date, I like to
chalk it up to the fact that I must have very bomb pussy.

After that, we were inseparable. He and I spent every moment we could together, work and otherwise. During that time,

Joshua introduced me to so much. He loved to cook, and made me all sorts of snacks I never would've tried, like peanut butter and berry reduction toast. He took me camping for the first time to Worlds End State Park, and showed me just how beautiful the earth can be.* He even introduced me to Bob Marley. Strange, right? I mean, you would think I would've been into Mr. Marley by then, having been both a college student and weed smoker, but I wasn't really. I knew the hits, but Joshua taught me the deep cuts: "High Tide or Low Tide," "Put It On," "Duppy Conqueror." Maybe you could've guessed this by the last few sentences, but Joshua also introduced me to good weed (I was smoking Reggie before), as well as *Game of Thrones,* disc golf (weird, but I like weird), actual good sex, and my own beauty. Sometimes, I'd catch him staring at me from across the room.

"What're you looking at?" I'd ask.

"You. You're the most beautiful girl in the world," he'd respond.

I'd just never heard my beauty stated like a fact before. He didn't even say it as a pickup line. He'd just say, "You're the most beautiful," and then continue with what he was doing. He didn't want anything from me; he just wanted me to know how he saw me, no more, no less. He was a simple guy, and I loved that about him. I was a complicated girl. He felt like clarity.

So, why'd we break up, you ask? Our relationship truly felt perfect, but as we all know, relationships are not meant to be perfect. They take work and sometimes long and exhausting

---

* Hey! If you want to try camping, go to Worlds End State Park. It looks like the freakin' Garden of Eden.

conversations. But we were just coasting. Eventually I was the one who brought the turmoil to our perfect love life.

One day, during lunch together at the mall, I was raving about the food court sushi when Joshua dropped a bomb on me.

"Hey, do you want to move in with me?"

It came out of nowhere, much like when he asked me out, or when he told me he loved me. In hearing this, I was blindsided. From day one, I'd told Joshua that I wanted to move to Los Angeles, and since then, my dreams of becoming a comedian were growing with my savings. When Joshua asked about moving in together, I got flashes of palm trees, sun, and stages. I did not see a life where I nested in his hipster haven apartment.

"Well, no," I said, picking at my California roll. "I'm planning on moving to Los Angeles, remember?"

"Still?"

I was hurt. It was clear from his reaction that Joshua hadn't taken my goal of moving to Los Angeles seriously. His view of the future had our same uncomplicated relationship in it, while my vision of the future consisted of me embarking on a successful comedy career, wherever the world would take me. These two views, it turned out, could not coexist.

"Yes, Joshua, still. It's what I want. What do you want out of life?"

"You."

"Besides me. Anything at all you want besides . . . working at Apple and eating sushi in the same mall where we work?"

Joshua sighed. "No, this is it for me, sweetie. This is all I see and all I want."

He broke up with me a week later. This time, though, I wasn't blindsided. Don't get me wrong, I still had feelings for him. At the time, I couldn't understand why he wouldn't try to do long distance or move to Los Angeles with me, why he was so ready to let all our love go, but I also knew deep down not to hold on to those questions.

Unlike my first relationship, I could reconcile with the breakup quickly and move on, and that's because he didn't play with my feelings at all. When he broke up with me, he told me that he didn't want to stand in the way of pursuing my dreams, and because of that, things had to end between us. He didn't see the point in standing in my way or stressing me out or keeping me from having a relationship with someone who could better support me.

I appreciated him for that. There was closure and no games with Joshua, which actually let me know that I would love him forever. When Joshua broke up with me, it snipped off one of the final threads from my safety net. Making a move to Los Angeles felt less like a dream and more like a reality.

Now we're on to my third and final great love. I know what you're thinking: *Quinta, you're so young, how would you know that this is your final love?!* First off, I'm not that young, I just have good skin and a small body. Second off, I know this love is final because I deemed it so.

My third and final great love is . . . comedy. Comedy was —and remains—the one constant through all of my most significant relationships. The first time I did improv, the only person in the audience who knew me was Malik. Joshua was the one who made me realize that it was time to take my comedy dreams more seriously. And I was the one who decided that comedy would be my final great love.

My affair with comedy began years before my romantic life did. It was truly my first love and will truly be my last.

I first started flirting with comedy when I was about six or seven years old. My parents have a VHS tape somewhere that has me walking around the house exclaiming, "Where's Ofra? Where's Ofra?" It's a line from *Martin*. Some big, huge guy says it in the show, referring to Oprah. My mom loved watching *Oprah*, so I started imitating it, and every time I did, my whole family would howl with laughter. In between gasps for air, my brothers and sisters would demand I do it again. "Where's Ofra?!" I'd exclaim and the laughter would erupt once more.

This was the first time I remember understanding what a joke was; if you said certain words at the right time in the right way, you'd get laughter. I wanted more of it, but I didn't know how to get it. For years, I quietly curated a mental collection of laugh points. If something made me laugh, or made others laugh, I noted it. Slowly I began building up characters and stories in my head, ones that I knew would get people laughing. It felt good to be loved, but it felt better to get a laugh.

When I got to Temple, I started watching *SNL* and quickly became obsessed with the show. Studying *SNL* every week opened my eyes to the fact that entertainment was a business where there were plenty of opportunities to support yourself while still doing what you loved. *SNL* showed me people performing for a living and making money. Like real money. Dance may have opened the door for my ambitions as a performer, but there weren't as many opportunities for financial security as I saw with comedy.

I began to research every single *SNL* player: Jason Sudeikis, Kenan Thompson, Andy Samberg, Kristen Wiig, Fred Armisen, Bill Hader, Will Forte, and more. Where were they from? Where did they go to school? Where did they work before *SNL*? I ignored my textbooks in favor of biographies and memoirs. Comedy became my new study.

During my research, a common thread kept popping up: the Second City. I very quickly decided that if I was going to take performance seriously, I'd have to take classes there.

After Malik moved to Chicago and we had broken up, I used our willingness to still be in each other's lives to finesse a trip out so that I could take a weeklong improv intensive program. The classes fell during Temple's winter break, so I told my mom I was going to go stay with a friend in Jersey for the week, and off I went, ready and open to start my career as a real comedian! All you need to do is take a few classes and then you're ready for *SNL*, right?

Chicago took my breath away. It was the coldest climate I'd ever been in. The icy streets sounded like shattering crystal as you sprinted from one warm place to another. The new, fresh air was filled with possibilities and I was ready to grab at all of them. When I arrived at 1608 N. Wells, the beautiful brick building that was reminiscent of the Philly Queen Anne rowhomes, I instantly felt at ease. For the first time in a long time it felt like I was exactly where I was supposed to be.

When I got to my ten-person class and removed about three of the seven layers I was wearing, I saw that I was the only Black person in the room. This would be a pattern in my life for years to come. As most Black people do, I clocked this fact and then went to find my seat.

I didn't quite know what I was in for, like, *What the fuck was a comedy class? You're either funny or you're not.* But I knew this is what all the people I admired did, so I had to see what was up. When my teacher, Shelly Gossman, came into the room, I had an immediate instinct we were going to get along. She was a pretty, young white lady with long brown hair and a pointy chin. Shelly had a silly vibe and I could tell she took comedy seriously, but not too seriously. And most importantly, Shelly was my first in-person example of someone who had made comedy their life.

Over the course of those five days, we actually learned a lot about the basics of improv.

Universal Principles of Improv

(that everyone who does it pretty much knows)

1. **Always say "yes, and,"** *not* **"but" or "no."** When you say "yes" to a premise, it adds to the scene and doesn't shut down the information your partner is giving you. You don't have to literally say it, but it forces you to keep an open mind when improvising/writing a scene.

2. **Think "today is the day."** For a scene to have good action, instead of just talking about doing something, you have to actually do it. Whatever your character is going to do, have them do it today, not tomorrow.

3. **Don't teach, do.** The beginner's instinct is to start a scene by teaching your scene partner how to do something, as if

that's enjoyable to watch. It may seem more comfortable to tell your partner how to act, but then you're not building the scene naturally. Just commit to what you're doing, and your partner will pick up your cues.

4. **You can't always predict, but you can always prepare.** Yes, even though it's oxymoronic, improv comedians—at least the good ones—practice a lot. They study each other's rhythms, they learn the tools for success, and then they hand the control over to the audience. Being prepared for the unexpected will help you not get thrown off by it.

5. **Improv is life.** Any of these factors, when used in your everyday life, will enhance it greatly. Improv is that girl.

At the end of the week, we had a final show where we'd perform in front of an audience. The crowd was mostly filled with students from other classes and family members. My only "family" there was Malik. When I ran out onto the stage with my classmates, a buzz took over my body. I'd been on plenty of stages before, but I was always part of a dance team, performing a very rehearsed series of movements. This stage was different. It was small, intimate, and there was no road map ahead of me, just a series of tools to help me perform. It felt like freedom. I fell in love in that moment. It was then that I realized that love, in any form, needed to feel like the freedom to be me, the all-in version of me, without any fear of what others would think. I had never had that before.

When our performance was over, Shelly pulled me aside. "Quinta, you have a real knack for comedy," she told me. I lit up. I'd been thinking it all along, secretly, but here was a professional telling me I had talent. "You should take the sketch writing course."

"Shelly Shelz, I ain't got the bread for that," I told her, in less absurd words. But it was true. I had spent all of my money to get to Chicago to take this class. Anything beyond it was out of my budget.

Shelly, bless her heart, gave me the five hundred dollars needed to take the writing course. No one had ever given me money to do anything. I applied for scholarships in college and never won any; same thing with dance. Comedy was the first thing where someone went, "You're so good, you need to be doing this. I'll help." Shelly Gossman is a living testament to the fact that not all influential teachers operate within traditional school systems. I felt so fortunate.

I took the writing course and learned the beginnings of how to write a sketch, how to write for TV, and how to write for film. Learning that there were methods to the comedy madness was exciting. I loved that I was getting to learn all the formal ways to joke around. At the end of my course, I was determined to learn more on my own, since I didn't have any money or time for more classes. But I knew then that this is what I wanted to do with my life. It's the craft I'm still working on today and that I'm committed on working on forever.

Each of my loves have taught me valuable lessons, but it's comedy that taught me the most. It taught me that love, at its best, is easy and kind. It's freeing. Through comedy, I learned that love isn't limited to human form. It exists all around us, all the time—you just gotta let it into your life, regardless of what it looks like.

Whether you're on your first love, your third love, or you're discovering your love of an art form, I wish you good fortune and, most importantly, lots of laughter.

7

Quinta's Classics: Part I

....

Growing up, my appetite for pop culture was insatiable. I didn't just watch movies, I rewound, rewatched, repeated every line, and continued to do so until every single moment from the movie was seared into my brain. Same thing with music. Music wasn't simply listened to, it was dissected, memorized, and turned into personal canon. And don't even get me started on TV. I'd marry TV if I could.

I dove so far into my pop culture interests that eventually, I was eaten whole by entertainment itself. Now, I live and work inside screens.

Because pop culture shaped and informed my entire career trajectory, I hold it very near to my heart. That's why I want to share with you the pop culture contributions that were very formative for me, just in case they might be formative for you, too. It's never too late to be influenced by a self-proclaimed anti-influencer!

"D.I.D.D.Y." — P. Diddy ft. Pharrell

The year was 2001 . . . a young Quinta, eleven years old at the time, entered her very first hip-hop class ever. It wasn't a requirement for my dance school, but since hip-hop, along with pretzels, was the main export of Philadelphia, it was kind of unavoidable.

Whenever a new song started getting play on the radio, that meant new dances would come out of it, so imagine how lucky I was to start my classes right around when "D.I.D.D.Y." dropped. I swear to you, the first time I heard it, I Harlem Shaked until my arms were numb. I mean, what an incredible flex to make a song spelling out your name—AND he doesn't even really spell it properly! The hook goes, "The D, the I, the D, the D, the Y, the D, the I, the D, it's Didddyyyy." No, it ain't, Diddy, it's technically DIDDYDID, but I still love it. The beat feels like an Adidas tracksuit—bouncy and a little too flashy. Diddy's song in honor of himself also features Pharrell, back when he was part of the Neptunes, which immediately elevated its status. If you feature Pharrell in anything you do, I'm automatically going to love it, because that man is sexy, a musical genius, and I think, above all—sexy.

The song is a reputable bop, and even the music video is incredible on its own. It opens on Diddy dancing in front of a large sign that also says Diddy (respect the branding), wearing a bomb tracksuit and a diamond cross. Then an adorable baby-faced Pharrell shows up, kind of chilling around. Add some hot girls without pants shimmying in the back and it's a flawless backdrop for a summer jam. But the best part of the video is when he internal monologues to a mirror about how people refer to him. He paved the way for many a mirror-talker, including myself and Issa Rae.

Everything about this video is perfect. There's even an outfit-change dance break AND his mom is in the video. Watching it still makes me happy to this day. There's so much macho culture with rappers, especially ones as successful as Sean Combs, yet he never felt the need to change himself to fit into that culture. Diddy was a dancer first, and I loved that about him. And if you don't 100 percent agree with me on this one, I'm going to have to ask you to find a mirror and give yourself a talking-to.

"Stand by Me" — Ben E. King

When I decided to learn to play guitar at age twenty, my friend Scott offered to teach me. He gave me his old string box and told me to pick a simple song from a list in a book for beginners. When I saw "Stand by Me," I was overjoyed.

That song. Man, what a classic. It is so quietly magnificent. Its purity always reminds me of the generation that came before us, parents dancing in kitchens, grandparents holding hands, bicycles with streamers on the handlebars. It exudes history but also timelessness. It's also one of my dad's faves. Some of my earliest memories of my parents involve sitting in the back of their minivan, listening to the oldies station together. When "Stand by Me" would come on, my dad would gently turn up the radio, which was a signal for me to get quiet and listen. The lyrics just stunned me. I found it so beautiful that a man could talk about a person being with him even if the sky fell. It hit that big imagination and lovesick part of my heart I had as a kid. I wanted to kiss a boy so bad, and wanted that boy to feel like he would stand by me no matter what, too. This song contextualized what love was for me: it's when someone will be with you until the end of the world.

"Stand by Me" became the first song I learned on guitar. It took me about an hour to learn the chords, and a week to make them sound good. I played the simplest version of it for anyone who would listen . . . like my parents, who were vaguely impressed. I actually appreciated their disinterest, because it showed me that I shouldn't pursue music as a career, just more of a hobby.

"Rhapsody in Blue" — George Gershwin

Jesus Christ, this song. A banger *for sure*. I found out about "Rhapsody in Blue" the same way everyone who is currently enjoying their thirties found out about "Rhapsody in Blue": *Fantasia 2000*. *Fantasia 2000* is a straight-up cinematic masterpiece. It's a 2D display of outstanding artistic and musical vignettes led by a wizard version of Mickey Mouse. Some might say *Fantasia 2000* is one of the last great 2D films. I might also say that, but I'm not here to start that fight.

The first time I saw that movie and experienced the way it visualized classical music, a distinct shift occurred in my understanding of movies. I had never seen anything like it before. Its opening montage of butterflies prancing around to the violins was hypnotizing; I was hooked from the get. Locking myself in our TV room and putting on *Fantasia 2000* was like the little-kid version of taking hallucinogens for me.

In the movie, "Rhapsody in Blue" plays over this classy New York City scene. Without having any words, it still tells a beautifully composed story of life in the big city. The jazzy animation takes its cues from this boisterous song, and what unfolds is a big and bold number giving life to the characters within the lines and colors of the animation. It's a song that made me realize that if someone could tell you so much about life only using musical instruments, then just *imagine* what a person could do with the power of words. It's a song that inspired me to look for the story in every piece of art, not just in writing.

Fantasia 2000 was the very first movie soundtrack I listened to. I'm not saying it's the first soundtrack I heard; I'm saying it's the first one that I consciously took note of in my brain. Before, I didn't really pay attention to the songs that movies chose to feature. But when I watched *Fantasia 2000* for the first time and heard "Rhapsody in Blue," it changed how I consumed music. It expanded its possibilities; it made me think more visually. Years later, when stealing music became a thing, I illegally downloaded the song on LimeWire and put it on my iPod. I'd listen to it while riding the El to school, watching Philly unfold the same way the city did in *Fantasia,* wondering how I could tell the story of city living in my own way one day.

Adding the soundtrack to my own life made me feel like I was living in a movie; and even more so, it made me feel like there were so many possibilities for creation. To this day, when I listen to music, I can get ideas for scenes; I've come up with whole plotlines to a movie based off one song. Music is incredibly crucial when it comes to storytelling. And I have Gershwin —and the fucked-up world of *Fantasia 2000*—to thank for this lesson.

"Isn't She Lovely" — Stevie Wonder

Hot take: Stevie Wonder is the most incredible musical artist of all time. The end. Okay, well, not technically the end, I have a lot more to say. His music heals me! I could be having the worst day, thinking the worst thoughts, and listening to him does for me what reading the Bible does for Christians — it gives me hope and clarity. Mr. Wonder's music is genreless and boundaryless. Every song hits. His production value is unrivaled; you can feel the care in each and every note. He . . . is . . . THE BEST.

Not only is Stevie a multitalented musician with twenty-five Grammys, but he's also a great teacher. Through his music, he discusses issues of the time, singing about politics, oppression, and the Black experience in America. He is never afraid to use his beautiful voice to share radical ideas, crafting songs like "Black Man," which taught everyone who listened about all of the good Black men have done in this world (and the not-so-great things white men have done). "Love's in Need of Love Today" touched on the HIV crisis, and "You Haven't Done Nothing" was an angry takedown of Nixon for all the lies that he pumped into the American people's lives. Stevie never just puts together notes to get to the top of the charts; he does so to make change, to keep the revolution alive.

While I think his songs that comment on society are genius, I love his songs about love. Stevie Wonder captures the feeling of love and puts it into words like no other. He turns love into an experience of the soul. "Isn't She Lovely" has always been my fa-

vorite out of his entire discography. It is the most beautiful song
Stevie Wonder has ever gifted us—and he has gifted us many.

When I was a kid listening to "Isn't She Lovely," I assumed it
was about a woman. But years later, after going on a late-night,
secretly-smoking-weed-in-my-bedroom-at-my-parents'-house-
induced Wikipedia binge, I learned it was written for his first-
born baby daughter. The song grew in meaning to me. When
you listen to the song knowing that it's written to honor the life
that he created, it takes on a pure spirit that's really special. It
always fills me with love and light beyond measure. I hope that
when I have a kid, I can make a piece of art that carries as much
love as "Isn't She Lovely" does.

"Happier Than the Morning Sun"—
Stevie Wonder (again)

I'm a huge Stevie Wonder fan, clearly, and even though it feels
a little wrong to have another one of his songs listed, I truly do
not care because I'm here to tell you my truth, and the truth is
that Stevie Wonder deserves two spots here on this list because
he is the GOAT. 🐐

I thought I knew everything about this musician whom I've
loved my whole life, but as it turns out, I do not. One day, when
I was crouched over my laptop answering emails, I had Stevie
Wonder radio on my Spotify. After a medley of songs by different artists, all of which I knew and loved, a song I'd never heard
before came on. It stopped me dead in my tracks. The intro had
this gentle guitar strum that carried a sort of warm innocence
inviting me to curl up within its hopeful notes. I immediately
recognized Stevie's signature *bum*s and *bop*s but was shocked

that between my dad's constant Stevie rotation and my own infatuation, this song had slipped by me. That's the thing about Stevie — no matter how much you love his music and think you're an expert on his entire discography, his work is so deep that a new track can present itself to you out of nowhere and make you fall in love with him all over again.

The song I heard that day, "Happier Than the Morning Sun," is a delightful and soothing gem. It is about loving someone so much that they make you happier than life itself. Its simplicity is beautiful, and it encapsulates what love feels like. It wraps up with Stevie repeating that he believes everyone should be happy. Every time I listen to this song, I damn near cry because of its beauty. It is the song I want played at my funeral. I know that's grim, but when I go, my wish is for everyone to be happy. And to me, Stevie and this song is synonymous with that.

"Don't Stop Me Now" — Queen

All right! Confession: I didn't really *know* about Queen until I went to see *Iron Man 2* in theaters. So yeah, I was about twenty years old when I found out about them. A damn adult. What can I say? I probably had heard some of their hits growing up, but my parents weren't big into rock, so I missed out on a lot of what people consider classics.

Anyway, there's a scene in the movie where Iron Man fights War Machine while a DJ spins a mash-up of "Another One Bites the Dust" and "It Takes Two," by Rob Base and DJ EZ Rock. For whatever reason, the remix made the bass line of "Another One Bites the Dust" stand out to me in a way it never had before. When I got home, I needed to know who the geniuses behind that song were. I know, I know, again: I was late to the game! But what matters is I discovered Queen, then discovered "Don't Stop Me Now," and then fell in love.

"Don't Stop Me Now" makes me feel like I'm on a ride every time I listen to it. It starts out slow, like a roller coaster making its way up to the first drop, stalling just a bit at the top of the peak—and then, it takes off. Every time I hear that takeoff, I become high on the thrill of it. I love Freddie Mercury's voice and I love the lyrics. I get the same feeling from "Don't Stop Me Now" that I did when I performed improv at Second City for the first time. That song just sounds like freedom to me. I know Freddie was a queer icon, and that song in particular inspires within me the freedom I've seen a lot of my queer friends display in their own expression of pride. They are free, they are themselves, and they can't be stopped.

Whenever I'm in a good mood, I like to put on this song. Between you and me, I often rock out to it in my underwear, because what did I say? The song is FREEDOM! And what's freer than doing topless high kicks in your Target-brand five-for-twenty-dollars undies? Nothing, I tell ya.

There you have it! Some of the most crucial tracks of my life. Quinta's Classics will be back after these brief commercial messages.

8

Hi, Handsome

....

After a few months of working at the King of Prussia Apple Store, I had socked away a thousand dollars, which I thought would be enough to make a life across the country. (Surprise! It wasn't.) There was no stopping young Quinta at this point. It was LA or bust.

Though I had this plan in my head for the entire time I worked at Apple, I didn't give my parents any sort of heads-up that I was not going to reenroll at Temple and would instead head two thousand miles away to try and make it in comedy. If I'm being honest, I never told them of my real plan because I didn't want to give them the opportunity to convince me otherwise. I finally brought them up to speed *after* I already had bought my ticket.

"Mom, Dad . . . I want to move to LA."

"No," my mom said flatly.

"Let me rephrase that . . . I *am* moving to LA."

My parents sighed. At this point, they knew that when I had my sights set on something, I was going to do it.

The night before I was scheduled to fly out, my mom sat in

my room on my bed with her arms crossed as I was packing my few things into one suitcase. ("Always pack light" is my mantra.)

"And where will you be again?"

"I'm going to stay in a sublet with Brittany."

My mom knew Brittany from my days of dance at L and L Productions. Brittany's friends were going away for three months to film something in Portland, so there was room for me.

"I don't know, Quinta," my mom reasoned. All of it sounded too whimsical for her.

"Don't worry," I told her, while she silently used her eyes to tell me not to go. "I'm going to save up some money and take classes at UCLA to finish my degree!" This was another one of those lies that everyone, including me, believed. I truly thought I might reenroll in school, even though I already knew what my real goal was, and a traditional college education, paired with traditional college debt, was not gonna get me there.

As soon as the plane wheels hit the tarmac, I felt like I had a shiny new start. No more lying, no more living multiple lives. I could now become whoever I wanted to be without the need to conform into what was expected of me. It was the start of the new me. I was a Philly girl in an LA world!

My future looked bright, especially since I was able to successfully transfer my Apple job to a store in Century City, which allowed me to cover rent and pay for classes at the Second City Los Angeles. I was getting closer and closer to living my dream.

The Apple Store at the Century City Mall was like the *Super Sweet Sixteen* makeover of my store setting back in King of

Prussia. The mall was outdoors, which turned my typical food court lunch break into an opportunity for fresh air and sunshine. There was a Coffee Bean and a Subway right next to my store, so I had a variety of options for breakfast besides the standard Starbucks fare I was used to back at KOP. And there was not one, but TWO yogurt shops—Pinkberry *and* Yogurtland! Pinkberry was still too bougie for me, so I went to Yogurtland when I could afford it . . . which was on payday . . . every two weeks.

I fell into a routine at this Apple in no time—I was an expert tech, after all—and became close with my coworkers. (Shoutout to Ikenna, Eric, Spoonz, Jean, and Jay for keeping me sane.) We'd work long shifts together, and then get dinner at Pink Taco afterward, joking about annoying customers while stuffing our faces with bottomless chips and salsa. It was easy enough to fall into this day-to-day. Sunshine, a solid job at a cool mall to work at (that I thought only existed on Disney shows), and good friends? LA was gonna be sweet forever!

A few months into working at the Apple Store, though, I hit a wall. Anytime there's this big, world-changing shift in my life —you know, like moving to the opposite side of the country— there's always a quiet period that comes with it. This slowdown usually happens after the excitement of the Big Life Change wears off. Where you kind of look around the room and think, "This is it?"

My look-around-the-room moment happened when I was helping an irate Apple customer. I was already having a shitty day; my bus passed me that morning, and because I was already running late, by the time I caught the next one, I had to sprint into work and couldn't get breakfast. My hair looked a mess, mainly because I couldn't afford to get it done. To top it all off, my shirt had a huge stain on it, which I only noticed midway into my shift.

When I first saw this customer, I knew she was going to be trouble. Draped in at least $50K of jewelry, she had one of those "I need to speak to the manager" scowls as she stomped up to the Genius Bar. Under her arm was what looked to be a 1960s muff? But as she got closer, I could see it was a tiny dog. *Sigh.* Little dogs in purses is like a warning sign that you're gonna be dealing with someone who is . . . difficult.

At the moment she arrived, I was helping another customer, but I could see from her dramatic look-arounds for assistance that she was going to be a headache. When I finished with my customer, I scanned the store to see my coworkers helping other customers. *How is this on me?* I thought. I glanced to Ikenna, who was purposefully taking a long time with his customer's broken headphones. That's like a two-minute appointment, and Ikenna was on minute nine. He shot me a "sucks for you" look. I almost pulled a muscle forcing a smile across my face, and walked over to the customer.

"How can I help you today?" I asked.

The woman dug around in her enormous designer bag, pulled out an iPad, and threw it on the table. "This doesn't work," she said as her dog tried to wriggle out of her grasp.

I took the iPad and examined it. It looked to be in good condition, but maybe it was something with the software or internal hardware.

"Okay, got it. What specifically seems to be the issue, so I can assist you in the best way?"

"It won't unlock. Watch this." She put the iPad flat on the counter, took her dog's paw, and pressed it onto the home button. The iPad lit up, and then nothing happened. I stared at the situation, trying to comprehend what I just saw.

"See?" the woman said, jamming her poor dog's paw onto the home button again. That's when it hit me: this woman was upset that the fingerprint recognition software didn't work on her dog's paw. Let me say that one more time for the people in the back: the lady was mad because her DOG could not unlock her iPAD.

"Ma'am . . . if you are insinuating that the iPad won't open for your dog, then . . . I would have to tell you that the fingerprint scanner wasn't created for animals. It only works on humans . . . if that's what you're trying to insinuate, of course," I said, trying to be as noncondescending as possible. I could not believe I had to use this combination of words in a sentence together.

"Well, she needs to be able to access it on her own," the woman seethed. "I downloaded an app to help with her separation anxiety. It doesn't make sense if she can't use it when she's anxious." Lol, sure, lady. That's what doesn't make sense in the scenario.

I mean, I could see why the dog was anxious. Three minutes with this woman and I was ready to inhale some Xanax. "Well, see, the app is meant for human usage. Not for animals. And also, I'm not sure if you saw the app, but it's got words . . . and dogs can't read," I said, trying to hold back my exasperation.

She moved her Pomeranian from one arm to the other and gave me an appraising look. "I don't appreciate your attitude," she sniffled.

"It's not an attitude, it's the truth." She was not pleased, and I knew that this scenario wasn't going to improve. "You know what, let me get my manager for you two!" I said, pointing to her dog. I turned around and yanked the smile from my face as I walked up to my manager, Jonathan, who was already aware of the situation. He had spotted it from afar and knew I would need relief. Bless his heart.

I highly doubt my manager coded some sort of "paw extension" to help her dog unlock the damn iPad, but I was grateful to get away from the woman. I also knew she'd be more willing to listen to him than me, since he was a large white man and I was a small Black girl who couldn't *possibly* know what she was talking about when it came to dogs using iPads! Ultimately though, the interaction left me stunned. This was a type of entitlement that I had never experienced before in my Apple Genius Bar days.

The Apple culture in Los Angeles was (and I'm assuming still is) *very* different from the Apple culture in Philly. I *understood* the people who came into the Philly Apple Store. Their problems made sense to me, because they were my problems. I knew that their phone was oftentimes their lifeline. I also knew that these customers didn't have a lot of time to get their phone fixed because they had to get to their lousy job or take care of their children. When someone came in upset or angry, I empathized with them.

In Los Angeles, it was a whole different bag. I was either dealing with a lot of rude, rich people, or their frantic and desperate assistants. No one wanted to shoot the breeze or even really make eye contact with me. They were busy, they were stressed, and they needed their phone fixed NOW. A few months after moving to Los Angeles and starting this job at Apple, I began to experience a bigger culture shock than I had expected. These people sucked!

Something broke in me that day. All of a sudden, the sunshine was bothering my eyes, the Subway breakfast started to taste . . . like . . . well, Subway breakfast. Even Yogurtland wasn't saving me . . . and I had a punch card! I stopped feeling that buzz of limitless excitement I first felt when I moved to LA. The routine was no longer feeling like a stable accomplishment, but more like a trap.

I started to shut down. When my friends would ask me to hang out after work, I'd dodge them and make excuses. While on the floor at work, I unknowingly stopped speaking unless spoken to by a customer. I turned into a zombie; I was so tuned out. One night, a kid dropped an iPad on my foot and I didn't even clock it.

The parent of the child went "Um . . . what the fuck? Did you not feel that? Timmy is sorry. Timmy, say sorry to the lady." It took Timmy yelling "Sorry!" for me to even realize I was in pain. Then it hit me, *I didn't come here to fix tech for Timmy, I came here to work in comedy.*

That evening, after my shift was over, I took a page out of Pomeranian lady's book and asked if I could speak with the floor manager, Diana.

Diana, a small mixed-race woman with the peppy demeanor

of a popular-cool mom, was very easy to talk to. When I sat down in her office, I explained that as much as I appreciated the job and how it helped me land softly into my new LA life, I needed to leave and focus on the reason I moved: comedy.

"Well, I'm sad to see you go," Diana told me. "But there's always a job here for you if you need it."

"Really?" I was surprised to hear that while I was quitting.

"Yeah! You're one of the fastest technicians we have! We'll take those East Coast quick-appointment skills any day!"

I took her kindness as a challenge. I was either going to make it, or I was going to be back at that store, telling Saudi princes I couldn't fix their gold-plated, completely customized "iPhones" because they'd gutted all the Apple parts, making them no longer Apple products. I vowed to make it.

That night I quit, I came home, packed a bowl, and wrote out a simple list of goals:

1. Take more improv classes.
2. Perform more often.
3. Get on TV.

At that point, I'd been at Apple for the better part of four years, and while I was happy with the steady paycheck, I was starting to get a little too comfortable. Success doesn't favor the relaxed; it favors the risk takers, and quitting liberated me to take those risks. It opened my schedule up for more classes, creativity, and comedy. I thought that if I put 100 percent of my energy into breaking through to the entertainment world, then I'd be successful and famous in no time.

Fortunately, before quitting, I'd saved up enough money to skate by for a few months. Sure, I had to cut down from four tacos at the truck near my house to two, but if that was the kind of sacrifice I needed to make to be a full-time performer, so be it. They call it starving artist for a reason.

After a few months of grinding on the comedy circuit, I could feel a shift within myself: I was getting funnier, making connections, and getting booked on more shows. My friend Heath invited me to join an improv group with our friends Danny and Warren. We called ourselves Simmercon (a mix of Heath and Danny's last names). We were performing at the iO West Theater* every Friday night . . . and people loved us! I was working around the clock on my craft. But this weird thing happens when you're spending all of your time and energy pursuing your dreams: you just keep running out of money.

Two months into my carpe the diem lifestyle, I was dead broke. I'd spent so much time on the art of comedy that I hadn't managed to book enough freelance work to last beyond the next three months in LA, even on a shoestring budget. A small bubble of panic (or maybe, probably, hunger) began to form in my stomach. So I turned to my dear old friend Craigslist for some fast cash. As I scrolled through the "Drive for Lyft!" and "Are You an Adult Tobacco, Nicotine, or Vape User?" ads, my stress grew.

One morning, in the middle of my daily desperation Craigslist scroll, I stopped at an ad that caught my eye:

---

* RIP.

★★ GET PAID TO DRAW $125 ★★

NOW CASTING artists and aspiring artists in an
art tutorial video. TODAY is your LUCKY DAY!
Get paid $125 to learn how to draw!
Send headshot and level of skill to:
04b8f43b9ede37baeb8982e1e0561t4@job.craigslist.org

I had taken some drawing classes in high school and figured
that at the very least, I could play a budding sketch artist for an
instructional video. I responded to the ad and continued my
freelance job search.

Within minutes, the account that posted the ad sent me a
location and shoot date. My drought had come to an end. Incredible! My first acting gig! AND I was about to get $125! Four
tacos at the truck for meeeee, baby! I vowed to be the best aspiring artist sketcher Hollywood has ever seen.

On the day of the shoot, I did my hair and put on my nicest
jeans, checking myself out in the mirror before I headed out.

"You look like a real professional fake artist," I said to myself,
nodding with approval.

I was so excited to be on camera that I basically heel-toed
all the way to the studio, which was conveniently down the
street from where I lived (another bonus: didn't need to use bus
money). When I got to the building, I saw there were already
a bunch of people waiting outside. The only discernable com-
monality about the diverse group of humans was that we all
looked like we were about $125 away from moving back home.

Eventually, we were let inside to a big, empty space, with a platform in the middle and a bunch of easels scattered around. One of the producers put me at an easel in the middle of the group. I pushed my purse under the chair and ran my hand across the paper they provided. It was super thick, which meant it was probably expensive. *Movin' on up,* I thought to myself.

When we were all settled, the doors behind us opened and a man in a toga walked in and scaled the platform. I let out a deep sigh. Not the kind of still life I was hoping for, but I was making paper, so who cares. I looked him up and down, and could feel my face start to scrunch up. Something was off about him. He just looked too fresh, like he'd been doing crunches in preparation for this video. His hair was done up, and he had the thirsty energy of an improv comedian. (I know the type well.) He just didn't look like someone interested in the arts; he looked like he was on his way to go crush some Natty Lights at a racist-themed party. Dumb as hell. I looked around to see if anyone else noticed that this dude looked like a joke, but everyone was focused on their canvases.

I shrugged and picked up my pencil. As I began to lightly sketch his outline, the dude's toga slipped and fell open to reveal . . . an abnormally large penis. Oh-no-oh-no-oh-no. I quickly pieced together what was going on. *I'm in the middle of a fucking prank show.* Still, no one else seemed to pick up on the fact that it was a setup, even with the donkey dick hanging out for all the world to see.

While my fellow artists continued to expressionlessly sketch away at their easels, I quietly began to pack up my shit. There was no way I would allow my first role in Hollywood to be "Girl

Who Was Surprised by Big Dick on a Prank Show." Wanting to be respectful of production, I made sure not to draw attention to myself and waited for the moment when the "instructional cameras" were pointed away from me. Sensing this was my moment to escape, I slipped out.

I hadn't even gotten halfway down the hall before a producer chased after me. "Excuse me! Hey! Um, you can't leave, we're in the middle of shooting," an extremely flustered man told me.

"This isn't really my thing," I said, trying to contain my annoyance that this stupid production ate up a whole day of job searching.

"Oh, that's okay! We accept artists at all levels."

"Turns out, I'm not that good at drawing and I don't want to do it anymore," I lied. I was trying to give us both the opportunity to save some dignity.

The producer furrowed his brow. "Let me level with you." He took a step closer and lowered his voice. "We're actually shooting a new prank show." (I told you.) "You can't leave because we already have you on camera."

"So what? Edit around it."

"We can't edit around it. Besides, you gave some of the best reactions. We'll give you $300 to sign the release form."

Of course my expressive-ass face gave some of the best reactions. Still, I wanted to be a professional actor; there was no way I was going to allow this clip to be my first on-camera experience—no matter how much I needed money.

"No . . . I'm good, man," I told him.

"Okay, what about $500?"

I shifted my weight from side to side. I wanted that $500. Do you have any idea how much spaghetti that could buy? How many taco truck tacos? Still, I just couldn't bring myself to sell out. I did not want some shady producer and shitty show having control over what they could do with my image.

"Nah, I'm good. Hope this turns out well!" I told him, power walking away before he could protest.

I left that dumb prank shoot with my head held high and my pocket held empty. Later that day, they emailed me offering $1,000 to use my reactions in their show. But at that point, I knew where my principles lay. I may have been desperate for money, but I was even more desperate to have complete control over my own comedic voice.

I was back on the job hunt that evening. This time Craigslist was looking even bleaker, since I had to be suspicious not only of sex trafficking, but possible Jamie Kennedy experiment wannabes. It was becoming soul-crushing to scroll and scroll, click and click, and find nothing.

A few days later, still dejected from dangle-dick guy, I found a posting on Craigslist that felt—I wouldn't say promising, but manageable.

~ ~ ** MaKe MoNeY U$iNg OnlY YoUR VoICE ** ~ ~

I clicked immediately, and nope—it wasn't an opportunity to work on *The Simpsons*! It was a "voice massage director" aka . . . a phone sex gig. According to the posting, I could make a dollar a minute talking to men. The longer you kept them on the phone, the more money you made. A simple business strategy I could get behind.

As I skimmed through the ad, I thought, I can talk to horny men, no problem. Plus, making up sexy stories on the fly sounded kind of fun, like a solid improv exercise. I could work on my craft AND make money—a win/win! I emailed to say I was interested and they accepted me right away; they didn't even bother making me record a sample. That very day, the company uploaded a profile for me. It included a fake name and bio along with a picture of a sexy and busty woman next to a number where "I" could be reached.

I got my first call within a few hours and was thrilled. I curled up in my bed and answered, excited to practice my backstory and crowd work skills.

"Hi, handsome," I breathed into the receiver. I was going for Marilyn Monroe meets Vivica A. Fox, like the picture suggested.

His response back to me was a little too vulgar to print. Just know it involved four of the worst words in the English language, and use your imagination. I was taken aback but managed to respond with a lie about what I was wearing . . . blue lace panties and a red bra. (Horrible combo, but that's improv, baby. Off the cuff!)

The guy on the other end of the line went on to emit the grossest sounds I've ever heard. It sounded like someone chewing on Jell-O after getting their wisdom teeth out. He mumbled something about his wife, and all of a sudden, nausea overcame me. I hung up. I couldn't do it. I stared at my phone, furious with myself. I was angry that I couldn't just suck it up and make money for the sake of survival. I was mad that I'd spent thirty dollars at Target on summer clothes that I simply didn't need. I was mad that I ever bought toilet paper! I could've just not pooped! All my anger funneled inward as I began recounting every financial mistake I'd made over the two months I'd planned to "make it."

Two weeks later, I got a check in the mail from the phone sex company for four dollars. A dollar for each minute, just like they promised. Guess I had no future in voice work.* I laughed as I mobile-deposited the check into my Bank of America account. It would take a day to process, and by then, the account would be overdrawn.

I weighed out my options. Yes, I wanted to spend every possible second pursuing my dream, but LA is not exactly a city where the average person can just coast and not have an income while they're grinding. I knew what I had to do. I went to Apple and asked for my job back that week. There was no way that Craigslist was going to lead me to find a stable freelance gig— or, at least, not one that I could stomach. I had to suck up my pride. You can imagine how humiliating it is to announce that you're leaving your retail job to pursue your dreams of becoming famous, and then come back four months later because you ran out of money and weren't very good at turning (any sort of)

---

* I write this shortly after lending my voice to the latest season of *Big Mouth*. So how do you like me now, past-Quinta?

tricks. Luckily, Diana was an incredibly understanding person and she hired me back on the spot.

Back at Apple, my schedule fell into the same cycle. I worked throughout the week, fixing electronics for rich people, and then on nights and weekends I did as much comedy as I could, daydreaming of the day I could just put all my focus into doing comedy full-time. Little did I know, that day was right around the corner.

9

Models and the Rest of Us

....

Your twenties are a series of crossroads, large and small, making it challenging to figure out which path is the right one. Day job or dream job? Wait on your crush who could care less or have sex with his friend who wants to marry you? Post a picture of your ass or go with a safe selfie with a smile that says "my ass is fat"? You're constantly bombarded with all sorts of decisions that pull your not-yet-fully-developed adult brain in different directions. When I first moved to LA, I faced one of these crossroads: swallow the weird pink pill or get out of the car. Guess what? I made the wrong decision.

My first few months in LA were mostly spent taking improv classes at the Second City and hanging out with my friends Gianni, Modi, Nadia, Quinn, and Aaron, who had also moved from the East Coast around the same time as I had. The environment was a stark change from what I was used to in the 215, but I was enjoying the warm weather, and I loved pretending that the apartment I was subletting, with its big open windows and nice furniture, was my own. I would host my pals over for dinner, pushing away the thought that I'd have to leave this perfect spot eventually. But before I knew it, I was getting a call from the previous tenants saying they'd be back from Portland in two weeks. All of this was further complicated by the fact that I had blown through most of my savings, and had only gotten a few freelance jobs working with Brittany as a fashion assistant, a job that sounds glamorous, but isn't. It basically consists of carrying boxes three times your size and getting yelled at for losing pantyhose. At one gig, I was asked to fetch strawberries for the models. I frantically searched the internet for somewhere else to live that was within my meager budget, knowing that whatever I'd find wouldn't be as chic or comfortable as my K-town spot.

After using up the full two weeks for my search, I finally found something I could afford, a room in a huge bungalow in Hollywood that I'd be sharing with a few other girls. The house itself was super cute. There was an avocado tree and a white trellis out front, French doors inside, and large windows that let in a lot of light. My room was smaller than the room I grew up in, but I made it my own with furniture from the Goodwill down the street and pictures of my friends and family back home.

From the Facebook photos I posted, my new spot looked superb, just what you'd imagine a "bungalow in the middle of Hollywood" would look like. But anyone who has ever lived in Hollywood, or even driven through Hollywood, knows that it's decorated with filth and heroin needles, and carries the stench of desperation (which smells like pee). Up close, Hollywood is (maybe predictably) a depressing place. But not to me. I was excited to finally be in the middle of the clogged heart of entertainment.

Even though my living situation was starting to feel settled, shady neighborhood or not, my social situations were starting to stall. I was a person who enjoyed meeting interesting people, and besides work and improv, the people I was meeting in LA weren't exactly that. When I'd go out to the bars and clubs, I was disappointed to find people droning on about status and hot people and other banal shit. If I tried talking to anyone about art, they looked like they were going to go get the bouncer to throw me out of the club. Everything seemed artificial, with way too much name-dropping. That started to bug me. It was nothing like socializing in Philly.

Philly has culture coming up through the cracks of the side-walks. It's the breeding ground for artists like the Roots, Jill Scott, Eve; people who are full of life, have something to say, and aren't scared to do so. My scene in particular was all about connecting people and pushing each other. Local creators would gather to support each other, debate, date, and everything in between at legendary parties at places like the Barbary, PIT, and the Blockley. These parties were a way to get to know people more intimately. They showed me people's essences and helped me build mine. Spending weekends with all these artists I loved and respected made me feel full of life.

Los Angeles parties, or at least the ones I was going to, didn't really supply the same kind of vibe. They seemed to lack culture, authenticity. To combat this, I decided I would throw a party to replicate the Philly feeling I'd been missing. Maybe I could teach LA how to properly party! I'd create my own scene, my own culture, right there in the middle of Hollywood! My roommates were down, so I started planning. I invited every single person I knew in Los Angeles: all my improv classmates, some musicians I met through my LA-based Philly kids (whom I also invited), a handful of Temple classmates. I wanted to have old and new faces at my Los Angeles social premiere. Facebook invites were very much the norm of the hour, but I took the time to individually text each person an invitation. All fifty of them. It was important to me to show that I cared enough to take the time to compose a text.

The day of the party, I wore a blue and magenta maxi dress that let my collarbones shine like the diamonds that they are. My hair was entering an aspiring Halle Berry (but realistic Rachel Maddow) stage, but I managed to sleek it back in a sophisticated way. My roommates and I readied the house, in the same way that all people in their twenties ready a house for a party: by pushing the furniture against the walls. That was about the only party "decorating" we did. I couldn't afford to go wild on streamers and shit! But it didn't matter, THE PEOPLE were what mattered.

I've always loved a good party and, on this day, I was buzzing with the anticipation about showing all of my LA friends a Philly good time. At the last minute, I even got my friend Abdul, another Philly native, to DJ, setting up two bamboo dinner trays as his "booth" in the corner. As he was cueing up a banger, our first few party people started to arrive. My roommates and I poured some drinks, sat back, and waited for the rest to roll in. And roll in they did. Instead of getting the fiftyish friends we were expecting, nearly 150 people showed up to this party. News traveled fast.

I know tripling your party attendance sounds like a good

thing, but for the person throwing the party, it's incredibly stressful. Things quickly started to get out of hand.

"Hi . . . who are you?" I asked one of the attendees who was standing in my kitchen with a group of people I also didn't know.

"I'm Shawn!" he said happily. "What's your name, sweetie?"

"No, I mean, how did you get invited to this? And I'm Quinta, I live here and this is my party, so it's weird that I don't know you!" I screamed over the music until I heard something crash—a table I had set up for drinks. Someone (I also didn't know) had broken it by accident but scurried away before I could call them out.

Things only got crazier from there. It took me a minute to catch on, but I realized that most of the people who showed up, 50 percent of whom I didn't know, were going straight to the bathroom to do coke. Cocaine?! In my pseudo-Christian, but mainly agnostic home?! I hadn't even done coke! If anything, *I* should've been the one to christen the bathroom with white!

More drinks spilled, more glass broke, and at some point, I just had to give in and accept the chaos. I had the best time I could after finding the friends I actually invited, but it wasn't the Philly-style party I imagined. I definitely wasn't having the types of conversations that bolstered my creativity, and instead spent most of the time trying to make sure we wouldn't lose our security deposit from careless people throwing elbows at our drywalls.

My house ended up surviving the party, but my relationship with Los Angeles almost didn't. I began missing Philly so much that I started to question whether or not I'd made the right move. Was this the type of city that was going to help me grow? Or was it all just a distraction? Was I going to get better at my craft? Or fall into the trap of looking cool without the substance? Would I change LA or would LA change me? Really though, who was doing coke in my bathroom? All this questioning led to a severe bout of homesickness, the type that colored my every move.

I realized that I'd spent my final year in Philly so focused on moving to Los Angeles that I hadn't thought about what I was giving up in the move. Sure, I had wanted to experience new places and things, but Philly had been my home for my entire life. That city held all of my stories, friends, and family within its unrefined edges. It wasn't until I moved into that house with three random girls and some rotting avocados that I realized I'd left a piece of myself on the East Coast, and no party was going to cure that feeling of loss.

In the middle of this homesickness, a girl I went to Temple with hit me up. She told me she was in town for a modeling gig, and asked if I wanted to hang. We weren't particularly close in college, but I jumped at the chance to spend time with someone else who was from home. Maybe she would help me find some of that creativity I was missing in LA.

Let me start out by saying, Drew is a nice person. But on the other hand, she is also a model. So is she nice? (Just kidding, sort of. No, she's great . . . but is she?) Drew has light skin, straight teeth, a perfect nose, and lush natural curls that are so impeccably styled, it makes me wish she made a YouTube tutorial I could watch every morning even though it'd never work on my hair but I would try anyway. She looks like a model in a Macy's mailer. You're probably like "that's not that beautiful," but I want you to go buy a newspaper, find that insert, and tell me that the only Black girl in it wearing this winter's pajama style isn't fucking gorgeous. By the way, the woman you're looking at is probably Drew, because Macy's is just one of the many places she's modeled for.

Drew and I had one class together at Temple: public speaking. As you can imagine, I fucked with public speaking—HARD. I was always speaking my mind anyway, so it was nice to get a credit for it. Drew was a natural at public speaking, too. And by natural, I mean she was a year away from being a professional model, so when she opened her mouth, the public listened . . . or at least they stared. Have I mentioned that she's gorgeous?

After that public speaking class, Drew and I went our separate ways. Still, I was always curious about her life. She was the only other person I knew who wanted a career more frivolous and narcissistic than comedy, so I was super interested in her life. When she messaged saying that she was coming to town and wanted to link up, I saw it as an opportunity to compare notes.

Not only was I hype that Drew was bringing Philly vibes with her, but also, she's a girl, and since moving to LA I had pretty much exclusively hung out with a crew of boys. Spending time with a human lady who was neither an Apple tech nerd, a fellow stand-up comic, nor a TV character would be a welcome change of pace for my social life.

I was looking forward to a girls' night so badly that I didn't

quite consider what kind of girl I was hanging out with. Instead, I just blissfully floated into work on the Friday Drew was
in town. At lunch, I ditched the coworkers and ventured into
the mall to get a new outfit for my big night out.

I wanted to treat myself to a smart and sexy look, since it
was Drew we were dealing with here, and she was both. So,
I took myself to ANGL. For those of you who are not familiar with ANGL, it's a Los Angeles clothing store that sells, as
they put it, "a wide variety of stylish garments appropriate for
the office but still let you slip away into a dinner party or a
night out with your girlfriends." Think Bebe's little sister. I
went there because everything was cheap, but looks legit in
super-dark lighting (aka: bar or club lighting). I wanted something that'd look like I'd "slipped away" from the office and
was ready to party it up like the sophisticated twenty-three-
year-old that I was not.

After searching for the least trashy things in the store, I found
a cool pair of jeans with red leather panels and a white billowy
shirt. At the time, I thought this was the pinnacle of sexy and
cool. Looking back, I realize that I looked like a metrosexual
pirate. In retrospect, I now understand that fake red leather,
denim, and polyester did not project the laid-back LA vibe I
was going for.

When it came time to head out for the night, I went to the
Apple bathroom and changed out of my T-shirt and jeans into
my evening-out lewk. (I always recommend changing into
your "going-out" clothes in the employee bathroom because all
your coworkers can be stunned when you walk out in your real

clothes.) When I came out, I saw a handful of coworkers look up from their screens. *I look hot,* I thought before waltzing out of those sliding glass doors.

As I strutted toward the Avenue of the Stars bus stop, I felt like I was killing it. To be fair, I did feel eccentric cute. My hair was growing back from the post-breakup pixie cut I had gotten, and I was wearing it in whatever cute little styles I could while managing "going natural," as the naturals call it. (To be honest, I wasn't going natural as a show of empowerment or anything like that, I just didn't have any money for a perm. But I know I probably should say that I was doing it because of the empowerment thing, so pretend I said that instead.) With my cute hair and dope clothes, I was ready to take on the clubs, model style.

When the bus finally arrived, I realized I'd never taken it beyond my stop for work in Century City before. Instead of going east back toward Hollywood where I lived, I went west toward Beverly Hills, where Drew was staying. Now, I was in for *real* culture shock.

Before Drew came to visit, I'd never had a reason to be in Beverly Hills—I mainly hung out in Hollywood and Downtown LA, where all the comedians, musicians, and crack pipes lived. I picked a window seat that day so I could get a good view of all the rich people and their cars, maybe a celebrity or two, but my sightseeing excursion quickly lost its fun.

For the first time since moving to Los Angeles, I felt embarrassed to be on the bus as it rolled into Beverly Hills. I shouldn't have felt that way, but I couldn't help it. Everyone on the bus was either homeless, a minority, or both, and as soon as we entered the notoriously wealthy area, it became painfully apparent that we bus people did not belong there.

I looked out the window, through the bird shit and other unidentifiable sticky substances, only to see that everyone on the street was disgustingly rich and predominantly white. As we drove past a stretch of Ferraris, Benzes, and other cars that were worth more than ten years of my salary, the wealth gap was so clear, it hurt.

I had never felt out of place taking the bus in Philly, but something about the emphasis on appearance in LA made taking public transportation feel really shitty. In Philly, the drastically different socioeconomic classes were separated by neighborhoods far away from each other, so you never really saw what richer people had, you only knew what *you* had, and that always seemed to be enough. Even when you did venture to the rich parts of town, they didn't feel egregious, because they're still relatively modest. In Los Angeles, wealthy people are extremely wealthy and flashy, driving their Bugattis right next to you on the road. People go through painstaking lengths to flaunt their shiny things and remind you of what you don't have. Sitting on the 704 bus as it rolled through the subject of a Weezer song, I couldn't help but start to think, "Damn, baby girl, you poor."

As I walked into the lobby of Drew's immaculate hotel in Beverly Hills, my shame spiral took a nosedive. It was clear that these carefree people in the lobby, sipping wine from *real* glasses, had not worked a retail job today like I had. You could see the freedom from consequences spilling from their smiles. Their clothes were stylish, they all looked hot, and they were happy . . . so happy. I mean, I was happy too, but not like that. I was more like "Woohoo, I'm doing all right! I've got one hundred and seventy-eight bucks in my bank account and the leftovers I had for lunch were actually edible" happy, while they were all "What are leftovers?" happy. It was nuts. I would later find out that kind of happy was called "being on valium."

When I got to the elevator, I realized that I truly did not know what Drew and I were going to talk about that night. My mind started to race. *Why did I commit to a hang with someone I don't know that well?! Am I dumb? I should've just stayed home and rewatched* Sex and the City *for the tenth time. Samantha, Carrie, and Miranda are the only friends I need!* At this point in my life, most of my conversational talking points consisted of iOS updates, Marvel, and *Adventure Time.* I panicked when it dawned on me that other than Philly, Drew and I didn't actually have very much in common. I didn't know anyone our age who could afford a real designer purse, let alone a swanky hotel, or "vacays." I didn't know what her favorite shows or movies were. I didn't even know what her favorite flavor of Cheetos was, a crucial fact that I know about everyone close to me. (For those wondering, I'm a Cheddar Jalapeño girl, myself.) Come to think of it, I doubt Drew even ate Cheetos!

I exited the elevator and tried to come up with conversation topics as I walked to her door: Kanye's new album? Adam McKay's career? Diamond Dollars, our college payment system?

Our hopes and dreams? My brain spun through all sorts of things as I knocked on the door and prepared to be hit with nostalgia.

Before I could even formulate my searing POV on Diamond Dollars, the door swung open, and there was Drew in all her model glory. She somehow got hotter since college, which should be illegal.

She gave me a huge hug and invited me into her room. It was a pretty standard hotel room, but whenever I think back and envision it in my head, I remember it being a cavernous spot with marbled floors, arched doorways, and Renaissance paintings on the ceilings.

"Remember Diamond Dollars? I sure miss them," I blurted out while Drew poured me some Cîroc. I scrunched up my nose, embarrassed I'd picked such a vanilla topic to dive into, but at least I knew it was relatable.

"Oh, yeah, miss those," Drew responded, handing me the drink. Okay, then. I took a sip of vodka, trying not to show my lack of hard-liquor experience.

"It's so amazing to see you," Drew told me, making intense eye contact.

"You too," I sincerely responded. Even though I didn't spend much time with Drew in college, I remember the kindness and warmth she always radiated. Drew was always quick to ask you about yourself, and even quicker to listen. She brought with her the exact from-back-home energy I was missing.

"Tell me everything. What have you been up to? Killing it in comedy?" she asked. As she sat waiting to hear about my LA life, I wondered if Drew and I would've been friends if I'd stayed at Temple.

"You could say that," I told her, beginning to relax. "I've been taking classes at the Second—"

Drew's focus shifted away from me and to her lit-up phone. "Actually, sorry, some friends are here," she interrupted, "I'm going to go grab them." Friends? Here? Who the hell? I sat in her room, alone, considering whether or not I had enough time to dig through her makeup bag.

She returned a few minutes later with two tall, well-built guys. The dudes, let's call one Idiot and the other Jason—because I hate the name Jason—were both wearing V-necks and the same fuckboy smirk. Idiot looked like he'd gotten his hair cut that morning, in anticipation of hanging out with a model and her friend. Jason looked like he told women he was close with his mom just to sleep with them. Needless to say, the two were also conventionally attractive. As I learned that night, hot people travel in packs.

Other Things I Learned about Hot People That Night

1. Instead of laughing they just say, "That's funny, you're funny."

2. They always keep one eye on the door to see if anyone hotter (than you) is coming in.

3. They don't like to sit down anywhere, even if there are seats available. It's like their hotness will disappear if they sit. I guess I can kind of understand this one, because I

love to sit, but when I look back at pictures of me where I'm sitting down somewhere, I always look like the Hunchback of Notre Dame's daughter. Not cute.

4. They have mastered looking like they are listening with an eye widening and a head nod.
5. They smell like Marc Jacob's Daisy. No matter what!
6. They hate short people.*

I could see the instant disappointment on Idiot and Jason's faces as soon as they caught a glimpse of me. I think one of them actually *sighed.* When Drew said it'd be her and "a friend," I'm sure they imagined someone equally as model-esque as Drew, but instead they got the girl dressed like a pirate wearing Rite Aid lipstick.

More drinks were poured and I tried to make conversation with Idiot and Jason. "You guys watch *The League*? I love Paul Scheer," I offered. Instead of responding, they gave me a "Yeah, heard of that" and continued on their phones, scrolling mindlessly. I felt like an extra wheel even though there were four of us. Their attitude made it seem like they were planning on creating some sort of tall-and-hot-person tricycle and my presence ruined everything.

It was clear Idiot and Jason were there for Drew, and I stopped being valuable the moment I wasn't the version of attractive they were looking for. Yes, the male gaze is problematic, but I have to admit, when that gaze goes straight through you,

---

* This last one is just a hunch.

it doesn't feel great. I took a big sip of vodka. Again, this scene did not bring in the down-home Philly vibe I was hoping for.

As they googled nearby bars, I shrunk in size. I'd never been dismissed on that kind of scale before. Connecting with people is my strong suit; I thrive at making friends everywhere I go. Remember when I told you I was prom queen in high school?! It's true! People like me!

Since I've always been pretty lucky in the social department, getting ignored by these two Drake impressionists hurt me in my heart.

"We should try this place," Drew said, flipping her phone around to the room.

"Sure, but let's go to the store first," Jason replied.

Drew linked her arm in mine and flashed a large Macy's-ad smile. "This is going to be so fun!" she told me. I believed her.

Minutes later we were in Idiot's car, headed toward a club in Santa Monica. I probably shouldn't have gotten in a car with dudes who were drinking vodka, but I'd already made so many wrong calls that night — what was one more? I tried my best to seem "fun and flirty," even though I was feeling "bothered and a little bloated."

When we rolled into the club, any sort of "maybe this will turn the night around" anticipation vanished. The bar was completely different from what I was used to in Philly, or even in DTLA. My ears were immediately harassed with EDM music; every song sounded like someone was repeatedly punching a synthesizer in the dick. The music was so loud, it was impossible to hear anything, so we all stood around yelling "WHAT?" at each other over and over again, aka pretty much the exact opposite of the fun and creative conversations I'd have at those Philly parties. To make matters worse, I was 100 percent the weirdest looking person in the club. It seemed like every girl got their bodycon dress from the same rack at the same store. I was used to standing out through fashion choices, but this felt different, not like a hip, unique moment, more of a "someone let a *Hook* cosplayer in here" moment.

I'm also pretty sure everyone in this bar was a model, too. You know how when you buy a new car and then suddenly you see that car all around town? This is what this bar was with models. I'd never noticed so many "beautiful" people before, but being out with Drew, it was like they were popping up out of nowhere, like we were in some sort of sexy horror movie.

Even though I was already pretty drunk, the guys tried to get us to drink more. I had work in the morning, and my interest to keep partying in this model-infested hellhole was waning, but Drew, on the other hand, was in full party mode. She was clearly in her element, giggling, flipping her hair, dancing to the repetitive droning bass lines of Avicii. It was like she was consistently in the slow-motion part of a birth control commercial. Drinks appeared for her out of nowhere and as soon as she finished one, a new drink was sent her way. Meanwhile, I stood around awkwardly, nodding my head to the spazzy beats.

Drew existed in a vacuum of attractiveness and therefore didn't understand the depth of awkwardness that is being a short, silly, young-appearing woman at a bar. I'm sure being that attractive brings in all sorts of unwanted attention for Drew, but on the other hand, I was making it my career to get attention, and so becoming invisible while standing next to Drew was confidence-crushing. I didn't want to bum her out by the fact that she was having a different night than me, so I slowly sipped my wine and pretended to be on her level.

After a while, the tall, sexy tricycle decided to head to a different bar. I thought about maybe calling it a night, but I hadn't matured to the point where I could just leave a social gathering without an excuse. I was too worried the others would think I was lame if I dipped out early, so I chose to stay. We all got back into Idiot's car and headed to a gas station for some water and snacks before continuing our bar hopping.

While at the checkout, Jason thought it would be a good idea to buy some of those knockoff Viagra pills. You've seen the ones with names like Rhinozen Black Fire, or Extenze, or Rising Phoenix—so that your boner presumably can rise from the dead? Luckily for Drew and me, Jason also bought the bright pink *for ladies!* kind.

"Wouldn't it be hilarious if we took these pills?" Jason asked.

Hilarious? Hm. Now, I wouldn't say I was a professional comedian at this point in my life, but I was in level two of improv at the Second City and, uh . . . taking sex pills with shallow drunk guys didn't sound like a hilarious premise to me. However, it did sound like a way to finally get some attention and feel like part of the elusive club of the Hots.

Drew and Idiot both popped a respectively binary-gendered pill. They had that "anything goes, I'm a different person tonight!!" kind of vacation vibe as they did it. I stared at my pink pill. Was I going to let these almost-strangers peer pressure me into taking dumb gas station drugs? With sex pills? Come on.

Why couldn't it have at least been something cool like shrooms or acid?

For the first time in the night Jason and Idiot turned their attention to me. I sighed and threw the pill into my mouth. Everyone cheered and for a moment, I felt back on my game. This is probably a good time to say that you should not do vague gas station drugs with strange men.

We headed to the next club as we waited for our "sex pill" experiment to take effect. I spent the whole time questioning myself in my head. I wasn't a sex-pill-popping, vodka-drinking club person. I was a perfectly acceptable fun person in my own way. I didn't need attention from these guys—I could get better quality attention from being on stage.

All these realizations hit me at the same time the pills did. My stomach twisted and I grew extremely hot and nauseous. I was gonna be sick. Whoever created these sexual enhancement pills had clearly never had sex. Or maybe they only had sex on rickety boats? I opened my mouth to tell the crew that I was done for the night, but what came out, instead, was vomit. A little hint for all you young ladies out there, an easy tip for stealing away male attention from a model is throwing up on the side of said male's car. Sorry, Idiot.

Drew thankfully insisted that Idiot and Jason drive me home. I'm sure it put a damper on their sexy LA club night, but at that point I didn't care. My legs were wobbly and my body was physically rejecting how dumb the whole situation was.

I don't remember saying bye to Drew or the guys, but I assume it was short. I'm not sure how the rest of their night played out, but I'm sure once the horny pills kicked in, it turned into a super-sexy tricycle orgy. Love that for them.

When I got home, I had a different type of super-sexy time, one that involved stumbling through my front door, avoiding my reflection on that wall-sized mirror, and falling into bed. I managed to undress while simultaneously loading *The Office* on my computer, which felt good. Like really good. It was the best night of *The Office* watching I'd ever had. So maybe those pills did work, a little bit?

The next morning, I woke up with a yeast infection and new-found understanding of what I needed to do to make the best of my life in Los Angeles. Even though I knew that those guys were yuck buckets, they were the first people in the city to truly knock me off my cloud of positivity and confidence. From my newly humbled vantage point, I realized that this wouldn't be the last time I'd feel like the odd girl out in a room, but it would most definitely be the last time I'd let my feelings of outcastness get the best of me. Even though the night kind of sucked, it reminded me that I wasn't in LA to party, anyway: I was here to work. And nobody was going to stop me from reaching my goals—even if it meant creating my own scene. Pirate shirts or not.

10

Girl Who's Never

··

The day everything changed for me started off as a day like any other. I left for my morning shift at Apple, carting my tattered H&M tote bag packed with a T-shirt, a banana, a joint, a ragged copy of Charles Bukowski's *You Get So Alone,* and about forty other things I didn't need to be carrying around.

I got my Subway breakfast, fixed phones, gossiped with co-workers, ate lunch, fixed some more tech, and then clocked out to prepare for a show I had that night. The whole shift, I played it cool, but the truth was, I was fixated on the show. This wasn't going to be some ordinary performance: Cristal, an improv friend, had asked me whether I'd be interested in performing at the world-famous Comedy Store. I nearly dropped the phone when I read that message. The Comedy Store? That was the place of legends. I immediately said yes. This would be an opportunity to show everyone what I could do, and I was game. Only problem was that it was a really last-minute ask: I only had one day to come up with a twenty-minute show.

After accepting, panic settled in. I wanted to do something special, something I could show off in front of a huge crowd, but lately I was in such a funk that it was making it hard to be funny. I was still feeling lonely in my LA life, and it was affecting my output. I was making people laugh at my shows with reliable old material, but a lot of my newer ideas were feeling flat or forced. I needed something to spark.

At the time, my dating life had ground to a halt, which was majorly contributing to my funk. In Philly, I was swimming in possible dating options. I could stop talking to one guy, and find another at a party in Northern Liberties later that night if I wanted to. In LA, the options were few and far between. Maybe it was because I was so focused on my career goals, and because of that it wasn't easy to be emotionally available. Or maybe it's simply because no one was really interested. According to the guy friends I asked about it, I was either too cute or not cute enough. They would go, "Quinta, you're wifey material, which kind of means you'd require too much responsibility and respect to date now, which is sweet but no fun for me!"

Around that time, I had reconnected with fellow Philly transplant and college friend Kate, who was also doing the LA comedy grind. We had reconnected because she wanted to collaborate, which was exciting because I really respected her as a performer, but we were also growing to be close friends, lamenting about our ambitions and the loneliness of LA single life alike. The night I told Cristal I'd say yes to the performance, I texted Kate to ask if she'd want to be part of the Comedy Store show. She was hype! She enlisted her friend Carrie, and I reached out to my friends Danny and Matt to round out the group. All people I knew who would be free and down to do comedy at a moment's notice.

I tried sketching out some ideas for my set, but I was coming up short. To distract myself, I went on Facebook and started clicking around, looking at old photos. I went down a rabbit hole, eventually getting into the era of photos that featured Joshua and me, laughing, hamming it up. It only made me feel worse.

"I miss dating, man. This sucks. I'm sick of being single," I texted Kate as I clicked through an old hookup buddy's profile. "You know that if we were in Philly, I'd be killing it right now."

"Yeah, true, but . . . dating itself sucks! You date, it ends, and then you have to do it all over again, trying to seem like the coolest version of yourself. An endless cycle. That sucks even more!" she typed back.

Kate was right. Dating did suck, even when there were more available options. In Philly, I'd barely actually get taken on a real "date"; it would usually just be us "hanging out." I mean, I'd get excited for the fact that a guy actually took me to the movies and paid for it. And if he paid for my popcorn . . .

Boom. I had an idea for what I was going to do to showcase my skill at the sketch show. Little did I know, it was going to one-eighty my life.

When I got home from work, I immediately prepped my living room for rehearsal with my last-minute team of comedic performers. I pushed all the furniture to the walls to make room for some creative thinking. I smoked a bowl (necessary), and around 2 p.m., my fellow underemployed comedy Avengers showed up.

Carrie had written an "Annie" sketch where Annie's dog

wouldn't stop humping her while she sung. Kate had a piece called "Conversations with Drake," where the rapper Drake's lines played anytime she asked him a question. Danny, a six-foot white guy with the spirit of a Labrador retriever, had prepared a controversial sketch where he wore a dashiki. I remember thinking, *I could stop this, but maybe he needs to learn this lesson in public,* so I let it fly. Matt, a sweet man with bright eyes, the best soul, and the ability to transform into any Victorian woman, had written a sketch about . . . being a Victorian woman. I loved them all, and was excited to share a stage with these weirdos. I was nervous too, sure, but deep down, something told me that the show would be a hit.

"Quinta, what do you have?" Danny asked me, gently folding up his dashiki.

I took a deep breath and smiled at Kate. "I've been thinking a lot about how shitty this dating scene is . . . so I'm going to be doing a character called 'The Girl Who's Never Been on a Nice Date.'"

I explained how it would be a girl that would be impressed by all of the small things a guy did on a date. Kate called it hilarious; Matt called it relatable. Those responses were all the reassurance I needed.

We all drove to the Comedy Store in Danny's Prius, pumped to perform at the place that birthed artists like Robin Williams, Richard Pryor, and Whoopi Goldberg. It would be my first time at the venue at all, so to be performing there before even being an audience member was completely surreal.

We walked up to a cloud of cigarette smoke on the outdoor

patio and said hello to the older white bouncer, who wasn't excited to see us, or anyone, it seemed.

"IDs," he said, as if it was the most exhausting two syllables in the English language.

"Yes, sure! And we're here to perform!" I told him, excitedly pulling my ID out of my purse.

He looked over our, let's just say, diverse group of oddballs, and raised his eyebrows. "You are? You sure?" Before we could answer, Cristal yelled my name from a different entrance down the street.

"Quinta, hey! They're with me!" The bouncer shrugged and sent us on our way. We excitedly met Cristal at the door and she ushered us into the theater's greenroom area.

"Okay, so you're the second act. You're on in five minutes and . . ." She stopped and eyed the group. "Wait . . . Quinta, you couldn't find one more Black person?"

"Uh, I didn't know I needed to? And I only had a little bit of time! Why? Does it matter?" I asked.

"You tell me." Cristal walked us out of the greenroom and pulled a curtain back so we could see the sea of an all-Black, uncle-and-auntie-age-group audience. The stand-up on stage was telling "bitches be" and "niggas always" jokes and the crowd was going wild. I gulped.

"Good luck," Cristal said as she went to go about her producer business. I turned around to see my team of Avengers looking more like they had just seen Thanos with all six Infinity Stones. They knew what I knew: Black audiences are the hardest to make laugh, and ultimately, these people didn't come to see sketch. They wanted stand-up, because that's what the Comedy Store was known for.

"We're gonna bomb. They're gonna hate us!" Kate said, looking like she was two seconds from passing out.

Matt chimed in, "Maybe we should just go home, or Quinta, maybe you just go out, do your thing?"

I gave it some thought. "Guys. Don't worry. We can do this. It may be hard, but we'll make them laugh. Trust me. Our stuff is funny. Maybe not 'bitches be trippin'' funny. But funny. *We can do this.*" I don't know where my confidence came from, but it seemed to have an effect. They all nodded and clapped, like we were an actual sports team and not a bunch of comedy nerds trying to string a show together.

The host of the show grabbed the mic and surveyed us. "And now before the real show," he told the audience, "we are gonna have some sketch comedy. Give it up!"

The crowd reluctantly clapped at the lackluster intro. Kate went up first with her Drake sketch. As she was setting up, a woman yelled out, "I'm bored!" and the crowd laughed. Despite that, Kate ran through it and managed to get a few good laughs. We were off to an okay start.

Next, Carrie did her Annie sketch, which also brought out a good number of laughs. People really enjoyed the dog (Danny) humping her leg. Slapstick prevails. After she finished, Danny went up with his dashiki on. I don't remember what his sketch was, and neither do my friends, but we do remember both "You a funny white boy!" and "Imma beat your ass, white boy!" being yelled out during his set. Danny rendered it a success.

Then it was my turn. I was nervous. This performance became an even bigger deal to me than it had been before. A Black crowd would absolutely make or break whether or not my character was funny. If they didn't like it, I had nothing. And if they did, I knew I had something special. I stepped onto the stage and positioned a chair in the middle of it, sending up a quick prayer to no one in particular before sitting down.

"This is . . . The Girl Who's Never Been on a Nice Date," I told the audience. I got no laughs, just one clap. I squinted to see that the clapper was my friend Abdul, who I'd forgotten I had invited and was a hero for actually going to his friend's comedy show.

As I smiled at Abdul, I caught a sight that shocked me: sitting right in front of him was American TV Judge Joe Brown! Internally, I freaked out seeing this huge daytime celeb in the building, but I didn't let that nervousness appear on my face. I had a show to do. This was my moment!

I sat up in my chair, tilted my shoulders back, and fixed my posture and face to be like a girl seeking to impress someone. I took a deep breath, and then launched into my bit. "This is a nice restaurant . . . what's it called? Cheesecake Factory? Oh . . . you got money," I said, acting as if the audience was the "date." I got quite a few laughs. I went harder on the impression, channeling all the Philly girls I knew, my younger Philly self, and the current version of me who was dying to go on any date at all, even one at a chain restaurant. I went on, waving my hand up in the air. "Excuse me, waitress, can we have some water? What kind of water do you want? Sparkling! Ooh, you got *money*."

The audience howled with laughter. They had spoken. It was funny. I was funny.

I ran through a few more date scenarios, until at last—the holy grail of date experiences. I closed with: "Dessert? YOU GOT MONEY!" The crowd lost it and cheered! I bowed, thanked them, and motioned for my team to join me on the stage. We all bowed in unison, beaming, as Abdul clapped extra hard and Judge Joe Brown threw us a huge thumbs-up. Kate and I looked at each other with glee. I couldn't believe it. My first time at the Comedy Store and I had crushed it.

Cristal paid me fifty dollars for the entire show and thanked us for performing. I thanked her for having us and split the money among my team. Ten dollars each! Showbiz, baby! We didn't care, though, we were just happy to hit a stage, and happy we all managed to get laughs (and threats of violence) from an all-Black crowd.

We were giddy as we headed out of the theater and back onto the smoke-clad patio. While pushing our way out, I caught up with Abdul, who was in love with our show, and my performance especially. "You should put that character on the internet!" he said. Before I could even tell him how internet comedy didn't seem like my thing, and that my true love was the stage, I felt a tap on my shoulder. Abdul, Carrie, Matt, Kate, and Danny's eyes all went super wide as I turned around. It was Judge Joe Brown!

"Young lady. You are so funny. You got a real future ahead of you. Very funny!" Joe Brown told me, a few friends behind him nodding and chatting in agreement.

I was elated! When I was a kid I used to watch this man judge people, and here he was judging me! "Very funny!"

"Thank you, Your Honor!" I blurted out, making them laugh even more. Then, one of his friends, who looked just like him and was probably also in his fifties, raised his eyebrows at me. "How old are you? Because, you know—you should let me take you on a real nice date!"

All of my friends laughed silently, and I blushed out of embarrassment. "I'm okay, thanks . . . as much as I'd love a nice date . . . I think I'm just really focused on my career right now." And just like that, my funk had lifted.

"Seriously, Quinta, put it on YouTube or something!" Abdul's words had been ringing in my head since the show all week. Then, when I met up with my friend Emebeit for dinner and told her how successful the sketch was, she echoed Abdul's sentiment. "Seriously, QBZ! You should try it!"

"I don't really want to put my videos on YouTube, though. It feels kind of hacky. I want to be the real deal, you know? I'm not sure that's the place for me," I said, chomping on a fry. I thought for a second. "Maybe I'll just put it on my Instagram page, since there's video there now."*

I hadn't really thought about combining the internet with my comedy; I had been so focused on the stage that anything less than that didn't seem worth it. But maybe there was some-

---

* That's right. Instagram had just gotten video, because there was a point where it was just pictures. Millennials, remember with me as we set up our retirement plans.

thing to it—it'd be a safe test ground. If it didn't land, I could always delete it. "All right," I said. "I mean, we're already in a restaurant. Why not try it out?"

And so right there, in the middle of dinner, I tried out the sketch in real time. Emebeit acted as my cameraperson, holding my phone as I treated the phone camera as the audience. She filmed me improvising he-got-money-esque lines from across the table, trying not to crack up the whole time. No one even noticed or cared that we were doing this, because it was in the time before Viners were running amok and disrupting businesses. Also, Emebeit and I were classy . . . we kept our volume low. Meb handed me my phone and I edited the video to my liking while she ate her dessert. "Here we go," I said, and posted it.

To my surprise, everyone who followed me—about a thousand people at the time—loved it! Comments like "lol" and "yo, this is funny" were racking up, and by the time Meb and I got our check, the video was getting more likes than anything I had ever posted. People were even commenting on it who didn't follow me, which had never happened before. *Maybe there's something to this Instagram video thing,* I thought to myself. I mentally made a plan to film another video.

A few days later, I called up my friend Aaron Ramey, a fellow Philly transplant, to join me for the next video. I figured if I wanted to take the character to the next level, I should have an actual guy present; this way, I could move around and do different scenes, having him be part of the adventure instead of always just talking to the screen. He agreed, and so the next day, Aaron, the "date"; my friend Samir, the "cashier" on our date; Emebeit, the "camera operator"; and me, the "girl," made our way to a movie theater at the Grove, a mall in LA that is a celeb hotspot and prime shopping destination.*

Emebeit found a partially hidden space where she could covertly film us as we played out a scene where Aaron and I went to the concession stand before a movie. I told Aaron to ask for candy, soda, and a popcorn, and I'd react to each with more and more enthusiasm. When Aaron asked Samir for a large popcorn, I turned to the camera and cocked up my eyebrow. "A large? He got *money!*" I exclaimed—loud enough that I caught the attention of a theater worker, who promptly told us to leave. But it didn't matter. We got the video done.

The three of us stood outside of the theater and watched the video together. We couldn't stop laughing, watching it over and over. That rewatch reaction was how I knew it was good. I decided to post the video immediately, before I had any second thoughts about it.

There was no way yet to see insights or even share the video at that time, but I was getting more likes than I had followers. Strangers were tagging their stranger-friends in the comments. People began writing things like "If that ain't me!" Or "I literally watched this ten times already!"

My Instagram follower count began to increase: 10K, then 20K, then 30K, and so on. This was taking off! I decided to make more videos, take this girl all over LA on different dates. I made a video of her on a rooftop, at a coffee shop, a theme

---

* Even though I think the Americana is better. More stores, more low-key. The Grove is actually trash.

park.* And Instagram was loving it. The comments kept rolling in; I couldn't believe it.

Then, a new level of internet notoriety happened: all of a sudden, my face started appearing everywhere. Someone had turned a still of me into a meme! I was so honored! It was surreal: I would log onto Facebook and then see my face float across the screen. Friends would send me a screenshot saying "look what my cousin just sent me when I told them I got a new car . . . you!" That's when I decided to make a Facebook fan page, so I could be in charge of sharing my videos. I also broke down and reposted the videos to YouTube, so more people could see and share. And, ironically, that's when the Girl Who's Never began to take a life of her own. The videos got nearly 900K views—which was unheard of for a fifteen-second sketch.

A defining moment in the whole experience was when Philly royalty and celebrity rapper Meek Mill posted the "He Got Money" meme on *his* Instagram. When he posted the clip of me, I was like, "Oh, damn, this is big. Okay." Seeing Meek post my video had a profound impact on me. When I was coming up, I used to watch him freestyle on these things called "Headshots" raps. They were short clips of people rapping in the neighborhood that were put on DVDs and handed out. Meek turned these low-production, high-talent street perfor-

---

* Which was my personal fave. The guy tells her he's going to buy the photo they take on the roller coaster and she screams, "He got money" as the roller coaster goes down.

mances into a huge career. Seeing my face show up on his Insta reminded me how powerful lo-fi and accessible creativity could be. I was inspired and ready to do the same.

As much as all of this notoriety was exciting, there was a downside: I was starting to get recognized. I would walk down the street to get a taco and someone would yell, "You're that girl from Instagram . . . can I get a picture?" It was cool at first, but then it kept happening to the point where I realized I couldn't leave the house looking a mess anymore.

Other times, someone would yell "he got money" at me and ask me to do the line while they recorded me. I always said no to that. In my head, I had already made a choice: I perform when I want, not when I'm told to, and I live by that today.

The worst, though, was that people started to recognize me while I was at work fixing phones at Apple. Having a customer shout "he got money!" while I was working a job that kind of said I didn't have money was mildly embarrassing. But I took it in stride; I was starting to care less about my day job anyway, with all of my focus on my next steps in the comedy world.

Now that I'd unlocked Instagram as a new tool for comedy, I put all of my energy into that. While that may seem pretty standard now, at the time, there wasn't a way to make money directly off going viral. I was glad people were digging my stuff, but ya girl still had to pay rent! That's when I learned about the weird job market of "appearance fees." Basically, a club or a conference can pay you mad money to just show up and say your catchphrase—so I did that for a while, stretching the character into new places. But the real moneymaker was merch. People were asking for it, so I reached out to my friend Jonny, who had his own clothing line, for his advice. He helped me design cool shirts based off the catchphrases and memes, and off the bat, I started making more money than I had ever made at Apple. It was crazy.

As my videos gained more and more popularity, and my bank account got fatter, I felt empowered to quit Apple . . . again. I walked into Diana's office, ready to break the news to her that I was moving on.

"You're out of here, aren't you?" Diana said, taking my moment from me.

"Yeah," I replied. "And I don't think I'll be coming back this time."

"I don't think you will, either," Diana said with a smile. We hugged. It felt good quitting that time, because I was leaving on a high note and happier in spirit, instead of being spiritually beaten down and angry. I felt that things would be good this time.

Meanwhile, there were more zeroes in my bank account than I had ever seen in my working life (three!). I began spending like a G: buying nicer clothes, paying for crab leg dinners, getting thirty-dollar bottles of wine instead of Two-Buck Chuck from Trader Joe's. In retrospect, it was not the best use of my newfound finances, but because I had never had real money, thus never learned how to manage it. I'd been broke for so long, I just wanted a taste of not being broke—and splurging on crab was the way I chose to do it.

Even though I was raking in cash, I began to get sick of the one-hit-wonder internet meme life. I was spending more time doing event appearances than making my sketches, having to cancel on live performances because I was traveling to block parties to "host." I was not fulfilled with that work, and it definitely wasn't sustaining my creative appetite. Doing appearances sounds easy and cool in theory, but it's also awkward and soul-crushing. Everyone expects you to repeat the same line over and over, which makes you start to feel less like a person and more like a cartoon character. I began to get scared that I was trapped in this one character for the rest of my life.

I knew that if I didn't want to get stuck in my fifteen minutes, I was going to have to level up. After an encouraging push from my newly acquired manager, Adam, I decided to explore stand-up. If I was going to get paid to show up in clubs, I wanted to do it as a comedian, not as a character. I found out that there was a stand-up night at an improv theater where my friends and I performed called the Improv Space. Fortunately for me, Kate wanted to try stand-up too, so I went with her to the show, on the fence about whether or not I would actually get up on the stage. I wrote some jokes just in case, but I was mainly going to support her.

I watched Kate triumphantly do stand-up for the first time in front of the thirty-seat crowd that night, which gave me the confidence to try it myself. I put my name in "the hat" to be called, and happened to be called up next. Fate! I got on the stage, told some jokes about homeless people and Barack

Obama . . . and I crushed. Maybe that doesn't sound humble, but it's the truth. Finding stand-up as another outlet to practice my comedy writing and performance skills reminded me that I didn't need to rely on gimmicks to succeed. I was funny. I am funny. I will be forever funny. I will always be good on the stage.

Now that Kate and I shifted our focus from sketch to stand-up, we began getting closer with some of the other improvisers who did stand-up at that theater, including my now good friend Justin Tan. Justin had great sets and a unique point of view, heightened by the fact that he was a tall Asian man. Overall, I loved his style and how he held his mic, gripped at the bottom and not at the center. We made it a tradition to get In-N-Out after sets.

"This Animal Style burger is getting pricey, man. God, I need more work," I told Justin, Kate, and our other friends jokingly while putting ketchup on my patty.

"Dude, but you're famous!" Justin said, stuffing fries into his mouth.

I laughed. "Yeah, well, famous doesn't exactly equate to money."

A few months later, Justin reached out to see if I'd be interested in filming something for a website called BuzzFeed.com. (Have you heard of it?) BuzzFeed Video had just started becoming a thing; at the time, they were mainly known as the website with clever lists. I recognized the spirit of evolution in their videos and wanted to be a part of it.

"I'm in!" I texted Justin.

"So all you have to do," Justin texted me, "is eat Doritos on camera."

"Tight. Sounds normal."

"Cool. We can pay $200."

Getting paid to eat chips? Fuck yes. This gig was already shaping up to be one of the best jobs I'd ever had.

When I arrived to the warehouse-like offices in Central LA, I immediately fell in love.

"Want a tour?" Justin offered.

"Let's do it."

As we strolled through the offices, I was floored by what I was seeing. The large windows and exposed-wood-beam ceilings gave it the kind of stylish start-up energy that every show makes fun of, but which I found pretty attractive. It was an open floor plan, too, so everyone sat at long white tables facing each other. Say what you want about millennial work environments, but to me, a person who had never been inside any sort of nonretail office, the whole place seemed cool as fuck.

The place was packed with young creatives who all looked hip and interesting. People were filming videos on Canon cameras right in the front open-space "lobby." Cameras, mics, and lighting rigs were scattered throughout—all the tools I was itching to get my hands on.

As we walked around, I noticed that these hip/interesting people were working on videos with all sorts of fancy editing programs open on their double screens, stuff I'd never even seen before. At home, I'd just been using iMovie on my laptop. It got the job done . . . but barely. I couldn't believe these fools were being paid to do the same things I did in my free time, for fun!

I immediately recognized the powerful opportunities that lay within those walls.

"Uh, yeah. I need to work here," I told Justin, who responded with a laugh. "No, seriously, can you hook it up?"

"Really? But you're crushing it on the internet."

"That's fleeting. I want to create at this level. And, I need a steady job." I fanned my arms across all the people working diligently at their computers. "You know I'd thrive here."

"Okay, okay, I'll put in a good word."

I knew I had to be strategic with what I did with my comedy, and getting a job with a stable paycheck, particularly one where I could learn how to edit and produce my own videos, would make me more valuable. BuzzFeed was the answer to everything my current career scheme was lacking. With Justin's assurance, I sat down to shoot the Doritos video, my entire body buzzing.

The shoot went off without a hitch. We ate chips, made jokes, and nailed it. I felt good. Beyond good. I couldn't believe I was making money and getting fed at the same time! It was my personal heaven. It took Justin two weeks to edit and upload the video and I bothered him every day until it was live. When he finally uploaded it on August 13, 2014, the video got over 7.2 million views.

With the video exploding on the internet (and finally with view counts I could see), my desire to work at BuzzFeed grew even more. I began straight-up bugging Justin about putting in a good word, because sometimes, you gotta be pushy and annoy your friends when you want something.

"Okay, okay, I'll put you in touch with Andrew Gauthier

(AG)—the head of BuzzFeed Video Division,"* he told me. Minutes later, an introductory email popped up in my inbox.

Like Justin, AG was also surprised I wanted to work for BuzzFeed, considering my face was all over the internet already. To them, it seemed like I'd found fame and fortune on my own. I had to really make my case, but at the end of our meeting, AG was convinced that I was serious about developing my skill set with BuzzFeed.

AG suggested I do a residency first so we could feel each other out, so I signed on to do a monthlong gig. For the first time in my life, I was actually getting *consistently* paid to be funny and creative. It was a literal dream come true.

I landed the internship in October, and threw all of my efforts behind my first-ever video, "The Actual Scariest Things on Earth." You know: things like dropping your phone, sending your parent a sext, checking anything on WebMD, etc. It was cute and short and ended up pulling over three million views. That silly video proved to me that I'd found a corner of the internet where I could thrive.

My monthlong internship eventually turned into two months, and two turned into three. At the end of the third month, AG called me back into his office to make sure I still wanted the job. "I see a big future for you," he politely told me from across his desk. "Are you sure you want to start that future working for a media company like BuzzFeed?"

"I am confident that this is what I want," I reassured him. And so, AG got Ze Frank, president of BuzzFeed Motion Pic-

---

* Now he's the director of video for Joe Biden.

tures, to meet with me. When I sat down with Ze, a large, intimidating man to most, he told me, "I keep hearing about you, and everything you built outside of here. I want you to understand the scope of the company and your responsibilities within it."

Luckily, I'd prepared for this meeting, so I had a response at the ready. It's important to never think anything is going to be handed to you, even if you're doing a good job. I knew Ze was a smart guy and he'd want to see what I was all about. I also knew that BuzzFeed was an environment built on innovation. I made sure to walk into the meeting with ideas to get more views for the company.

"I have a vision for BuzzFeed Video," I told Ze. Even though I'd only been there for a handful of months, I made sure to spend a portion of my time thinking about the scope of the company and who I wanted to reach with our videos and how we wanted to do that.

At the time, I was working on *BuzzFeed Violet*, a bunch of short videos on topics that were all super funny/relatable. "I see a world where these videos are serialized. Where we write characters and story lines that people will follow, much like they follow TV characters," I continued. Ze, who had already discussed this direction with other creators there, was impressed with my foresight and ability to speak with confidence. I got the job.

During my time at BuzzFeed, I wrote, produced, and directed content that help bring in more than one billion monthly views. My viral videos alone brought in more than 138 million views. I could have never expanded in this way on my own. Before I took the job at BuzzFeed, there was no way of knowing that it'd actually make me even more famous on the internet, but I did know it'd teach more than I could learn on my own, shooting from my iPhone. The gamble paid off.

When I hit my stride at BuzzFeed, I began to truly, madly, deeply feel myself. If you've ever had the pleasure of working a job that aligns with your interests, then you too understand the feeling of showing up to work and thinking, "Holy shit. I like my job." Of course, not every day was sunshine and accolades, but at a good job, there are enough of those days to keep you happy.

BuzzFeed provided a built-in community that supported and respected me. It gave me an elevated platform where I could experiment with my humor and sharpen my editing skills. Everyone may not have always agreed with my perspective, but we had respectful conversations about each other's viewpoints. If you take one career tidbit away from me, it's that whatever it is you want to do with your life, make sure you have a strong community around you while you're doing it.

Getting that job at BuzzFeed taught me so much, and also marked the last time I'd let myself get in a bad situation with money, too. No more crab leg dinners just because. But even though I've learned how to make smarter decisions, I still slip up now and again. For example, a few weeks ago, I bought the Le Petit Baci raffia tote from Jacquemus. When I saw its straw tassels and gold-plated name tag, I thought of summer, luxury, happiness. I wanted to give myself all of those things. So I spent an embarrassing amount to do so.

The bag itself is ridiculously small, no bigger than a Chinese takeout container. It barely fits my phone (my lip balm can forget about it). Totally useless, but I love it. I scheduled a whole trip to the park just so I could show it off to the world.

As I struggled to fit my phone into the purse, I let out a few choice words in frustration.

"Why did you buy it if it can't hold anything?" my fiancé laughed.

I looked at him and thought about when my only option for an LA boyfriend was Judge Joe Brown's friend. Then I looked at my purse and thought about my ratty H&M bag that held all my worldly possessions inside of it until the day its seams burst. How far I had come since then.

I swung the bag over my shoulder, looked my boyfriend square in the eye, and said, "Because . . . she got money now."

11

MAC

....

That's a picture of me in 2009. I was nineteen years old, at a college party called Dripping Like Water. Its name was derived from a Snoop Dogg song, but was earned by the fact that the party would get so packed and sweaty that the ceiling would actually drip moisture (college is gross). Why did I wear

a hat to that, you ask? I don't truly know. College Quinta loved hats even when they weren't cute, complementary, or necessary.

You might look at this picture and go, "aw, young Quinta, looking cute, go, girl!" You'd be right, I was cute. But I look back at it and think, *I'm so happy I've grown from then, and love myself more.*

I look at the heavy eyeliner that doubled as shadow to make me look more emo. I look at the weave that I begged my sister to put in after I permed my own hair (against her advice) and damaged it badly. I look at the top I was wearing, which was actually a dance-costume leotard that I decided to wear under a skirt because it could unzip and show off my boobs. I look at this picture, and I see a girl who was happy her skin looked lighter than it usually did in photos, because that meant people would like her more. Sure, I was cute, but to me, this picture represents a girl who was trying to be someone she wasn't— someone who was leaning hard into what the media was telling her she should be, rather than celebrating who she was.

When I was younger, first establishing my mark in dance classes, I wanted to be exactly like the girls in *Bring It On:* tough, spunky, and talented. All of my classmates felt the same way. Of course, me and my all-Black-girl class identified with Gabrielle Union and the Compton Clovers, but we really wanted to be the lead-in-the-movie and lead-in-life star: Kirsten Dunst. She got the gold and she got the guy. Whether we knew it or not, she was who we wanted to be . . . the main character. The hot one who stole the show and won the competitions. I remember watching that movie over and over again, wishing I could get my hair to bounce around the way hers did when she flew through the air.

Kirsten Dunst wasn't the only star to influence me, of course. As I got older and became more aware of the trends in pop culture and entertainment, I absorbed everything, paying close attention to who was in which commercial, watching every show through the last credit, practicing impressions in the mirror, just generally trying to figure out how to be them.

During my studies, I saw the same types of images flash across the screen: the stars were thin, white or light, and if not that, thick and voluptuous but with perfect features. Anything that fell outside of those conventional standards was not represented in the mainstream, so I assumed it was undesirable. I subconsciously accepted that, and committed myself to working harder to get as close to the norm as possible. I couldn't be white or blond, but I could keep my hair cute, my body under control, and my style on point.

All the media messaging I was taking in began to take its toll when I was eighteen. I went from rolling out of bed and high-fiving the mirror to wearing extra tights under my school pants to make my butt look bigger, or straightening my hair to make it look more Kirsten-y. Playing with makeup is fun, and something a lot of girls do, but I began caking my face in too-light foundation so that my natural skin would not be seen to the world. I started using Nair to get rid of my face hair, but sometimes left it on too long and got unflattering chemical-burn mustaches that made me look like a tiny Black-girl Alex Trebek. I even started wearing a magnetic nose ring (because, of course, my mom would never let me get a real one). One time, while laughing too hard at *Family Guy*, I snorted and accidentally inhaled the magnetic back. I think it's still somewhere in me. Basically, everything about me became fake, high maintenance . . . and sometimes hazardous.

I distinctly remember being a nineteen-year-old at Urban Outfitters one day and trying on a cute yellow dress. I liked the way it fit and decided I was going to buy it. I wanted to go out to show my friend, Lauren, but I realized that I hadn't shaved my legs in days. I can't go out there like this, I thought to myself. People might know that I, a human, have hair on my legs!

"What's taking so long?" Lauren called from the other side of the curtain divider.

"Chill! I'm coming!"

I searched my bag for a razor, since I always had a ton of toiletries on me while traveling back and forth to campus. I found one and started to dry shave my legs in a hurry. Of course, I cut myself and started to bleed on the dress. I told Lauren I couldn't come out (why didn't I just do that in the first place) and would DEFINITELY be buying the dress. But when I went to take it off, I was horrified with what I saw in the mirror: an abstract version of myself, with a bleeding leg, smudged makeup from struggling, and my straight weave tangled across my face. Who was I? My obsession with not looking like myself worked, and had transformed me into an unrecognizable person. My hair wasn't mine. My eyelashes weren't mine. And while those things are okay if you make conscious choices to do them, they're scary when you don't. I just didn't look like myself anymore. I was actually startled by my reflection.

How had my self-perception gotten so bad? Like, how did I go from someone who would wake up each day with the goal of projecting my purest self into the world, to someone who didn't want to leave the house because I didn't have Buffy the Body's butt or Buffy the Vampire Slayer's cheekbones? I went from feeling like I was a charismatic magnet to a sad-face person-repellant. The culprit? Materialism, advertising, and consumerism, or what I'll refer to from here on out as MAC.*

MAC releases a toxic energy that infects the brains of strong but vulnerable people. It can take a confident person and boil them in self-doubt. It corrodes their common sense and decision-making skills, telling them they need to buy more to feel better. And that's because the business of beauty thrives on nasty business practices. You can't sell cover-up if people like their natural skin; you can't sell lip fillers without making someone feel that their lips aren't full enough. It's advantageous for advertisers to break down consumers' self-esteem, make people focus on their "flaws," so that these same advertisers can promise to rebuild that self-esteem with the shiny and expensive products they're pushing on you.

I spent years quietly ingesting the MAC messaging that told me I wasn't cute enough, I wasn't interesting enough, I wasn't Kirsten Dunst–y enough. But no matter how much I spent on makeup, I was never going to look like Kirsten Dunst, or even Gab Union. I can only look like Quinta. When I was a teenager, this was a hard reality to face. It made me feel like I simply wasn't born with what's needed to succeed in my dream of being that main character.

The truth was, the more pop culture I ate up, the more I wasted away as a person. I wasn't me anymore. After that day

---

* Not to be confused with the makeup brand. Don't sue me, please.

in the Urban dressing room where I lacerated my leg, I decided to start from scratch. I liked who I was before I fell for the ads and commercials that pushed this nasty POV on me. I wanted to go back to viewing myself with the same enthusiasm and self-assurance I had when I was younger.

So, from that day forward, I went through the hard process of relearning myself in order to figure out how to like me the way I came out into the world. Here's some tips for how I did it, in case you find yourself in a spot where your own negativity is eating you up. It's hard, but it's worth it, I promise.

How to Relearn Yourself

1. **No idols.** And yes, I know idolization is an unavoidable part of human nature. People have idolized others at least since Jesus dropped, so it's nothing new. But try doing it less, or emphasize looking up to yourself and your peers ahead of someone famous who has an entire hair and makeup team on staff. If you can manage, have no idols at all. It's possible.

2. **Shop small businesses if you're able.** Large brands will do anything to get you to buy their products (including brainwashing you into self-hatred). Faceless corporations should not be the ones in charge of what's beautiful—you should decide that for yourself.

3. **Reevaluate your relationship with makeup.** Try to be sure you're wearing the face, and the face isn't wearing you. Are you ashamed to leave the house without makeup? Maybe look into that. You need to be cool with your own face—it's the only one you've got, after all.

4. **Listen to the song** "I Am Not My Hair," by India Arie. Follow it up with "Unpretty," by TLC.

5. **Ask yourself "Why?"** When you see something you want, ask yourself why you want it. Is it to fit in? Is it to feel better? Is it to fill some sort of void? Most of the time the things that we buy won't solve any of these problems.

6. **Diversify your content.** It's very easy to follow the same kinds of people on social media, which only serves to reinforce the same kinds of imagery. You should intentionally diversify your feed so that you're seeing all types of bodies, fashion, people—that way, you won't fall prey to one type of look or way of being.

7. **As corny as this sounds:** remember that no one's perfect, and that no matter what image they're projecting out into the world, they're probably worried their skin is too dry, just like you.

Obsessing over the entertainment industry from such a young age may be what led me to scrutinize how I looked, but it's also what pulled me out of that cycle of self-doubt. When I realized I was going down this path, I had to take a hard look at myself and say, "If I want to be someone who finds common ground with people in my work, I have to be cool with who I am first. I have to like the person I am, and trust that I'm good enough, or else who am I asking people to relate to?" In other words, if I wanted to create from an honest perspective, I couldn't do it without total self-acceptance and assurance. Respecting and appreciating yourself helps you create from a more stable place, and helps you create more timeless work.

I'd be lying if I said that the day I decided to ditch my MAC-influenced additives was the day that my life improved and Mr. Hollywood called to offer me a job. That's just not how it happened. It took a lot of work to deprogram what the entertainment and advertising industries taught me. I started from an internal place—going easy on myself, focusing on my strengths, forgiving my weaknesses. Early on, a friend from college gave me a bunch of affirmations to say in the mirror. At first, I thought it was kind of bullshit, but I'll tell you what . . . it worked! If you say something kind to yourself enough, it helps you believe it. And trust—that repetition has the same effect for negative thoughts as well. Don't get caught up in the spiral of being your own worst critic.

Even though I ditched a lot of the negative thinking that comes with consuming pop culture, I still slip up every now and then. But sometimes these incidents end up humbling me. One time in the fall of 2013, I was hanging out with my friend Sarah, getting ready to go out on the town, when I began joking about how my butt just wouldn't clap. The joking came from a place of insecurity. As a Black woman, I used to feel weird about not having a big butt—it seemed like a thing I should have. God just never sent mine.

As Sarah was doing her hair in my full-length mirror, I began yelling at my butt, "Clap, damn it. CLAP!" Sarah immediately began cracking up. Laughter is my fuel to go harder, so I began yelling louder. "IF YOU DON'T CLAP RIGHT NOW . . ."

"Oh my God, Quinta, this is hilarious," Sarah said, reaching for her phone. She hit record. "You have to put this on Instagram."

And so I did. By that evening, once again, my comments section was flooded with strangers tagging their friends in the comments section. It was another viral success, built off something that seems trivial, but hits deep.

Sharing an insecurity with the internet is how I learned that people were craving more authenticity in what they were consuming. People on the 'gram liked what I had uploaded simply because I was being myself. Seeing how many individuals related to, loved, and shared my short little video made me realize there may be a larger need for more videos like the "Butt Don't Clap" one. People wanted to see themselves in what they were watching—not just trivial stuff and overly produced, perfected celebrity.

Learning to stop comparing myself to whatever image was coming out of the screen gave my mind more room for creativity. As soon as I figured out how to swim against the tide, I became more empowered and more impenetrable. It wasn't easy: I was still living in LA, after all, quite possibly THE MOST vain place in the world. Being here means I had to turn my MAC defenses up even higher.

After learning how to be happy with myself, I translated that into a few concrete actions, standards I held myself to and continue to uphold to this day. First, I made the call to only hang out with people and at places that made me feel good about myself. Don't need any bad vibes from people who aren't committed to your best interests. Next, I consciously decided I wasn't going to reshape my body to fit Hollywood standards. That was a trap, and I knew it. Lastly, I made the personal decision to stop going to auditions. I didn't want to contort myself and torture myself and then have to wait for approval from the gatekeepers in the industry. Doing so only ever made me feel bad about myself. Instead of waiting for someone to give me a chance, I was going to create my own opportunities for success. It's worked for me so far, and I think it'll continue to work for me, so long as I stick to these principles.

When it comes down to it, I'm not against makeup, extensions, or any of those fun things. I still love getting glammed up in the right circumstances. In 2019, after we wrapped filming *A Black Lady Sketch Show*, I had the opportunity to do a press junket and a few red carpet events. It was all so fun and exciting; it was like prom Quinta times ten. In the beginning of the press run, I let the teams do whatever they wanted, since they were the experts. They threw me in cool clothes, styled my hair in cute ways, and gave me the hottest trends in makeup. I looked great, but even with that, I'd still see Getty images of myself and go—wait . . . who is that?

Now trust me, I don't want to hit a red carpet with a bare face and my regular-ass clothes. Some occasions call for some extra care. However, I realized my relationship with my stylists would have to be just that—a relationship. It would require conversation and some work on my part to help them understand how I wanted to look and how I wanted to be perceived, so that I could feel more like myself, and less like whoever was blowing up people's timelines with their OOTD. Again: it's all about making sure you're the conductor of your own narrative. You gotta be true to yourself above all.

It takes constant work to love yourself. Self-care is not something that can be bought. The creams, the gels, the drinks, the . . . crystals? They are all just twenty-first-century versions of those awful magazine ads. The only difference is, the Photoshop technology is a little better these days.

Liking yourself takes a lot of inner focus, reevaluation, and dedication. It takes drowning out what MAC says you need to be whole and figuring it out yourself. But I promise if you put in the work and start liking yourself, the rest of the world will have no choice but to live with it — and that, reader, is the true path to self-love.

12

Quinta's Classics: Part II

··

Hello and welcome to part two of Quinta's Classics. Thank you for joining me. Without any further interruptions, here are some more of the pop culture goods that got me to where I am today: trapped inside the internet. Just kidding. I'm not trapped, not really. I can leave when I want. I think?

Jurassic Park

Jurassic Park is the first movie I remember watching. I was four years old and immediately became obsessed with it, thanks to the fact that my brother Kwei was obsessed with it. He was the last sibling still living in the house full-time, and so like most kid sisters, I trailed Kwei around, absorbing everything that he did and said. His interests became my interests, and so I became the little girl who got into wrestling, video games, and most of all: dinosaurs. He'd read books about them, watch shows —we even had Jack and Jill bedrooms with dinosaurs all over the walls, like some sort of prehistoric shrine. Growing up with all this exposure created a deep reverence for dinosaurs within me. I was probably the only kid in my class who knew that the Troodon was the smartest dinosaur. It was the CC of dinosaurs.

Given that he already was pro-dino, when *Jurassic Park* dropped, it changed Kwei's life, and therefore mine too. Even though I had the attention span of, well, a hyperactive four-year-old, I watched *Jurassic Park* from beginning to end. I even learned how to rewind the tape so that as soon as the movie finished, I could rewatch it immediately. That's because even young Quinta knew that this movie was cinematic gold.

Let's get this out of the way first: the movie was and still is incredible. At the time, its special effects were groundbreaking. I legitimately thought they used real dinosaurs in the scenes; *that's* how good Steven Spielberg was. (I'm not going to admit exactly how old I was when I figured out that they weren't real, but I'll just say I was around "too old" years old when this realization dawned on me.) Steven Spielberg was able to humanize these dinosaurs in a way that got a little Black girl in Philly thinking they were creatures worthy of empathy.

Through the perfectly woven plotline of *Jurassic Park,* I learned that just because you can do something doesn't mean you *should* (e.g., just because you can create dinosaurs doesn't mean you should create dinosaurs). This is a very powerful lesson to learn as a child! And because the movie does such a good job setting it up, you don't feel like Spielberg is shoving his morals down your throat, which is not an easy thing to pull off. So, thank you, Steven, for teaching me to take responsibility for my actions and the power that comes from making the correct (or incorrect) decisions. I promise not to let you down when I eventually make my blockbuster hit.

Even Stevens

Here's the thing: if you grew up watching and loving *Even Stevens,* we're gonna be friends. That's because it's an underrated comic gem. *Even Stevens* was the first TV show that blew me away with its humor. It wasn't just silly kids' jokes, like "Oops, I slipped and fell in this puddle!" It had an *evolved* sense of humor.

This sitcom was truly the *Frasier* of children's television. It followed the traditional three-act structure with lots of hijinks, but the creators respected their viewers enough not to dumb down any of the humor. Each episode was packed full of jokes, each character had a sharply outlined personality. Even though I had a crush on (Alan) Twitty, I couldn't get over how incredible Shia LaBeouf was in his role as the annoying but intelligent little brother, Louis. Even at that age, Shia clearly had the chops to be a mega star, and he inspired me to be funny, too.

The best part about *Even Stevens* is that it went out on a high note, which is not something many TV shows do. The series did a contractually obligated three-season run, and then instead of trying to draw the plotlines out further, they ended its run with a feature-length film that had millions of viewers. In it, Louis and Ren Stevens resolved their sibling rivalry through being stranded on an island, which turned out to be a fake setup for a reality show—a nice nod to where the culture was going, if I do say so myself. Innovative.

Watching *Even Stevens* made me a bit of an outsider in my house. The other comedies were watched together with others: my whole family enjoyed *Full House* and *Family Matters,* while

Sister, Sister and *The Steve Harvey Show* were for me and my siblings. Occasionally, I could convince them to watch *That's So Raven* with me, but no one was interested in the world of *Even Stevens,* not even kids at school. It was "white shit," according to Jia. I had to respect her opinion, and so, eventually I stopped trying to get anyone to watch with me, and just took *Even Stevens* for myself. It was my own little comedic gem that defined what I thought was funny, and I became okay with that. It meant I truly had my own taste.

The Office

Confession: I was five seasons late to *The Office.* People couldn't stop hyping it, but I heard about its premise and was like, "An office? Sounds boring as hell. White Shit. Next."

My attitude changed when I was watching the Steelers square off against the Cardinals during Super Bowl XLIII.* I saw a teaser for the show and was like, "All right, maybe I'll check this out, see what everyone's been talking about." Immediately after the game ended (the Steelers won, 27–23) and my dad left to go to bed, *The Office* "Stress Relief" episode aired.

Before I could change the channel, I was hooked. Thirty seconds into the cold open, Dwight sets the office on fire and chaos ensues: Angela throws a cat into the ceiling, Kevin throws a chair into the vending machine, Stanley grabs his chest and collapses on the floor. It was insane, ridiculous, absurd. I was like, "Hold up, this is *not* some boring Staples commercial

---

* Bruce Springsteen and the E Street Band was the halftime show, so you don't have to look it up.

shit?" I didn't leave my seat for the entire two-part episode. I immediately became a fan.

I watched every single episode from then on, and when the final episode aired, I went back and watched the whole series starting from the beginning, falling in love with the characters all over again. It is my professional opinion that *The Office* is the perfect sitcom. The show's ability to balance comedy and heart makes it exceptional. It goes deeper than just laugh lines — it reveals what makes us tick as humans. The fact that a show can have zany characters like Michael Scott, rom-com story lines like the plot of Jim and Pam, and adult journeys of queer characters like Oscar proves that you can write things with humanity, love, and not compromise any of the humor. *The Office* made me want to make TV shows, and I will continue trying to make TV shows that measure up to *The Office* for the rest of eternity.

Napoleon Dynamite

The year 2004 will go down in history as one of the most formative years for the blockbuster comedy movie genre. I could not go to theaters fast enough to see all the movies coming out: *Anchorman, Dodgeball, Mean Girls, White Chicks, Harold & Kumar Go to White Castle.* They were all spectacular. I was always fiending for the next hit, constantly checking the "comedies" section of the newspaper to see which movies would be out next. Naturally, *Napoleon Dynamite* caught my eye.

Napoleon was me! He was the odd man out who thought he was cool. While watching the movie with Njia, I realized that she was laughing *at* Napoleon, while I was laughing *with* him.

I would definitely put Tater Tots in my pockets if given the chance!

The humor in *Napoleon Dynamite* was like nothing I'd ever seen before. It was so irreverent and wacky. The movie took big comedic risks and only asked that you come along for the journey. That's probably why it wasn't the big, genre-changing blockbuster that I thought it should be; it was just too weird for some. I don't care though; *Napoleon Dynamite* will always be close to my heart because I had such a deeply personal connection to it. When I saw it in theaters for the first time, I felt like it was my civic duty to tell everyone about this movie.

When I came home from the movie that night, I immediately began quoting lines to my family. "Tina, you fat lard, come get some DINNER! . . . Tina, eat. Food. Eat the FOOD!" I said in Napoleon's dork voice. No one laughed. I chalked it up to my family not being up on the hot comedy of the moment and decided to take my new Napoleon impression to school the next day. "Eat the food, Tina!" I repeated at school. Again, nobody laughed. I quoted lines and explained scenes. "But he draws a liger!" I kept explaining to my classmates, but no one was interested. People just weren't into absurdist white humor the way I was. My classmates were more interested in *Soul Plane, Barber Shop 2* — all good movies with huge comedic merits, but they didn't surprise and delight me the way *Napoleon Dynamite* did.

I was so determined to make my classmates like *Napoleon Dynamite* that the next time our school had a movie day, I brought in the DVD and demanded we watch it. I was going to make them understand this weird little indie corner of the comedy world if it was the last thing I'd do. And you know what? People loved it! They finally understood all my nonsensical lines. Their laughter washed over me and confirmed that I should trust my gut, no matter how weird it might be.

Anchorman

I know I mentioned *Anchorman* in the list of blockbusters that came out in 2004, but I just had to give it its own little section, because *Anchorman* changed the game for comedy.

I first discovered *Anchorman* on DVD in 2004. I didn't see it in theaters because, well, no one wanted to see it with me. But I had a feeling that I'd like it, so, when the movie came out on DVD, I bought it and watched it maybe ten times in a row. I couldn't get enough of the absurd racy humor bridled with how it made grown men look so terribly and unknowingly insecure. Soon, I wasn't the only one recognizing its genius. Before long, at school, everyone was quoting *Anchorman*. The low-key internet memes of the moment didn't lie, either — Ron Burgundy was everywhere.

Anchorman was the definition of good comedy. First of all, the writing was so unique, with strong, well-developed, and memorable characters. And the cast is *flawless*. It was so fun to see the actors take on the weird personalities of their characters and run with them. (Well, the male characters were fun. Christina Applegate's character was kind of flat, but she had a few heaters.) Even though the movie was live-action, it somehow managed to seem cartoonish with the larger-than-life personalities they had dreamt up.

But the ultimate test of whether comedy was good or not? It had to be something that bothered my mom. Her tolerance for wacky comedies is so limited that when I am nonstop quoting one and she hates it, I can tell it has staying power. When I saw *Austin Powers* for the first time, she hid the DVD in her room because I was annoying her so much with my constant quoting. My brother managed to get *Ace Ventura* banned from our home altogether because he was talking out of his butt so much. With me doing nonstop impressions of all of *Anchorman*'s best moments, my mom almost wrote a letter to get Adam McKay himself to ask me to stop.

Anchorman changed the standards for humor in pop culture, and it was so cool to see that cultural effect happen for the first time in my life. It must've been what the world felt like when all of a sudden, the Three Stooges started smacking each other and redefined what was funny. No doubt about it, *Anchorman* helped expand the scope of comedic boundaries, and I wouldn't be the same without it. Still in a glass case of emotion about how much it changed my life.

Lars and the Real Girl

Ooofff, man. Now that we know more about mental health, I'm not sure this film quite holds up, but I had to include it on this list because of its impact on me as a person. *Lars and the Real Girl* was the first indie movie I ever saw. I remember being on my mom and dad's couch, flipping through the movie channels, being all sad after my breakup with Malik. I flipped past Ryan Gosling's face, then flipped back because he was looking less hot than usual, and I found that interesting. I, too, felt less hot after my breakup. *Representation!* Fortunately, it was the beginning of the film and I got to watch his character fall in love with a sex doll in order to get over his own trauma. He projected what he needed onto her, and through that found peace. Was it weird? Yes. Was it soothing? Absolutely.

Part of my affinity for *Lars and the Real Girl* is that I saw it at a time in society where you could still walk into a movie without knowing anything about it. Those were the golden years of being surprised when the lights went off and the projector turned on (or in my case, lying on the couch, in the dark, with sour-cream-and-onion chip crumbs all over me). What a delightful experience to watch without expectation! Something that has subsequently been ruined by everyone spouting off their opinions on Twitter.

I went into the movie without knowing what to expect and came out feeling heartwarmed to my core. *Lars and the Real Girl* was so well-written and so sweet. Seeing a whole town nonjudgmentally support a man and his delusions* reminded me of the good of humanity. For one hour and forty-six minutes, I got to live in a world where an entire community rallied around a person in need, and it didn't seem unrealistic. I wish that was more common in our culture, but sadly it seems our walls are getting taller and our divides are getting wider.

Lars and the Real Girl opened me up to the fun of telling softer, quieter stories. Ryan Gosling may be superhot, but he's also a fantastic dramatic actor; his role as quirky Lars showed

---

* Especially when that man and his delusions are not oppressive or seeking to hurt anyone. Ahem.

me that an actor's best performances aren't always the most sale-able. Importantly, it left me with this: just because your movie is small, it doesn't mean the message has to be.

Bossypants, by Tina Fey

Where would I be without this book? I probably would've been a lost soul, floating around Hollywood without a plan and with-out direction. Tina Fey's memoir taught me everything I needed to know to break into the game without it breaking my spirit.

Initially, Tina Fey was important to me for one reason: *Mean Girls*. I saw it with my girlfriends when I was fourteen simply because I was a Lindsey Lohan fan and because the trailer looked funny, but by the time the final credits rolled, I was changed. My friends went on and on about how funny the movie was, but I needed to know *why* the movie was so funny. I committed the name of the writer to memory: Tina Fey.

When I got home that night, I turned on the family laptop and started to research her. Google told me that Tina Fey was a writer and performer for *Saturday Night Live*. Wait a minute—she did sketch comedy *and* wrote movies? How cool! I thought to myself. One day . . . I just might want to do that! A light bulb went off in my head.

A few years later, I picked up her book from the Barnes & Noble bookstore on Temple's campus with the last bit of Dia-mond Dollars I had left over after I bought all the textbooks, clothes, and food needed for school. Sure, my parents had loaded my Diamond Card with money for education, but I fig-ured I should treat myself to my forbidden fruit at the time:

comedic education! I suppose I expected to read a fluff piece by my favorite comedic writer; I was okay with that because I needed something to balance out reading about American history's effect on Black people. A white lady's memoir would be perfect for that!

But instead of fluffy, shallow tales of making it, *Bossypants* was full of honest stories about Tina's experience in the industry, both good and bad. It was exactly what I needed to read at the time: I knew it would be difficult to become successful in this industry, but to hear it from someone whose accomplishments I admired was an extra reminder to stick with it when times were tough. She was a person who knew deep down that she was good at what she did, and she never doubted that. That's what inspired me the most—to always have faith in myself, even if others didn't. Thanks, Bossypants.

Crooklyn

Ay, go take your ass to watch *Crooklyn* right now. It's an underrated but beloved gem by American director Spike Lee, about a little girl named Troi who experiences a summer in New York where she loses her mother.

I saw *Crooklyn* for the first time because it was on TV and my sisters refused to change the channel. At ten, I begged Njia and Kiyana to put *SpongeBob* on when we had to share the family TV that winter night, but they told me to shush and watch the movie they were watching before they beat me up. Now, I'm grateful for that threat, even though at the time, I only listened to them because I was scared as hell.

Crooklyn is a beautifully shot and beautifully written movie, but it stuck with me for much deeper reasons. Before *Crooklyn*, I had not seen an honest portrayal of the relationships between Black people on film—mothers and daughters, fathers and sons, friends hanging out with friends. Troi was around the same age I was, with the same hairstyle. She moved through the world like I did. She talked like me, had friendships like mine—it was like we grew up together. I had never experienced that before. *Crooklyn* was an honest portrayal of me and the people around me, and I don't know if I've ever seen another movie come close to that humanity.

True authenticity in film is rare to come by, but it is essential. *Crooklyn* put me on a mission to tell authentic stories about Black girls. I gotta warn you—it's pretty hard to get these stories to hit the screen, even now, nearly thirty years later. Hollywood is playing catch-up, and executives are somehow still just learning that Black people's experiences are not only worth sharing, but that people will pay to go see them. I'm not gonna give up my fight, though. I'll continue writing good and funny and true things about the Black experience until I'm cryogenically frozen next to my boy Shia LaBeouf.

Don't touch that remote! There's more of Quinta's Classics coming up!

13

Rough Edges

'vc spent a large portion of my life sitting still: in makeup chairs, kitchen chairs, salon chairs. This butt has known some chairs, and loved all of them deeply.

The first chairs I got to know well were the ones my parents had crowding around the kitchen table, wooden ones with engraved details running across the backs. For as long as I live, I'll never forget what it felt like to spend hours sitting in one of those chairs, with my feet propped up on the seat and knees hiked up to my chest, as my mom did my hair.

My mother made sure I was born into a family that knew the importance of keeping one's hair convenient and presentable. She had two daughters' worth of practice before I came around, so she had the hair routine down to a tee. Every two weeks, like clockwork, my mom would tell me to bring my hair accessories into the kitchen. My shoulders would slouch when I'd hear the scrape of the wooden chair against the floor's tiles, knowing I was about to be sitting in that chair for hours. The only enjoyable part of the process was picking out accessories; at least that meant I had some say in the pulling and prodding that was about to take place on my head.

I had a clear plastic *Little Mermaid* pouch that held all my ballies, plastic barrettes, and elastics, which I'd obediently bring to my mom as she was getting my wooden throne ready. We'd dump the contents of the pouch onto the plastic tablecloth, sorting through all the hair accessories, picking out my favorites.

"Sit still," my mom would warn before using some grease to soften my hair. It was called Blue Magic, and it turned my kinks into something that could be brushed.

"Quinta, stop moving! Or we're going to be here longer," she'd grumble as I squirmed, already pre-uncomfortable for what was only the beginning of a long stretch of pain.

Sitting still and getting my hair done felt like torture. I was always sweating because my mom would simultaneously be making dinner, occasionally calling in a sibling here or there to help stir something on the stove. I'd spend most of that time daydreaming about being somewhere else, either digging up worms from the sidewalk cracks or practicing somersaults off the couch.

To pass the time, I used to trace the roses on the tablecloth with my pointer finger. I could probably air-draw them from memory. Other times, I'd tune into *Oprah* with my mom and find interest in whatever issue the fifty-year-old lady in the audience was having that day. But as much as I wanted to wriggle out of that chair and go outside, I never moved too much, knowing full well that if I threw my mom off it would add precious minutes to the chair (and maybe also a pop to the back of the head). Little did I know that those early days of my mom doing my hair were about the quickest it'd ever take to get my hair done.

You probably won't be shocked to learn that baby-girl Quinta was always on the go. Being active was my identity as a child. In the winter, I practiced my Kristi Yamaguchi twirls on the ice (mostly falling). When it was warm enough, I'd go for swim lessons at the YMCA (mostly sinking to the bottom of the pool because I was a big block of muscle). I had dance classes two to three times a week from first until twelfth grade, and to top it all off, I was also a cheerleader in both high schools I attended because I'm that bitch.

Being in constant motion required some extra work in a way most Black girls are familiar with: basically, there was no way I could do all of these activities and still look presentable if my ac-

tual hair were out. If my natural hair was left to its own devices, it'd become puffy, frizzy, tangled, and just rough to look at — I'd look like an adorably sloppy little Honeycombs mascot. The only way I could wear my natural hair while still being athletic would have meant having it done after each and every activity. And by "having it done," I mean having my mom do it with a hot comb in the kitchen, which would be damaging for my hair. On top of that, if your mom had four kids and a full-time job like mine did, then that meant there was no *way* you could have your hair done daily — too time consuming. Therefore, it needed to be done in styles that could last for a long time and maintain their shape. My style of choice? Braids. When I got them put in, or *installed,* as I like to say, they'd last for one to two months, sometimes three if I slept in a scarf, put a bonnet over that scarf, and said a little prayer.

Now, my relationship with braids wasn't all easy, breezy, beautiful CoverGirl. Because, like I mentioned, they had to be *installed.* Oh my God, did that shit take for-ev-er to put in. Cornrows took the least amount of time, however, if I were getting individuals, I'd be sitting there for about three hours. And if I was getting micros? Throw the whole day away. Of course, micros were my favorite braid, because they're small, versatile, and also, I like my hair like I like my life: complicated and gorgeous.

I started dance classes around the time Jia and Kiyana were in high school and getting good at doing their own hair. I remember my mom pushing me toward Jia's bed with its butter-fly sheets and saying, "You want to go to cosmetology school, right? Practice on your sister."

Kiyana, who was especially good at braiding, came in from her room, which shared a door with Jia's. "I got it, Mom. I can braid!"

Jia was relieved. Both sisters had been helping my mom with my hair since I was a child, but as I got older, the styling I wanted got more complicated. Kiyana took me down to the living room, laid out packs of hair onto the back of the chair she sat me in, and pulled out her rattail comb. "Come on, I'm gonna give you some box braids."

"Okay! Can I pick what we watch on TV?"

"No," Kiyana said as I sat down. She flipped through the channels to find an episode of her favorite show, *Friends*.

Unlike my mom, who was always doing ten things at once and had six lives to track, Kiyana had a more laid-back braiding style. It may have taken her longer than my mom, but in those extended periods of sitting for my sister, I was exposed to the best pop culture of the era. At first, I hated *Friends*, but after watching a few episodes with my sister, I thought, *this Phoebe is pretty funny. "Smelly Cat" is hilarious!* And it didn't stop there.

Sometimes, Kiyana would let me spend the night in her room after getting my hair done. I loved it up there, on the third floor of our rowhome, because her room was really big, with windows overlooking our block. There was enough space for me to do approximately six cartwheels, *plus* she had her own TV. I would take my blanket up there, lay it on her floor, and watch whatever TV she wanted, since she had such good taste, judging by the Phoebe factor. My favorite nights were the ones that we'd catch *Conan* together. Those seemingly endless hours with Kiyana shaped my comedic tastes for years to come.

Years later, when Kiyana was married and had her own home, she was still doing my hair. At fifteen, I'd go visit her in Germantown to get cute cornrow styles, and even then, she was still teaching me the best of pop culture. It was in that era that she introduced me to what would become one of my favorite albums: *The Miseducation of Lauryn Hill.*

Kiyana had her CDs in one of those big, black zipped storage pouches, and I remember her flipping through page after page of loose CDs until she found it and popped it into the player. The intro came on, with that school bell ringing up top, and I was hooked. Ready to learn as my sister went to work on my hair.

Now, my sister Jia also did hair, but she specialized in straightening and styling. If I had an important event coming up like prom or a dance recital, I'd go directly to her. When Jia did my hair, I looked like a teeny-tiny news reporter ready to break a story in my bob or curly look. I loved it because a part of me felt like I was a little Black Marilyn Monroe. Until I moved to Los Angeles, I had never even gone to a styling salon that wasn't Jia's. (She actually went on to open two of her own, like the boss that she is.)

Sometimes my activities piled up, and the women in my family could no longer keep up with the braiding demands of my hair. It was then that my mother would load me into her Plymouth minivan and cart me to Forty-Sixth and Walnut, aka Philly's Ethiopian part of town, to go to a braiding shop.

The first time I went to one of these shops, I was about ten years old. We walked up to the brick building with a neon red

OPEN sign where the *P* was always burnt out. The doors and windows were papered with photos of Black women with different hairstyles, each with a number in the corner, so that you could tell the stylist which number you wanted. On that day, I knew I wanted micros.

My mom, way past the stage of getting any kinds of braids herself, quickly disappeared as my braider took me over to a red leather chair—much more comfortable than my parents' wooden kitchen stools, or my sister's apartment floor.

The woman braiding my hair was fascinating to me. Even though we shared the same skin color, she had these uniquely distinctive Ethiopian features that I just fell in love with. Her face looked like a painting; she was beautiful.

"Okay, your mom says micros," she said, her accent coating each word. I nodded my head yes, taking in the new rhythm of language I was hearing in person for the first time. Before visiting the salon, I'd only heard people from Africa speak in movies, and usually by an American impersonating an accent. At that moment, I was experiencing a rich accent that sounded like it had more of a beat than mine. I loved it.

I flipped through a hair magazine that was next to my chair. The pages revealed Black girl after Black girl, with elaborate braids, each style more incredible than the last. When I was finished reading the magazine, the braider wasn't even a quarter of the way done, so I settled back into the chair and turned my attention to a small TV perched in the corner of the salon. Playing on it was a Bollywood film that all of the braiders in the shop were *very* invested in. After about five minutes, I understood why—this movie was incredible! The colorful cinematography, the extremely dramatic acting, along with the singing and dancing—it made *Singing in the Rain* look like child's play!

"Saif Ali Khan is so handsome," my braider said to no one in particular. She didn't take her eyes off the TV the entire time she was braiding my hair and still somehow managed to get the job done.

From my first visit I knew better than to get in the way of these women and their Bollywood films. I could tell it was an important part of their job; a meditative experience that allowed their minds to disconnect from their bodies. Sometimes they'd suck their teeth and let out a "That is *so* wrong" when a character was doing something they didn't agree with. Sometimes they'd say something in their own dialect, which I could usually decipher from context clues based off what was happening in the movie. But mostly, we just sat and stared up at the TV. The hours would melt away as I watched, with bated breath, to see whether or not Rahul and Anjali would end up together.

Getting my hair done may have been an exhausting process for me, but it must have been even more exhausting for my braider. She'd work from start to finish with no break. It is my firm belief that the women who work in African braiding salons can do anything in the world. Their patience is astounding, their focus is unmatched—they could probably dismantle a bomb with one hand if they wanted to. Instead they were using their gifts to make women look good, quietly make their money, and take care of their families in and out of this country. All the respect to them.

The best part about getting my hair done was not only looking cute, but being able to really go my hardest without worrying about what was happening on top of my head. I loved the freedom that came with having braids—I felt truly invincible in a way I didn't when my hair was out. With my natural hair, I would always have to worry about looking a mess and getting matted. With braids, I was able to thrive, do my very best at everything, and look good while doing it. Sounds dreamy, right? Little did I know that there would also be a dark side to braids. A point of contention that revealed itself in the most horrific of ways: publicly.

So, you probably have heard a lot about edges recently. "Edges" refers to the hair at your hairline, and it's come to mean a few different things in our modern-day lexicon. Basically, if your hair is healthy and full around your hairline, then dammit, it shows that you're doing well. "My edges are laid" means "I look good." Or maybe you've heard the term "my edges were snatched." That means you went to a Beyoncé concert and it was so good that your edges and wig are now gone from the brilliance you witnessed. Like most trend-setting phenomena, the edge-specific phrasing came from the Black LGBTQIA community.

I have been immersed in hair culture alongside my two sisters since before I could form memories, but I must say that for most of my life edges never really were a huge part of our conversation. But at some point, probably around 2016, I started hearing about them more and more. "Edges" was trending on Twitter, edges were posted to Instagram, tutorials on how to lay edges were uploaded to YouTube. Even though I felt a little out of the loop when the term first exploded, I welcomed the trend. I thought, *Cool, the conversation about Black women and hair has gotten real cute and open.* The more conversation, the better.

When I was younger and had permed hair, Jia would take the time to lay down my edges with Murray's Beeswax, so, keeping up with the trend, I attempted to replicate her techniques. Worked like a charm. Being able to dive hair-first into the edges trend may seem vain or insignificant, but I built myself up on keeping my finger on the manic pulse of the internet; it felt good to look good and to know what's good in the Black girl community.

Even though I'm not as physically active as I once was, I'm constantly changing up my hair for different projects, photo shoots, or just plain old fun. That's the amazing thing about textured hair; it single-handedly gives Black people the opportunity for rebirth, for evolution, for looking hip, cute, and fly. Black hair is art. It binds our community together. It creates conversation. It creates controversy. It demands skill. It demands patience. It demands respect. So yeah, if my hair is looking good, you know I'm going to post it to Instagram.

One such instance of this is when I posted a side profile of me with two big cornrows going back. I had done my hair *myself* and was proud of how it looked. If you don't think it's that big of a deal, please reread the previous twenty-five paragraphs.

This shit took approximately one Bollywood movie and 1.5 Netflix Comedy Specials to pull off.

I snapped a pic and was pleased with what I saw. My neck looked long and sophisticated, I wore a red lip, and had an *American Gothic* look on my face. You know that stern, "I am above it all" look that gives off an air of strength? That's the vibe I had. Joke's on me because I was not above it. I was not above it at all.

After I posted the photo, a bunch of nice comments rolled in about how pretty I was, and how other people would be trying to do the same braids. Then I saw it. *The* comment. This was before I learned that scrolling through comments is like playing emotional Russian roulette; most of them are filled with empty validation, and then there's always the one bullet that tears through the confident facade you've spent so much time building.

"Where are her edges? She doesn't have any," it read. Now let me tell you, I've since had way worse comments than this one. I mean, just the other week someone wrote, "That cat is not cute," on a photo of me cuddling Jack.* But this comment came at a time when I was just starting to get attention on the internet. Before, my Instagram followers were mostly friends and former classmates who showered me with the familiar kindness that comes with knowing what a person looks like IRL. This comment was from the first negative stranger (of many) I'd encounter on the internet. And so, it stuck.

Not only did it stick, but it stung. No edges? What did that even mean? Everyone *has* edges! I decided to investigate the photo. This was before Instagram allowed pinch-zooming in, so I had to take a screenshot and *then* blow up the screenshot.

I squinted at my hairline and realized my edges *were* really thin. I ran to a mirror for a real-life look, and boom. There it was, or, I guess I should say, there it wasn't — my edges were considerably insignificant compared to the rest of my thick hair.

Growing up with Jia and Kiyana literally hovering over my head, I'd always felt like I had all the tools to take care of my hair. Everything to make sure my hair looked on its game all. the.damn.time. Having good hair was always my thing. This comment ruined me. I was spiraling. I FaceTimed Jia.

"Heyyyy." Her face filled my screen.

---

* Who is the cutest cat on earth so what are you even talking about?

"WHAT IS WRONG WITH MY EDGES," I yelled, shoving the phone into my forehead.

Despite being a professional hairstylist, Jia also hadn't heard "edges" discussed much before that year. She was so used to seeing all different types of heads that she didn't really think about there being a "correct" way to wear one's hair—a very comforting stance when you feel like you're going bald.

Jia managed to calm me down and give me advice on how to fill out my edges: namely using Jamaican Black Castor Oil on my hairline, which is thick as molasses and boosts regrowth. I vowed to do anything to get my edges to come back, even if it meant ruining a few pillows in the process.

After getting off the phone with Jia, I immediately deleted the photo. I know that you're not supposed to let the haters get to you, but I'm human and I'm vulnerable. I grew up in a society and an industry that consistently reminds me that I am outside the norm. I am other. I don't look how I'm supposed to (which is: four popsicle sticks jammed into a Slim Jim). So yeah, the comment hurt my feelings, and so I took down the photo so I didn't have to think about it. I'm confident, I love myself, but I still waver. Everyone does.

And on I went with the nightly head slatherings, hoping for growth. During the great castor oil regrowth experiment, I vowed to no longer wear my hair in a way that might show I didn't have any edges; I put that shit on lockdown until the situation improved. No luck. A few months in, it became clear that the oil wasn't working, so I spent a whole day researching and buying up every single product that the bloggers told me to get: walnut oil, hair growth serums, even a derma roller (which is basically a little contraption with spikes that jam into your follicles). My bathroom was overflowing with masochistic machines and expensive goo, none of which worked.

It was time to get scientific about it. I googled "why don't I have edges?" and down the rabbit hole I hopped, until I found an article describing something called "traction alopecia." Definition: "A form of gradual hair loss caused primarily by pulling force being applied to the hair. This commonly results from the sufferer frequently wearing their hair in a particularly tight ponytail, pigtails, or braids." BRAIDS. Bingo.

I shut my laptop and stared at the wall. Flashes of my childhood flitted through my brain. There I was doing a backflip on the football field, my micros brushing the ground. There I was at the pool, stretching a swim cap over my cornrows. There I was sitting in the red pleather chair of the Ethiopian hair salon getting individuals installed.

The very thing that saved me during my active younger years had robbed me of being able to shine on Instagram. I grew furious. Furious at my hair, at my younger self, at everyone who had ever braided it, at the internet. I was ready to punch something. It was poetic injustice! Janet Jackson would be pissed.

What sucked most was it didn't seem like there was much I could do to get my edges back. From my research, it looked like the damage was permanent. But this knowledge didn't deter me from trying. I continued buying the creams, serums, and oils—I even began looking into platelet-rich plasma therapy, a procedure where you get your own platelets injected into your damn scalp to stimulate regrowth. Sorry! I know this is terrible! I just wanted to at least be able to wear a ponytail without a fear of shaming!

The only thing I could do was prevent further damage, and the only way I could do that was to stop wearing braids. So, I did. But it was beyond hard. I felt like I was limiting myself by not being able to throw my hair back into an easy updo. Braids meant I could make videos without worrying about needing to spend hours on hair prep; they allowed me to roll out of bed and start the day as soon as my feet hit the ground. I even exercised more when I had braids in.

Months went by since "the comment" and I settled into a life of twist-outs and headscarves. The same rotating cast of hairstyles over and over. No rebirth. No evolution. No looking hip, cute, and fly. Then, I decided to book a trip to Hawaii.

As I envisioned days filled with white sand and clear water, I kept coming back to braids—how good they'd look, how easy they'd be! The more I tried to push the thought out of my head, the louder it got. I was like an addict, struggling with something that I knew wasn't good for me, but craving the immediate gratification. I wanted to look cute and have maintenance-free hair on vacation.

So, I broke and got braids for the trip. I Ubered down to an African braiding salon in the middle of Hollywood and sank into the familiarity of the cushy chairs and Bollywood films. As the braider tugged at my hair, I asked her not to braid too tightly around my edges, because I was attempting to grow them back.

"Mmm," she acknowledged my request, but I knew it was

kind of a moot point. Braids have to be done in a way that is secure, so that they don't, say, fall out and embarrass you while on a plane with a bunch of confused white people and other Black people who will pray for you, but also be ashamed. But still, I figured, no harm in asking.

My trip was amazing. I swam and swam and swam. I biked. I hiked. And after a full day of sweat-inducing activities, I was able to go to a luau looking like a princess. *Thank you, braids. Bless you. I won't care about my edges thanks to your goodness*, I thought to myself.

When I got back to LA, and subsequently back to reality, I immediately took my braids out, hoping that if I took them out early enough it'd be easier on my hairline. I was wrong. The hair around my edges was coming out in small clumps, leaving them thinner than before.

I was devastated. I scrutinized my hair in the mirror, I-told-you-so-ing myself the whole time. When I went to go get the braids, I *knew* this would be the outcome, but I did it anyway. That's the thing about me: I have one side that whimsically does things pretending I don't know the outcome, and another smug Princeton-professor logical-scientist Black-mother side that's like "hypothesis was correct, experiment complete, and yes, you are a dumb bitch."

I went back to the regrowing drawing board, this time buying more products and being a bit more vigorous with my plan to change things. I dedicated time on the weekends to caring for my hair and my edges in a way I hadn't done before. It was a whole process. I deep conditioned with the hopes of making my hair stronger and revitalizing my scalp, I used peppermint and castor oils just the way the girls on YouTube did, I soaked my scalp in oils before bed, and used a massager to make sure they really got into my pores. Still, it didn't work. My edges were snatched, and not by Beyoncé.

In the midst of all of this, I began to do some budgeting. In order to have a successful and sustainable career, I realized, I needed to organize my finances rather than spending blindly like I had been. This meant looking into my spending for the years prior. I accounted for everything from clothing (boy, did I help ASOS thrive) and eating out (boy, did I help the entire RESTAURANT industry thrive) to beauty, where I was hit by a hard truth: I had spent a grand total of five hundred bucks just trying to grow my edges back. That may not be a lot of money to some, but to many, that's something significant. Half a thousand dollars could feed someone's family for a month, change the lives of the less fortunate, get someone back on their feet. And I know all this mainly because I've been in those vulnerable positions, where five hundred bucks was a golden ticket out of a bad situation.

As I looked at that *five hundred* number in the spreadsheet, my brain exploded with questions: Why was I spending so much on something I hadn't cared about before 2014? Was it really that big of an issue? Did I care about my image too much? Most importantly, why was I letting one Instagram comment start to control how I saw myself? My hair didn't put me in this position, my brain did. And so, in that moment, I told myself to stop resenting the way my hair grows or doesn't grow. I decided to be proud of where my edges came from, and to be proud of the braids that created them.

Because of my braids, I learned to be brave and fearless, I learned how to push my body beyond what I thought it could do. I did backflips and dance routines, I ran, I hiked, and I jumped into oceans. For that, I'm grateful. And if edges had to be sacrificed in order to obtain that freedom — well, then so be it. But, edges . . . if you're reading this and you want to come back, that would be fine, too!

14

How to Mind
Your Own Damn Business

....

*"As a Philadelphian and fan of his shows and comedy, I
can say that Bill Cosby deserves every ounce of that jail
time. #dontdruggirlsmaybe #dontrapeperhaps"*

I sent this tweet in the middle of 2017, right after Bill Cosby
had been arrested for drugging women. After sending it,
I clicked my phone off and tossed it onto the couch next to
me. I had about twenty minutes to kill before an appointment
with the gynecologist, followed by a trip to the DMV (I like to
schedule the worst errands back to back so I can just get them
over and done with, like ripping off a Band-Aid), so I turned
the TV on and put on an episode of *The Office*.*

Jack began licking his paw and using it to clean his face. It

_____

* I had already seen the episode thirty times and it was still as fucking hilarious as the first time.

was cute as fuck. "Stay there, Jack, don't move," I told him, because he clearly understands English. "I need to put this on Instagram."

I picked up my phone, clicked it open, and found that it was still on Twitter. My eyes widened at the sight—my tweet had 232 RTs and 123 favorites. It had only been a few minutes. Reader, I don't know if you know this but to have this type of retweet-to-fave ratio in such a short amount of time usually means you've caused some trouble on the app, and that others had something to say about it. My cheeks grew hot and my body filled with dread: I was being called out. The response was so strong and so swift, it was disorienting.

When I first downloaded Twitter in August 2008, the platform was not what it is today. My friend Aden told me to get on because it was where she was posting her status updates, instead of Facebook, and I needed to know everything she was doing because she was one of my best friends. Once I got on, I also realized she and other kids from Temple were just writing their thoughts and talking about music, and that was cool to me. I sent my very first tweet—"FUCK THE POLICE"—after adoring how James Franco yelled the line in *Pineapple Express*.

From there, things would pop into my head and I'd send them out into the world via Twitter.

But after I joined BuzzFeed and became more recognizable on the internet, I realized I couldn't just say the first thing that popped into my head. It wasn't just me and Aden and other friends tweeting our own reviews of Philly block parties, it was me and a bunch of people who liked me from videos where I played "Quinta." They expected me to say the things that "Quinta" would say. Not me, "Quinta," internet "Quinta."

I decided to use Twitter to share broader thoughts and general jokes. The interactions on there were mostly encouraging and exciting. It was awesome to tweet about being short and have 30K other people like it and engage with it! Having something get that type of traction felt similar to telling a joke on stage that really makes the audience laugh. But there was another side of the platform that I hated to experience, and that was: criticism.

My Cosby tweet, which was picked up by *The Shade Room* (a popular celebrity gossip blog), had unexpectedly opened up a Pandora's box of anger on Twitter. There was such an enormous torrent of rage being funneled at my account that you would've thought I slapped somebody's mother! As I scrolled through the comments on the tweet, they began multiplying like some sort of cancerous e-growth. I would try to reply to one, but then ten more would pop up. The fury wasn't something I could even get a handle on. People were getting mad at all sorts of things: comedy, me, each other, women, Black culture, grammar. It felt impossible to keep up with everything.

> *"turning on a brotha for this white woman? How could you!"*

> *"this is the problem—you're giving up on bill, yet call yourself a comedian!"*

"How can you be from Philly and do this? Are you really from Philly?"

That last one fucking hurt. I didn't duck gunshots on Forty-Ninth and Chancellor to be called out as someone who didn't rep my city.

Trying to grasp at the collective anger of everyone weighing in on my tweet was like trying to hold on to Silly Putty: the tighter I held, the more it dripped out of my hands. In the real world, I would've at least been able to speak to the intricacies of the Cosby case and what it meant for Black America, but on Twitter it was impossible to have a nuanced conversation.

I stepped over Jack, who was still washing his face, and headed to the bedroom, where I could get into a better position to handle all the poison coming at me. When you build an existence around making people laugh, and suddenly a large group of people become very angry with you, it's really destabilizing. All I want in this heinous world is to spread joy, and it felt like Twitter was ruining that for me. Lying in my bed, knees to chest, phone pressed to face, I continued to watch as the comments rolled in, and made a snap decision to delete the tweet. It just wasn't worth it to have something like misinterpreted intentions throw off my entire day. As I got ready to put my phone down and shake off the experience, I noticed my name was still blowing up.* People had turned from criticizing the

---

* Another funny thing? You are never more famous than when you're being called out by people in your mentions commenting on your non-fame by listing your credits in the comment. It's nuts!

tweet to criticizing my choice to *delete* my tweet. You just can't win, can you?

I held my finger on the Twitter icon until everything jiggled and then I clicked the X, deleting the app from my phone. I was frustrated with Twitter, but mainly I was frustrated with myself. I was mad that I felt the need to delete the tweet, and I was also mad that my statement about something that was happening in the atmosphere of Hollywood was now being taken from me and repurposed to fit other people's narratives on unrelated subject matters.

From my years of social media usage, I've learned that when massive conversations get limited to a small amount of characters, the communication tools can often become more dangerous than helpful. There are millions of people trying to jampack emotions, knowledge, and background information into tiny clips that are just too easy to misinterpret. It becomes an endless cycle of someone tweeting a thing they feel passionate about, then other people coming in and tearing apart their idea because it doesn't exactly align with their own. That's not a dialogue; it's an argument into the void.

Let me give you another example. A little while ago, I was reading story after story about young Black girls getting kidnapped. I was furious, reading about these missing teens who were most likely being sex trafficked, and wanted to use my platform to draw attention to the issue. I thought maybe if more people knew about what was going on, we could group our minds together to find a solution. Rally our leaders, or communities, or something.

I composed a tweet that addressed the issue, carefully considering my wording. A little part of me worried that posting such heavy content might end up being turned against me—I am a comedian, after all, and one of the most common criticisms we can get is to "stick to the funny stuff." But the thing is, sometimes I personally can't stick to the funny stuff. Sometimes the darkness of the world seeps into my soul, and I need to let out my emotions somehow. So, I tweeted:

"I'm seeing more and more posts about missing Black girls . . . there seems to be a surge. Ladies, let's protect ourselves until something is done about it."

Short, simple, and direct. To me, it seemed bulletproof. "No one can pick apart this argument," I told myself, before pressing send.

Within seconds I got a response from someone saying, "Well, this is reductionist thinking because sex trafficking of young Black girls actually has been happening a long time."

WHAT. THE. ACTUAL. FUCK. How did I mess *this* up? But, according to the internet, I did. It wasn't enough to draw *attention* to this issue; apparently, there wasn't enough nuance in my 140 characters to satisfy everyone. Stuff like this happens on Twitter all day. Everyone wants to be the most right, the most nuanced, get the most reactions. But the chances of that happening all the time are impossible. The platform doesn't always allow you to try out new thoughts, or workshop anything —it's all reaction, all the time.

I don't blame the people on Twitter for feeling the need to respond, correct, or argue. It's the nature of the platform. Twitter was constructed to have people share bite-sized opinions, and it's evolved to hook our attentions and provide an addictive gamelike quality to conversing. And what's better for engagement than an argument? I'm just saying that even though I know better than to let a platform like Twitter take over my emotions, I still get caught up in it. That's why I've started old-school journaling again when I need to get my thoughts out. It's not worth it to raise my blood pressure just because of strangers @ing me in the comments.

I go back and forth with having Twitter at my fingertips. No matter how often I delete it off my phone, I'll inevitably get annoyed at the inconvenience of checking it on my laptop and download it back onto my phone. I'm telling you this because it is the truth that I haven't really figured out a way to have a healthy relationship with Twitter. Just because I'm good at the internet doesn't mean I'm always good *with* the internet.

Ultimately, this isn't a story about whether or not it was my place to weigh in on the Cosby trial, or about sex trafficking, or about how to optimize your Twitter usage. This is a story about what I learned — How to Mind My Own Damn Business. The internet has normalized a tendency for those of us on it to always be up in each other's and strangers' business, and I'm not sure to what benefit. It might be bad for society and communication to get this riled up about what strangers on the internet are saying.

I honestly believe that Minding Your Own Damn Business is the salvation and pathway to peace that we all need. We, all of us, could stand to chill out and mind the business that minds us. If we spent half as much time concerned about our own villages, maybe the entire town wouldn't collapse when one house was set on fire. Maybe we all would have the resources to help that house, because we'd been harnessing our own tools for months. I've clearly thought a lot about this, and naturally, I have some tips for you.

How to Mind Your Business

Hello and welcome to the Quinta Brunson School of Minding Your Own Business. I'm Quinta Brunson. This multipage course will teach you how to protect your sanity and learn how to coexist with the internet, and subsequently the world, in a mature and healthy manner. After all, you have your own business to mind; you don't need to be minding other people's. You don't have time for that!

Ten out of ten scientists agree that this approach to minding your own business will lead to a longer and happier life. #science

Step One: Are you about to speak on something that doesn't concern you? You *could* do that. But wait! Is your laundry done? Have you paid that bill that's about to go to collections? Instead of talking about what Cardi should do with Offset, have you ONSET working out your own relationships? Consider taking care of yourself before you start putting your nose into the goings-on of others.

Step Two: Does the word "selfish" carry a negative connotation for you? Well, stop thinking that way. I am

here to tell *YOU* that you need to be selfish! The more
you think about yourself and your community, the easier
it'll be to stop caring about what random other people
think of you. This will lead to more freedom of expression and better actions on your part, which only work for
the good of yourself and the people you know in real life.
Which, especially in these times, is the only thing that
matters.

Step Three: Unfollow blog sites. Right now.

Step Four: Don't give your opinion as fact on the
internet unless you're an expert. If you have a PhD in
whatever the subject matter is, then go crazy! Otherwise,
don't tweet your opinion presented as fact. I find that
opinions are like glasses of wine: best shared with friends,
best given some time to air out. If you want to exercise
your freedom of expression and you want to talk about
something you're not versed in, then be open and ready
for the fact that you might get schooled.

Step Five: Is all of this just a little too hard to do?
Then delete the Twitter app off your phone and down-
load an addicting game app instead! Might I suggest
Homescapes? It's this great game where you get to reno-
vate an old home by winning *Candy Crush*–style games.
No one's going to call you out for being a hypocrite on
Homescapes! Plus, it's free.

Step Six: I already told you to unfollow the damn
blog sites. Don't make me come grab your phone and do
it myself.

Step Seven: At the end of each day, put your phone in a drawer. You're going to break this rule, and that's okay, but at least try doing it tonight and tomorrow and a couple of days in the upcoming weeks. When you feel yourself getting worked up, just remember —drawer. The drawer is a psychological jail for your phone.

Step Eight: When someone does something that gets your blood pumping, or gives you the urge to gossip, subtweet, or be nasty, just write it down on a piece of paper and then forget about it. And fine, if you want, set the piece of paper on fire because it's fun and looks cool, you little pyro!

Step Nine: Evaluate why you care so much about what other people are doing on the internet. Is it because there's something missing in your life? Are you projecting your own insecurities onto someone else's digital presence? Make it your personal mission to fill the empty space of whatever it is that's missing in your life, and I *guarantee* that things will improve.

Step Ten: Hang out with a friend and remember what it's like to talk in real life. Challenge each other to talk about anything but what you've read on social media. It's a game changer, I'm tellin' ya.

That's it for the Quinta Brunson School of Minding Your Own Damn Business. Thank you for taking the time to read. Come back next week for my talk on wearing flower prints, and not letting flower prints wear you!

I know that a lot of the reason I'm successful is because of platforms like Twitter, and I don't take that for granted. I understand the value of having a platform and using it wisely. But I can be both grateful and tired — and those are usually the two feelings that coexist within me when it comes to my relationship with social media. Sometimes I wonder what this app is doing to my ability to connect with people in the real world. Like, is it possible to be both good at the internet and good at real life — or does one cancel the other out? What a scary thought.

I used to look at conversations on Twitter as if they're the sole reflection of our society, when the reality is that less than a quarter of the world's population is on Twitter. Using Twitter as your primary lens for how to view and interpret the world will put you in a bubble, wrongly enforce the thought that your bubble is the best bubble, and make you angry when anything challenges said bubble. It's one big repetitious cycle, and it's not a smart way to advance thought or create empathy.

In the future, I'd like to see less social media engagement; a world where people understand that it's not the best thing for our mental health or our collective well-being. If I'm being real, I hope social media can go the way of plastic straws. Everyone will know its downfalls and try to limit their interaction, like, "Aw, man, I can use social media if I *have* to, but I *prefer* not to." I am currently starting to create this world for myself by limiting my social media usage and staying put in the present. Conversing with people about things like books and sustainability of life. I'm hearing different types of people out and am forming more nuanced opinions about the world because of that. And less time on social media means more time to do my work, and relax with my family. I am quite literally minding my actual business, and I feel way better about it. Please join me —well, kind of—in minding your own business.

15

Work. Life. Balance.

....

When I woke up one February morning in 2017, it started off like any other: debating whether or not I could sneak in a few extra minutes of sleep. Knowing what I do now, I should've thrown my phone out the window and stayed in bed. But that's not how the world works. So, grumbling, I got up and went to work for what was supposed to be an average-ass day.

This was during my second year at BuzzFeed, an experience I was enjoying after years of that comedy/freelance/Apple grind. There were lots of things happening in our offices as the site became more and more notorious. We had just moved into Siren Studios, a multibuilding production space in the middle of Sunset Avenue. This new studio was big enough to house all of the employees and the new sets where we could film our growing number of shows and videos. It was an interesting transition, because we were previously in a building where everyone was basically sitting on top of each other all day, and getting to your shoot was just a desk away. This change felt like we were creating boundaries between teams.

Working at a successful start-up is exciting, but simultaneously disorienting. I loved that it felt like we were all growing and evolving together—but I missed the early days, when it felt like work was just a bunch of your friends hanging out in a basement, competing to make each other laugh. In the old offices, I spent most of my time with Justin, who helped me get the job, and my friend Zack Evans. We were our own little pod in charge of pitching and producing sketches. It was the dream. Our three-person department was called "Neon" and our only objective was to make funny sketches for various Buzz-Feed channels. We worked best when it was just the three of us, and for the most part, our bosses let us do our own thing. We basically rolled into work and shot Nerf guns at each other until we came up with a funny video idea.

The only editorial requirements for our videos were that we start from a very human place and build up to the most relatable concept that we could from there. We called our sketch concepts "Moments Inventories." They were based around these small parts of your day where you take stock of the human experience. One of our most famous sketches was a video called "Wedding Season Is Coming." The idea started with Zack, Justin, and me complaining on a text thread about all the weddings we had to attend that year. Bingo. When the three of us found a common emotion, like the existential dread of having to hear "Love is patient, love is kind" for the tenth time in three months, that was usually a good starting point for a pitch. We sent out an email across the BuzzFeed listserv to see who else felt the same way we did.

"Y'all stressed about wedding season?" we wrote to our co-workers. "Do you think it's worth making a sketch?" We got back an unequivocal "Yes" and it was off to the races. Once we got approval, we'd head down to the front lockers, fill out an equipment rental form, and check out a camera. Then it was: shoot, edit, upload. I don't mean to be flip about the process, but it truly was that cut and dried. BuzzFeed was one of the rare places that trusted its employees with the voice of the company. As of this writing, "Wedding Season Is Coming" has 3.3 million views. Before BuzzFeed, I had accidentally figured out how to draw the attention of the internet a couple of times. But as I continued to work at BuzzFeed, I began to learn how to be more intentional about what I created. Having a substantial platform and boundaryless creative control taught me how to relate to people on a massive level.

We were required to put out six Moments Inventories videos a month. Agreeing on six ideas a month took a lot of collaboration, which just made us closer to each other. It is so rare to do what you love with people you love. Zack, Justin, and I spent so much time together that we mind-melded to become one functioning creator. I have yet to find another such a cohesive working unit. Those two guys were my brothers. I couldn't think of a better crew to navigate my early years in the biz with.

The blessing and curse of working at a start-up is that nothing stays the same for too long—even the good stuff. As I delved further into my career, I began to branch beyond my daily duties. When the execs at BuzzFeed encouraged everyone to pitch their own shows to partner companies like YouTube Red, Go90, Facebook, I jumped at the opportunity. I wrote and edited pitches, sent them off for consideration, and you know what?

The partner companies began buying my shit. I sold a show called *Up for Adoption* to Go90, a show called *Broke* to YouTube Red, and one called *Quinta vs. Everything* to Facebook. After selling these three shows, I got a promotion. BuzzFeed essentially created a new title for me: development partner, making me the youngest showrunner at BuzzFeed. Becoming a development partner was a huge step forward for me, but it also meant I had zero time to work with Justin and Zack. I had to shift my attention to writing and producing for these other projects.

My move within the company was hard for Zack, Justin, and me collectively. I knew I needed to branch off and do my own thing to move forward, but it was difficult to feel like I was leaving my best friends. We were all evolving in our careers, so it was a natural change, but still bittersweet. Luckily, we respected each other so much that our individual moves were celebrated, and ultimately, we're still close because of this mutual respect.

Shortly after I began working on my own stuff, Justin guilted me into coming back to shoot a video with him and Zack. The idea was originally Justin's baby. He wanted to shoot this sketch where kids are asking their teacher stupid questions. The teacher responds saying there are no stupid questions, but the sketch is furthered by having the kids fire off more and more ridiculous questions at the teacher. In the improv world this is called heightening. By the time we finally coordinated all three of our schedules, months had passed since I last worked with Justin and Zack. I missed my boys and was excited to get back to what we did best together.

Usually, we would've worked on an idea like this together,

but since I was tied up with my other stuff, I only had time to pop in to play one of the main students. Justin and Zack wrote out the questions and all I had to do was deliver my lines. It was kind of weird being disconnected from the creative process, but I was looking forward to taking a back seat. Without the added responsibility of conceiving the sketch from beginning to end, I could just goof off and focus on being as funny as possible.

On the day of the shoot I showed up in a floral top, loose pants, and box braids. I felt cute and confident. I grabbed a snack from the kitchen* and headed across campus to meet up with Zack and Justin.

Being in that room and feeding off Justin and Zack's energy made it feel like no time had passed since we last collaborated. Justin was in the corner setting up the camera and putting on his serious director persona. He is a fantastic director. Justin is so connected with his own emotions, and it really comes out in his art. Even if he's shooting a silly video, he puts 100 percent of his soul and talent into what he's making. Meanwhile, Zack sat next to me and tried to get me to crack up between takes. Zack does a great job of making you feel relaxed and funny. He'd push me to be as silly as possible and usually got the best results that way.

The sketch that day was an easy one. It had one location, few shots, and a simple concept. The vibe was very relaxed. As we settled into our respective roles, Justin called action and we were back at it.

---

* I was always eating Pirate's Booty, so much so that I can't eat it without getting sick anymore.

"Are dogs boys and cats girls?" Zack asked.

"Is Bon Jovi the same guy as Jon Bon Jovi?" I deadpanned.

"Is Swaggy McGee a cool rap name for me?" Justin added.

As we were firing out questions, I felt my phone buzz in my lap. I looked down to see it was my oldest sister, Jia, calling. I declined the call and flipped my phone over so it wouldn't distract me.

"If I'm ugly, does that make me my daddy's son?" I said on cue. My phone buzzed again and I silenced it.

When Justin was filming his lines, I peeked back to see it was Jia calling for a second time in a row. Weird.

Jia and I are super close. Even though she's in Philly with the rest of my family, we talk all the time. But I'm the one who typically calls her, which threw me off. On the rare occasion that Jia does call me, she usually calls in the evenings. After all, she's a hairstylist who owns two businesses—she doesn't really have time to chat during the day. Also, Jia never calls more than once because she's an OG and OGs don't do that. Something felt strange here.

My mind raced. But maybe there wasn't anything wrong? Maybe I was just being paranoid? Maybe she was just calling to tell me some good gossip? I didn't want to mess with the energy of the room, so I talked myself out of the negative thoughts and focused back on the shoot.

"Was Waldo ever reported as missing?" I asked, getting back into character.

After an hour of filming, we took a break before improvising some stuff. I pulled my phone out of my pocket and scrolled through the notifications. I checked my emails, read my tweets, and opened Instagram. As I mindlessly scrolled through the photos of food and selfies, I kept thinking about Jia's call. Normally, I'd wait until after work to call a family member back, but I couldn't get the bad, anxious feeling out of my body. I stepped out into the hall and dialed her. She picked up after the first ring . . . also not normal.

"Hey," she said. I'd heard her say "Hey" thousands of times, but this sounded different. It was curt. Her "Hey" was coated in anger and sadness. I sensed pain in her voice. I walked farther down the hall, away from the shoot.

"Hey, I saw you called, sorry I didn't answer earlier, I was filming," I explained.

"Yeah, I have bad news. Tyrese was shot and killed."

My seventeen-year-old cousin was dead.

As Jia told me the few details she knew, all I could think about was this black-and-white photo I snapped of Tyrese years earlier. I was very into photography at the time and had just gotten a new camera. I was running around our family picnic, all like, "I'm gonna capture life in action because I'm a serious photographer now."

As I danced around with my new camera, I looked to get candid moments with my family. I knew Tyrese would be a good subject because he was always exploding into big fits of giggles, and I wanted to get his enormous, beaming smile on camera. So I snuck up next to him and brought my camera to my eye, in the hopes that I could catch him midlaughter. Tyrese saw me trying to take a photo and immediately mean-mugged for the camera.

I sighed and dropped the camera. "Tyrese, why?"

He broke into laughter right after that. I still managed to snap a photo. In it, he's scowling but there's a mischievous glint in his eye. That photo is my go-to visual when I think of Tyrese. Young. Carefree. Happy.

Everyone liked Tyrese. I know that's what you say about a person when they pass, but it was true about him. He was a level-headed kid with good energy, always a bright spot in my visits home.

At seventeen, Tyrese was doing well for himself. He was pulling straight As in school, working at American Eagle as a manager, and he had a beautiful girlfriend whom he loved. He had a full-ride scholarship to a school in Pennsylvania and couldn't wait to start college. Tyrese was cool. He was neat. He was smart. He was a son. He was a brother. He was a kid. He was too young to die.

I guess this is the part of the story where I'm supposed to tell you how he got murdered, so that you can form a logical understanding of it in your head. So you can justify why something like this would happen to a good kid. But what if there's no logical justification? What if he wasn't a "good kid"? What if it just happened out of the blue, in the middle of the day, for no good reason? What if I don't owe you more details? What if I didn't want to give you any more details than that because I have an issue with how Black death is handled in this country?

I guess I don't feel the need to lay out a full portrait of what happened, because if I write about it here, in this book, and you do nothing about it, then what's the point of sharing this trauma? Telling stories that do not result in action turns those stories into entertainment. I don't want to titillate anyone with the gruesome details of a tragic death.

We've seen the documentaries. We've read the think pieces. We've watched it unfold online. We've heard enough. But we're not doing anything about it.

I can't help but think of the Romans; how they would go to stadiums in order to be audiences for gladiator fights. Spectators from all over Rome sat in the privileged stadium seats, high above the arena, and watched men fight to the death. Other humans would die in front of their very eyes. And for hundreds of years, those spectators didn't do anything to stop it, they just sat there, eyes transfixed on the murder of their fellow humans. How is Black death different? If there's no plan to change the daily numbers, no resolve, then how is it not just a sick form of entertainment? People are losing their lives and we're watching all this from our phones and computers.

I'll tell you this much, though: Tyrese did nothing wrong. Nothing. He was simply walking down the street one morning and a stranger opened fire. He was a good kid and he didn't deserve it. My cousin was not the first young Black kid to get shot and killed, not even the first in my family, and he certainly won't be the last. He was just one of many during one of the bloodiest summers in Philly. The next day, his story was over-shadowed by another child that was shot and killed.

Before I could process what Jia had told me on the phone, I was snapped back to the present. A production assistant approached the bench I was sitting on and tapped my shoulder. "Quinta, we're ready for you on set."

"Jia, I gotta go, I'll call you later," I told my sister before hanging up.

"Fuck," I thought. My stomach churned; I thought I was going to be sick. It felt wrong to be standing in the middle of that brightly lit hallway, palm trees swaying out the window, the California sun highlighting everything it touched. "No one here is going to understand this," my brain screamed inside my head.

Here I was at my predominantly white company, in the center of Hollywood, feeling the entire weight of gun violence in America, and being Black, and being from the hood, and being different from everyone around, sitting on my chest. I looked down the hall to where we were filming, acid burning in my throat.

"Fuck." I shook my head. I can move across the country, I can work in comedy, I can make money, but I'll always be dealing with the effects of being Black and being from Philly. I can't outrun where I'm from.

I gave myself a little pep talk, forcing myself to orient my headspace. "Pack this up, Quinta . . . put it in a suitcase, shove it in a closet in your mind, finish what you were doing." I immediately decided I was not going to tell anyone on set what happened. I didn't want to ruin the good mood of the shoot; I winced at the thought of bringing the room down. Sure, I knew that gun violence in America wasn't my fault, but in that moment, had I brought it up to the room of people I had been joking around with just an hour ago, I felt like this experience would be inextricably connected to me. It wouldn't just be Quinta, comedian. It would be Quinta, comedian, and what a tragic thing she's lived through. I didn't want that. This was my burden to carry and I was going to carry it alone.

But the biggest reason I didn't want to tell Zack and Justin what I'd just learned? I didn't want to make them uncomfortable. Simple as that. I didn't want to see them struggle with how to comfort me, or hear their fumbling attempts at condolences. No one wants to experience that, even if the reactions of sympathy come with good intentions. There was no way I was going to put the weight of "understanding" on them.

Up to this point, Zack and Justin only knew as much as I was willing to share with them about my family and life in Philly, which was pretty limited at best. They knew that my parents were married and that I was the youngest of five. They knew that I had a ton of funny nieces and nephews, all of whom I was close to, but other than that . . . they didn't know much about my family life. Instead, they knew things like what album I was listening to, my lunch order from Noodle World, and an endless list of random facts that you learn about someone when you work together so closely. But when it came to anything serious, they were kept in the dark. I guess I always just wanted to be the chill one, the one who could turn anything into a joke, who could light up a room with positive energy — in order to do that, I had to handle the unfunny stuff on my own.

I realized in that moment that I had spent my entire life separating my personal life from professional, creating invisible barriers between who I was with my family and who I was in the world. It started in school, and it was continuing with my work. My "job" was to be relatable, and the deeper I got into my family dynamics, the less relatable I felt. Sure, everyone's family is wacky, but there is something so uniquely specific about the Black experience that is very hard for the white-majority demographic of this country to understand. Can you imagine if I uploaded a BuzzFeed video about my teenage cousin being murdered in broad daylight? It's not the type of "Moments Inventory" you really want to document.

This death had layers. It was gun based. It was "hood" based. And though my coworkers weren't familiar with that side of my life, it was very much a part of who I was. In a way, I was hiding part of myself and what made me *me* because no one could relate. I didn't do this intentionally; I was like a chameleon changing colors to suit my environment. But now my past had caught up with me.

It didn't matter that I was in LA, that I was working at Buzz-Feed, or that I was somewhat famous with a little bit of money. The reality of it is that systemic problems follow you. It doesn't matter where you go or how much you try to escape them, you will always be affected by those elements of your life. And sometimes, it will come in the form of death. Senseless, tragic death.

I took a deep breath and started to walk back to the shoot, information in my head, heart in pieces. My legs were moving, I was in motion, but it felt like I was on autopilot.

I walked back into the classroom and plopped down at my desk ready to play a kid, immediately after one I love was just taken away from me.

• • •

When we were done doing final takes, I gathered my stuff and headed to my next shoot for the day. I walked quickly and kept my head toward the ground—hoping to avoid eye contact with my coworkers.

Siren Studios owns a house on the lot that looks like a normal house, but is actually a space used for filming. As I headed toward the fake, real house, my phone vibrated in my hand. The hair on the back of my neck stood up. More bad news? I looked down to see that my dad was calling.

"Hi, little girl," he said on the other end of the line.

As soon as I heard my dad's voice, I began to cry. My dad is one of the few people whose voice and presence can do that. It's because he's a strong person, and his ability, or need, to constantly be that strong opens up some sort of deep sadness within me. But it's the role he plays in our family and he plays it well.

My phone conversations with my dad typically revolve around finances and life planning. He is a student of order. When disorder is thrown into his life, he's always the first to logically make sense of it all, and then comfort his family. That's what gets me. It's not a fair place for a dad to be put over and over again.

My dad spoke about the possible circumstances surrounding the shooting; the logic, or lack thereof, of what happened. He told me everything would be okay, and that the family would cope. But even with his calm, measured presence on the other end of the line, telling me I'd be fine, I can't say it made me feel better. It just made me feel like I was very far away from home.

Anyone who lives in a different city from their family can relate to that feeling of helplessness that occurs when bad things happen while you're so far away from everyone else. It sucks not being physically present to process those things with the rest of your family, but it's the reality of following your own path in life. It's easy to let the guilt eat away at you, but I find guilt to be unproductive, so I don't allow it for very long. At that moment in my life, I was literally living out my dreams; I knew I was in the right place. But the weight of my situation still affected me. Feeling secure and feeling awful can exist side by side—I'm proof of that.

At the end of our call, my dad reiterated that there wasn't much I could do from Los Angeles and that I should just carry on until there was more information. Carry on. Ha.

In an ideal world, everything would've come to a screeching halt. I wanted everything to be shut down so I could mourn the loss of my beautiful baby cousin; until we as a society could find a way to make sure that this type of loss never happened to any other family again. Figure out how to stop gun violence from tearing through entire communities, empowering poisonous people, and creating irreparable aches along the way. But that's not realistic. Tragedies happen, and the world keeps spinning.

As I approached my coworkers, fear was holding my hand. My job was a place I loved very much. It was a space where I felt safe, a space where I had friends and people I consider my family. It was my creative playground. It gave me hope for universal unity. However, I didn't feel like anyone could relate to the very tragic death in my family, and that made me sad on top of the grief I was already feeling. I could sense the walls between my work life and family life beginning to erode.

Seeing my coworkers standing around and chatting made me

realize that I couldn't reveal any information about what was going on, but I also knew I couldn't keep my worlds separate if I stayed at work. I told the person running the shoot that I needed to go home because of a family emergency. "Emergency" sounded better. It made it seem like swift action could solve the problem. Wouldn't that be nice?

I couldn't bring myself to specify what was going on beyond that. Maybe I shouldn't have felt that way; maybe I should've let my coworkers into what was happening in my world. But at the moment, I felt disconnected from everyone around me. Completely alien.

The truth is, no one wants to hear about death by gun. Old age, we expect. Cancer—awful, but not unheard of. A shooting? No, thank you. A Black teen shot and killed? No way. No one wants to unpack it and start asking the real questions to actually enact change. Questions like:

"Why does this keep happening?"

"What's up with gun laws?"

"Why do people take the lives of other people?"

"What can a Black kid do to be safe?"

"Is this an effect of systemic oppression?"

"How do we stop it?"

To be clear, I don't blame my coworkers. It's not their fault that their life experiences likely hadn't brought them to a place where they'd have to confront these issues head-on. But I resented that the burden was on me. I didn't want to have to step up and become the face of this problem. The "it happened to me, to my family" person. Especially when all you want to be known for is being quick to crack a joke. I just wanted to be me. And "me" just wanted to go home, and go to sleep, and not have to think about any of this anymore.

When I got home, I dragged myself inside my apartment, dropped my bags, and plopped down on the love seat closest to the door. I was alone for the first time since I'd gotten the news and wasn't really sure what to do. What do you look at to feel better, in these circumstances? I instinctively reached for my phone and stared at the home screen for a bit. Completely unhelpful. I also dreaded any other phone calls, I realized, so I turned my phone off and threw it on the couch. Instead, I just sat there and focused on the dark screen of the TV. It was somewhat soothing to look at something I was familiar with: I knew the mechanics of that TV, how it worked, what was in there. All that stuff made sense to me. I needed to be around things that made sense.

Los Angeles has a weird way of getting extremely quiet when you're dealing with something horrendous. It's like the whole city dims around your sadness. At that moment, I was longing for some kind of connection but felt incredibly alone. Then I remembered my boyfriend. We were supposed to hang out that night. Fuck.

I'd just started seeing this guy; we'd only been together for three months, and had just decided to become exclusive a few weeks prior. It was so new. On top of the newness, he was white, and I was almost certain he'd never dealt with anything like this before. My sadness exploded into anger. It just felt so unfair that I had to have this conversation with him.

I was supposed to be forming new inside jokes with him, not testing his capacity to handle an emotional bomb like this. Up until that day, our relationship was sunshine and roses, just enjoying each other's company and laughing together. Now, all of a sudden, I'd have to get real, whether I liked it or not. I DON'T WANT THIS TEST RIGHT NOW, my brain screamed at me.

I'd barely had enough time to grieve, and now I was navigating yet another awkward conversation I'd be forced to have. If my boyfriend didn't respond the right way, I knew it'd be over. And I really, really didn't want it to be over. But I also knew he wouldn't know how to respond, because how do you?

I leaned over, grabbed my phone off the couch, and dialed his number.

"Heeyyyy!" came his chipper voice. His naive, upbeat energy made me angrier.

"My baby cousin was shot and killed," I blurted out.

There was silence. I could hear the wheels turning as he tried to grasp for the right words. I'd just sliced through our honeymoon phase and threw him into the deep end. Here it was, time to show his true colors.

"Oh my God . . . I'm . . . so sorry. That's terrible," he said.

It was the wrong answer.

"Yeah, well, that's not really what I want to hear right now," I told him. "I'm just really sad and need some space."

"Sure, of course. Whatever you need," he responded. I could tell he was hurt, but I didn't care. I was hurting more. I hung up the phone.

"Ah shit, I gotta break up with this guy," I thought. The night was getting worse. I headed to the kitchen and poured about half a bottle of wine into a mug and dug up some old cigarettes that someone had left at my place. I sat in my window and smoked cigarette after cigarette, watching the sun disappear and the evening bar crowd tumble into the street. The whole world had shifted, but it also remained the same.

I spent the night sitting in my sadness and allowing myself to feel terrible. My mom called, and her frank attitude oddly calmed me down. It felt almost as if she had predicted that something like this would happen. "Something like this was bound to hit at some point. That's the way it is in Philly." I cried more. Drank more. I wrote in my journal. Things became blurry.

At some point, I'd fallen asleep. I woke up, still in my clothes from the day before. I felt like shit, but at least my physical feeling matched what was going on inside my head. I didn't go into work that day because I just couldn't bring myself to face my coworkers. My head was not in a space to be in such a vibrant environment; my head was in a "stay under the covers" space.

As I lay in bed, craving the routine of my previously unexceptional week, my phone rang. I look down to see it was my boyfriend. I answered, ready to tell him he hadn't given me enough space, but he cut me off.

"I'm at your front door."

I crawled out of bed and threw on a hoodie. I didn't bother to check my makeup and slinked down to the entrance of my building. When I opened the door, he was standing there with flowers.

"I'm sorry I didn't know what to do or what to say. I wish I were better," he told me. It was like the most fucked-up roman-tic movie moment ever.

"It's okay," I told him. "No one on earth knows what to say." And I meant it.

"Well, I just wanted to be here," he responded, and once again, I burst into tears. Big, sloppy, wet tears.

He led me to the deli below my apartment and that's where we sat, holding hands, for a long time. There, at the deli, I real-ized that all I needed was someone to sit with me and to word-lessly hold my hand. That's it.

My new boyfriend had to go from thinking I was cute, smart, fun, and sexy, to having to be there for me in a real, no-fun way that came without a rule book. It felt like we added six months to our relationship, there at that table. This experience was aw-ful, but it made us closer in a deeply human sense. He learned to care for me in a very mature way early on, and it made us even stronger as a couple.

After I allowed my boyfriend to react to the death, the veil had been lifted. I realized that Zack and Justin and my other coworkers *did* need to know about this. This is the reality of my life and where I'm from. I respected these people and I should give them the respect of telling them what's going on.

I went to work the next day and told people what had hap-pened. Everyone was kind and gave the standard, shocked "I'm so sorry for your loss." A small part of me was like, does this just sound like an episode of *The Wire* to you? Is the death real to you? The *I'm so sorry*s had an underlying vibe of "I couldn't imagine" in them instead of "I've been there." I don't blame anyone for that; this is just my lived experience. I know many other people can relate. If that's you, I hope this chapter makes you feel less alone.

When you're going through loss, trauma, or other difficult personal circumstances, sometimes the feeling of isolation that accompanies it is almost more powerful than whatever sadness you feel. Loneliness can eat at you in a way that's even more complex, even more difficult to show, than immediate grief. If someone you know is going through it, and you don't quite know how to handle it, keep that in mind, and just . . . be there for that person, in whatever way you can. My boyfriend couldn't quite understand every layer of my pain, but he showed up without being asked and held my hand. That was enough. I felt loved and supported, and because of that, I was able to open up to him, even though I was scared to do so. That support was everything to me. That's all I needed. Not questions, not stares. Love. We could all use more of that.

16

Quinta's Classics: Part III

....

Well, hey there! It's the final installation of Quinta's Classics. We've talked oldies, dinosaurs, and *Napoleon Dynamite* so far. Now it's time to talk the final wave of things that shaped me into the semi-recognizable person that you know and love!

Mario Kart

I started playing *Mario Kart* on a Nintendo 64 when I was about ten years old. It was my favorite video game, because it was one of the only ones my brother Kwei owned where no one died or bled ever. Enjoyable and never gruesome — that's how I like my games. Fun!

When I first picked up the controller to try *Mario Kart*, I had no idea I'd be hooked for life. Since then, I've played by myself, with friends, with boyfriends. I've played when I've needed a break from responsibilities and to celebrate accomplishments. I'll basically play for any reason. It soothes the soul, that *Mario Kart*. It ties me to the past while entertaining me in the present.

In all the years that I've been playing *Mario Kart* I've learned a lot about living life. It's taught me the art of strategy, confidence, and competition. That's right . . . all of the answers to this thing we call life can be found in a game where a banana is your worst enemy. For example:

If you're in first place, people will be mad about it. Being in first place in *Mario Kart* makes you pretty vulnerable to attacks. People want to take your spot, and they'll do anything to get there. Whether it's a red shell from the second-place person, or a blue shell hitting you and everyone else from the back —you're a target. Prepare accordingly! Basically, never get too comfortable or complacent in your success—it can be taken from you at any moment (also, people are haters).

You must always protect yourself. Regardless of whether or not you're in the top spot, you should always be on your toes. Sure, you might be fine in third place one minute, but then you all of a sudden get knocked back to ninth by someone who has it out for you. Make sure you always have a banana or a shell (or a well-timed insult) to take the blow of an attack coming your way. When you're prepared for someone else's nastiness you're more likely to be unfazed by it.

Don't get stuck. When you're in first or second place in *Mario Kart*, the game will give you items to protect yourself with, such as a green shell. If you're in last or second-to-last, you probably don't have a shot at winning, but the game's algorithms will at least help you get further with big-ticket arsenal items like a bullet or the golden mushroom. But if you find yourself stuck between fourth and tenth place, aka coasting in the middle, you may end up there for the rest of the game. In the middle, they treat you like a crab in a bucket. Don't get stuck, and if you do, fight your way out. Use your items wisely. Drive smart.

Trust women. Peach is the best *Mario Kart* player, and that's that. Stop sleeping on my girl.

The bad guys are fast, but heavy. The bad guys in *Mario Kart* (Bowser, Wario, Waluigi) may be fast and have other advantages when it comes to their maneuvers, but they're also heavy as hell and can get weighed down by their own bullshit. Playing as one of these characters might feel like it'll give you an advantage; but it's a quick fix—ultimately, not worth it. Stick with the players that are the good guys—even though it might take longer to get to number one, it's better to be on the right side of history.

Basically, you guys, play *Mario Kart*, and you'll learn how to play the game of life.

Mario Party

Yes, I have two Nintendo games in a row, but like I said, I don't make the rules . . . I'm just here to tell it like it is. Despite being a huge fan of games like *Mario Kart* and *Super Smash Bros.* when I was younger, I never quite got into *Mario Party*. My brother didn't have the game, and since I only played the games that he played, it was never on my radar. Once I got into my twenties, I stopped playing games entirely. I didn't have my own Nintendo 64—it didn't rank at the top of my priorities, like, I don't know, paying rent and buying groceries. Eventually though, I treated myself to a Nintendo Switch via my boyfriend's wallet. We downloaded *Super Smash Bros.* and *Mario Kart* and went to town. My love of video games returned and my urge to procrastinate for hours instead of doing any work was alive and well.

During my last visit to Philly, my brother brought his son, Nasir, over to visit me at my parents' house. Nasir is a smart and adorable kid who I haven't gotten to spend much time with, because I moved to LA before he was born. However, I see him every time I visit, and it's been such a pleasure to watch him grow into a thoughtful, intelligent, and inquisitive little guy. The last time I visited, he was grown enough to have his own Nintendo Switch. I was excited to bond with him over our newly found shared interest. He didn't have any of the games that I played, but since he's a kid, and kids have game rights, we decided to play his favorite—*Mario Party*. Only his adorable face could get me excited about a game I hadn't even considered before.

He gave me a controller and we played as partners; he used his kid know-how to show me how the game worked, which not only helped us win but gave me the opportunity to see just how smart he was. He explained the motives, the dice, the boards, and the games like a total pro. "We have to work together to win!" Nasir exclaimed as we started the game. He proceeded to high-five me every single time we won a round. It was so sweet, it almost made me want to cry. I even got a chance to teach him to be kinder to the losing team, letting him know that kindness and humility go a long way in the game of life. I enjoyed sharing that. "You're really good at this," he told me. His little voice saying that meant so much to me.

I now play *Mario Party* pretty much every day because it makes me feel closer to Nasir . . . closer to home.

"Excuses (Yours Truly Session)"— The Morning Benders

At twenty-one years old I was bouncing back and forth from my college apartment on Temple's campus to my parents' new home in Lansdowne, PA. It was a very fractured time in my life for sure. On campus, I had boys over and smoked out of a homemade bong; at home, I watched *Family Feud* and read the Bible with my parents. One thing that stayed the same for me in both worlds was my music. I loved spending time alone on the internet, discovering my own tunes. I loved the thrill of finding another thing I loved, another thing to add to my "taste bank," so to speak. Discovering music on my own made me feel like I had a special connection to the song, like we were meant to find each other. I spent a lot of time on YouTube watching music videos of all kinds, but was especially drawn to the ones that looked as if they were put together by a group of friends. At the time, YouTube was a place where smaller bands could find new audiences through low-budget music videos. It was inspiring, knowing people could be that good on their way up, and that they felt free to experiment and live in a world where they could practice their art. It was everything I wanted and what I had hoped for myself one day.

One night in my room (read: my parents' attic) I came across a video called "Excuses" by a group named the Morning Benders. The thumbnail showed a bunch of happy-looking people in a room with instruments. I was still getting over my breakup and was fairly miserable. Escapism was near! I clicked, watched, fell in love, and then watched it approximately twenty-seven times afterward. It was the most beautiful song and video I had ever seen.

The video, which has a behind-the-scenes element to it, begins with the singer talking about getting the song and band together. Classic creative footage about the hopes for the video. Then it heads into the studio, where the sound kicks in with a bang. Now, I smoked a lot at the time, so my best memory from my first time watching it is actually closing my eyes and feeling like the song was a big ship rocking me back and forth on big blue and white waves, with the singer's whimsical voice acting as the breeze that soothed your soul. Add the pounding drums and soaring violins against the lyrics that sounded innocent but were in reality kind of sexual, and that was it. I was in love.

Over the years, I've watched that video countless times, and I always go right back to my desk in the attic any time I hear it, transporting to that time in life where I was rocking back and forth like an innocent sexual ship. Nowadays, it's used in commercials for brands like Oreo and Samsung, but I remember when it was just my little escapist song.

"The Making of Addiction"—Ryan Leslie

Continuing with my love for videos that show the background on an artist's process brings me to a notorious video for any young Black creative: the behind-the-scenes look of Ryan Leslie making his future banger, "Addiction ft. Cassie." "Addiction" is a track that tore up the radio stations in the summer of 2008;

you couldn't escape it. The song is amazing, but the making-of video is what's stuck with me all these years.

The video starts out with an intern filming Leslie as he gets into an SUV, promising that he has a surprise. Then we see him in the studio: Ryan goes from the drums to the piano to the synthesizer, crafting the beat by hand, simultaneously mixing it all together, like a one-man symphony. At one point, he asks the intern what time it is. "Five twenty-one a.m.," the intern responds. The video continues with him singing and playing instruments until the song is done in what looks to be one very long night.

This video has since been cut up and turned into a hilarious meme: "Me When I Walk into Guitar Center." But it's so much more than that. It taught so many of us that we could do whatever we wanted to do, as long as we had the talent to back it up. It turned many of us into the types of creatives the world wasn't ready for: the types who wanted to do everything themselves, and who knew they were good enough to do it.

I watched this video over and over in my twenties, outdone by Ryan Leslie's skills. I couldn't take my eyes off him. He was pure talent, Beethoven-level to me, and inspired me to have a new respect for loving myself and my art for whatever it was. Leslie was an artist, straight up, and even though I possessed none of his musical abilities, I wanted to be just like him.

"I'm Calling the Police" — Shrek

Okay. This is dumb. But this is a book about a girl who started out her career as a meme, so I feel like I'm contractually obligated to tell you about one of my favorites.

All right, so, the year is 2018 and I am downloading memes to my meme folder on my phone to share with friends and/or on Twitter [dot] com at the perfect moment. In my meme travels, I came across a gem — Shrek's head on a woman's body standing in a kitchen alone with the caption "I'm calling the police."

The second I saw this image, I laughed out loud. Sometimes memes hit a funny bone, a part of your soul where things can't be put into words. I call it the uncanny valley of humor. It's the type of thing that when you share it to someone else who gets it, they appreciate it just as much as you do, but if you try to *explain* why it's funny, it sounds flat. This meme falls into that category. Trust me on this: this shit is *funny*. Years before it became popular to name scared white women who called the police on innocent Black people "Karen," this meme existed and made the same point. It perfectly encapsulated the gross practice of white ladies calling the police on Black people, and it added an absurd element on top of it to really emphasize how awful this is. It's simple, it's genius, it's in my pop culture all-time canon. It may not hit you right away, but the depth is there. It has layers. Like an onion. :)

"people be gay" meme

I've mentioned before that I've been a meme more than once, and arguably the most popular one is the "people be gay" meme. Like most memes, this one makes little sense outside of context, but I love it because it hits home for those who need it. Buckle up for a story.

In 2018, Vulture published an interview with Quincy Jones

where he spilled a lot of tea about what he knew about Hollywood, including a story about how Richard Pryor had slept with Marlon Brando. The internet was in shambles over it. People couldn't believe that their beloved Richard Pryor was queer, and because of that, homophobic rhetoric started flying on my Twitter timeline. I didn't like it all, and decided to respond. It's now deleted, but I tweeted something like: "I can't believe all of the homophobia I'm seeing on my timeline in 2018, the year of Rihanna's thighs. People be gay." Gayness wasn't new, and if people could be comfortable with newer artists like Frank Ocean being gay, then they should be comfortable that the artists from our past may have been queer, too. Simple point, no? Anyway, the tweet was so impactful that legendary tweeter and excellent friend Zack Fox took my Twitter avi at the time, which was a matte glamour shot of me looking like an R&B indie cover singer, and superimposed *people be gay"—Quinta Brunson* over it in yellow letters. I retweeted it, it gained traction, and boom—a meme was born.

Of all the memes I've been in, this one is my favorite. Every June, members of the LGBTQIA community share it to help kick off Pride Month, which is amazing. I feel honored to be part of something that makes people feel proud of who they are, especially in a society that somehow manages to still be so intolerant. It's humbling to me that my face and simple words are representative of something so moving, daring, and courageous. People have even used the meme to come out to their parents and friends! I can't express how grateful I am to be part of people's journeys in that way.

• • •

There you have it. The list of pop culture items that made me into the Quinta I am today. I truly do not think I could've become the creator I am without having these shows, songs, movies, and memes guiding me along the way. I hope you're inspired to make a list of things that made you who you are, too. I think sometimes we forget them, but in reflecting on our influences, we figure out a lot about who we would like to be in the future. Thanks to making this list, I know who I want to be: a hybrid of Peach, Ryan Leslie, and a dinosaur from *Jurassic Park*!

17

On Cooking

··

When I started writing this book, I had a standard LA kitchen: cute, small, practically begging you to leave it alone and order takeout instead. Despite all of this, when I started dating my boyfriend, I decided to get all domestic and learn the art of cooking. It's been a long-ass journey, and although I have learned a lot, and can finally eyeball a teaspoon, I'm no Julia Child . . . and don't think I'll ever be.

The first time I told my boyfriend I was going to make dinner, it was pretty spontaneous. We had been dating for about three months, and so we were at stage two: a stage where we were pooping in the other's home. I wanted to do something special (but not too involved) to celebrate our three months of love, so I put on my cutest cooking outfit (a little black dress, very practical), opened a bottle of wine, and went to investigate what I had in the fridge.

The truth of the matter is, I wasn't that close with my fridge at the time; we didn't really know each other outside of the fact that it was a great place to store my leftovers. I scanned the shelves: grapes that should've been thrown out a week before, a half-eaten salad from Tender Greens, a ridiculous number of

Chipotle bowls, some greens, chicken breast, eggs, extra salsa from my favorite taco truck, and tortillas. Chicken it is.

I pulled out my laptop and put on a cooking playlist, aka Thundercat radio. His station brings a healthy mix of artists such as the Internet, Anderson Paak, and Phony Ppl—in other words, excellent music for making a meal with love. I pulled out my phone to google "easy baked chicken recipes." An hour later, I'd learned about the history of communism in Laos, responded to Gabrielle Union on Twitter, and uploaded and then deleted a cute photo of myself to Instagram. Cooking was going great.

When I pulled together enough focus to find a recipe that felt relatively easy—baked chicken and rice, thanks to some Uncle Ben's I found hanging in the back of my cabinet alongside spices that I never used—I got to work. I pulled the chicken from its thin plastic container and immediately scrunched my nose. The truth of the matter is, I'm terrified of raw chicken. It's a simple food in theory, but the preparation feels way too high-stakes. If you get remnants anywhere, you can get salmonella, and if you don't cook it properly, it can kill you. Why aren't more people terrified of raw chicken?! Again: It can KILL YOU. For just trying to cook your little-ass dinner. I didn't want to accidentally poison my boyfriend to death!

An uncomfortable feeling began to form inside of me. "Ah, I know you, bitch," I thought. It was anxiety. Trying not to touch the chicken's gross skin, I plopped it into a mixing bowl and decided to take a break to add a little more wine to my glass.

I consider myself to be a pretty fearless person. I don't think twice before getting on stage, I love roller coasters, I'll swear in front of my mom. But cooking scares me more than public speaking, nuclear war, and leaving my phone in an Uber combined. Every time I put together a dish, I worry that whoever eats it is going to get sick, or worse: they'll hate it. I once saw one of those Live, Laugh, Love Instagram quotes that said "Cooking is love made visible." For me, "Cooking is panic made edible." My heart rate goes up whenever I'm in charge of a meal. Yet here I was still doing it.

After looking at the simple recipe twenty times, I got to work. I was in the middle of looking for the paprika, which I didn't really have a relationship with outside of knowing it was the name of Pepper's wife on *Blue's Clues*, when I got a text from the boyfriend:

> THE BF: be there round 7
>
> need anything?

I looked at the bottle of wine. There was no way that thing was going to make it to dinner for two.

> QB: Wine please🍷?
>
> THE BF: sure thing!
>
> QB: thank you! I'm making something special over here ;)
>
> THE BF: 😻

Dammit. I didn't want to disappoint.

I can't remember the first time I met my boyfriend, specifically. We had mutual friends, so it always seemed like he was just around, when I think of it. Then one night, during a friend's birthday party at a brewery downtown, he caught my eye. I don't know what made this one night different from all the other times we shared a space, but there was an electric vibe between us.

At the time, I was dating a guy in Philly long distance, and, besides that, was uninterested in being with a white guy. But despite those two factors, something about him drew me in. He had always seemed to have a good energy, and I did think he was cute. So I thought, *Why not see what this guy's about for the night?*

I pointed to my future boyfriend and asked my friend, "What's that boy's name?" Before he could answer, my future boyfriend saw me pointing and came over to introduce himself. I had a few drinks in me and was feeling bold.

I served him some flirtatious fun: "Hey! Every time I see you, you make me smile." Reminder, I had a few drinks in me.

He responded with "That's great, because your smile brightens up my day."

Mentally my jaw dropped, but I kept a stone face. At first, I was like, "Um . . . no, this white boy did not just use this corny-ass line on me?" It was a little sweet, though. When the guy wasn't paying attention, I told our mutual friend, Adam, the one who I asked his name, that I thought he was cute.

"Him?!" Adam exclaimed, almost spitting out his beer. Then he thought about it for a second and went, "Actually, that could work."

With what I considered to be Adam's blessing, I went on flirting with this guy for the rest of the night, cracking jokes, knocking glasses, still thinking that I was just going to have a bit of fun. But at the end of the night he got my number. He didn't want to leave without it . . . and I liked that.

On our first date a week later, we went to a bar called 3 Clubs. The conversation was so easy, it was scary. We talked about likes, dislikes, jobs, and family. I noticed he was really listening to me and interested in knowing what I was going to say next. He wasn't just waiting for me to finish talking so he could insert himself into the conversation, but instead he let my words hang there in the air before offering a thoughtful and attentive response. During the whole date, he was alert, meaning he never touched his phone once.

At one point, one of my favorite songs, "Across the Universe," by the Beatles, started playing on the speakers. John Lennon's delicate guitar strums floated down from the ceiling and I closed my eyes.

"I love this song," I told him.

"I have this album at home! I play it all the time," he told me.

Cute. I was starting to like this boy more and more with each new fact I learned about him. The first date led to a second, a second led to a third, and before I knew it, we were a real-ass couple. Then I screwed myself over.

"Okay," I said one night, about two and a half months into our relationship, "if you had to eat the same type of food for the rest of your life, what would it be?"

"Oh, I love Italian food. Especially home-cooked," he replied.

"Me too! It's my favorite type of cuisine. Yessssss!"

"Nice! I also just love home-cooked meals, in general."

"Me too!" I exclaimed, and it's true—nothing sparks pure joy quite like a home-cooked meal.

"You cook?"

I didn't skip a beat. "Oh, yeah . . . I can cook!" It was true! I had cooked in the past, I had even boiled an egg that very morning.

"I'd love to try your cooking sometime." He smiled. I melted.

"I'd love to cook for you sometime," I said. *Shit,* I thought. *Now look what you did, Quinta.*

So here's the truth: at the time, I don't even know if I'd even turned on my oven besides that one time a friend of mine stayed over and cooked chicken wings for the both of us. Technically, *I* had not used that oven yet. It's not that I didn't *want* to cook. But spending the majority of my adult years focused on climbing the ranks of the entertainment industry didn't really leave me much time to learn how to cook. And in LA, there's really no need! You can usually find the best taco of your life from a truck down the street for under two dollars aaaaand it's served in tinfoil so you can just eat it and toss it. No dishes! Taco trucks are the poor woman on the go's fuel.

But now that I'd stupidly promised my boyfriend a home-cooked meal, I was going to have to learn . . . and fast. Which brings us back to my kitchen.

Feeling a little wine-tipsy, I stared yet again at the recipe on my phone. I had already seasoned the chicken like it told me to, but then wondered if I was using too much seasoning. Like, is "a pinch of onion powder" a literal pinch? Was my small-fingered pinch different from the pinch of the normal-sized adult who wrote this recipe? Should I add two pinches? I'll add two pinches, I thought. Then I added double all of the seasoning and threw the bird in the oven, feeling like I did something wrong. To make sure there was no risk of death, I decided to leave the chicken in the oven double what the recipe called for. I figured the extra cook time would sufficiently murder all the salmonella molecules.

When my boyfriend came over, bottle of red wine in hand, I had my meal ready and waiting. It wasn't the most beautiful thing in the world, but looks aren't everything right?

"Ooooh, smells good!" my boyfriend said as we sat down to the table. I poured us a couple of glasses, and proceeded to watch in horror as he threw his entire shoulder into cutting the inedible chicken.

"You know what," I said, trying to conceal my panic. "You don't have to eat it."

"No, I want to!" He put a piece of chicken in his mouth. "So, how was that thing you had this morning?"

As I forked a hunk of overcooked chicken into my mouth, my heart sank. It tasted like how I'd imagine a sneeze would taste like. A little salty, and mostly disgusting. This was a disaster. My boyfriend insisted it was fine, but it just made me feel worse to know he was being quiet because he didn't want to hurt my feelings by telling me what I knew was the truth. Would we ever have an honest relationship?

I looked at my boyfriend attempting to chew his chicken like it was a jawbreaker.

"Baby. It's bad." I gave a sad face and then laughed.

"It's . . ." He stalled, trying to find the right words. "Just a little rough . . . but you'll get better! And I'm excited to see you do it. I'll help. I'm just happy you're trying for me. I know you're a busy woman."

He knew who and what I was. He accepted it . . . and even managed to be kind about it. On top of that, he looked at how things would get better if we worked together in the future. I loved him even more.

A few weeks later I did what I do whenever dealing with the uncharted waters of womanhood: I called my mom.

"Mom, why didn't you teach me how to cook," I whined into the phone. "How am I supposed to follow in your footsteps if you didn't leave me any instructions?"

My mom sighed. By this point, she was used to me calling at all hours of the day with random thoughts and accusations.

"I don't know, Quinta, I'm sorry, I just kind of forgot about you. You were last, and . . . I don't know, I just missed you," she laughed.

It's true. I was totally missed! Everyone in my family knows how to cook except for me. They're experts. Meanwhile, whenever I attempt to cook, I spend most of the time frantically scrolling through the confusion that is a cooking blog, and getting oil on almost every piece of technology that I own.

Being the youngest child of five, I felt like basic life skills weren't really passed down to me the way they were for my siblings. By the time I was born, there were enough people in the house to make sure I was taken care of, so I didn't really need to learn how to do anything myself. I was simultaneously spoiled and ignored. My mom figured that if she didn't have time to show me something, surely she had birthed someone who did. But they didn't! And I never requested to learn to cook, because it was done for me. By the time I needed to learn, I was in college and it was too late.

I don't really blame my mom, especially now that I know what a straight-up burden it is to operate as a fully functioning adult. I don't even have kids and I'm barely feeding myself. My mom had five! How she got anything done is beyond me. I ask her often how she did it. She tells me she has no idea how, and I believe her.

My mom made being an adult woman look easy. She would spend all day controlling thirty screaming kindergartners and then she'd go to the grocery store, come home, and feed a family of seven. And she didn't pull any punches in the kitchen. She made simple, efficient dishes that kept us coming to the table night after night—your spaghetti, your fried chicken wings, your greens, and your rice.

On Sundays, though, we'd get special meals. She had her mac and cheese recipe down to a science. Macaroni. Milk. Butter. Flour. Sharp cheddar. Salt. Pepper. Mix it all up in an oven-safe dish and bake at 350. It was a straightforward dish that is the perfect partner to her baked wings, which are also a specialty. (You can't have that recipe; that's for family.)

For six out of seven days a week (Saturday was pizza), my mom cooked for survival, to feed her tribe, and that's it. She didn't have time for that "try new recipe" shit. The children (and husband) were hungry and on a schedule. But the meals were always delicious and made with love.

There is only one time I remember my mom making a bad

meal. I was about eleven years old. Kiyana, Jia, Kwei, and I all gathered around the dinner table for spaghetti and salad. I set the table with forks and knives, and my sisters did the plates. (Kwei didn't have to do anything. Boys, man.) We sat down, my dad prayed, and we started to eat while watching *Jeopardy!* on the family TV.

As we dug into our meals, my siblings and I began shooting looks at each other. The pasta tasted off. Not bad, just . . . off. I shoved another forkful into my mouth, trying to place it.

"Mom, this . . . tastes weird," Kiyana said, sniffing her pasta.

"Yeah, it's . . ." Kwei put more pasta in his mouth to try and figure out what made it taste different. "Sour?"

My dad was silent. So was my mom.

I took another bite and it clicked. "Oh no, Mom. Is this ketchup?!"

"Ketchup, that's it!" Jia nodded.

"AWW, YUCK, mom." Kwei laughed.

"I ran out of spaghetti sauce! I didn't think you'd notice. You know what . . . Make your own dinner next time," she said, seeming embarrassed as we all gagged.

It was a story that we kids giggled about for years to come: the day Mom served us a home-cooked meal of noodles and ketchup. But now that I'm older and I can so clearly see all the steps in my mom's day that led to that moment, I do feel a little bad for laughing and blowing up her spot. She came home from work, exhausted, and got ready to go through the added work that would result in a fed and happy family. She probably put the water on to boil, threw in a bit of salt, and then went to the fridge to pull out the pasta sauce only to see it wasn't there. There was no time to change the plan or go to the store, so she just made do with the red tomato-based sauce she had. I can't imagine the hurt and frustration she must've felt for dropping the ball ONE time.

My mom always provided for us, no matter what, because I think family is what kept her and my dad grounded. I go back to this thing that my dad once said: that he wouldn't have made it in this world as a single man. "I would've done stupid things because I would have no focus, no center of gravity, nothing to try to be better for," he told me in his gentle and calculated manner. "I experienced that early in my life and I'm glad my ship finally got a rudder. The rudder of my life has been my family." It's the perfect analogy for what my family has been for me, too. Growing up with such a strong familial foundation, including nightly home-cooked meals around the dinner table, is what made me want to have the exact same experiences with a family of my own. I wanted to at least be able to crank out a few reliable meals like my mom, even if I couldn't be the next Top Chef.

My inability to cook is a flaw for sure, and I don't know if you can tell this about me yet, but I don't do well with flaws. I have this inherent drive to be the best at the things I do. I hold "cooking" on this pedestal that unlocks the necessary elements for me to be a grown woman. That pedestal currently feels out of reach, and that is driving me crazy. Every time I see a beautifully cooked meal, I take it as a personal insult to my capabilities. I know I can do well on screen, but the fact that

I'm not able to be as natural in the kitchen has always felt like a huge hurdle to me, something that was holding me back from achieving the well-rounded life I wanted.

Growing up, whenever I imagined what my adult life would look like, it always included being a provider for my husband and children. I wanted to be a good wife and mother just as much as I wanted to be a successful comedian. This statement is always received in a revolutionary manner. People react as if I've just said something extraordinary, when in actuality, women have been doing this shit for-ev-er. But when you're a woman in entertainment, this statement *is* extraordinary.

Up until recently in the entertainment industry, the women who survived were the ones who learned how to act like the men. We still struggle with equality in the workplace, which means muting the things that make you a woman. So even today, when more and more women are entering the field, people look at me funny when I say my goal in the next five years is to have a baby. Women in creative industries have been conditioned not to be so open about a desire that's rooted in femininity and time off from the grind.* But right now, I don't care what anybody says: I want to be a working comedian and I want to be a mom. Those two things can and should exist together more often.

There's this perception in Hollywood that you need to go "all-in" to chase your dream, that the only people who succeed are egotistical workaholics who treat other people like disposable objects. That's just not a personality trait that I want to

---

* I do think things are getting better, especially with Gen Z coming in hot, starting revolutions on TikTok and all that shit.

adopt. I believe in the sanctity of family/community and the virtue of hard work—but you can't have any of these things without first finding balance in your life. I don't think I can be as a strong of a performer or worker if my home life isn't strong too.

So yes, it's just as important to me to sell a show as it is to know how to whip up a meal for the person I care for. The problem is, I'm a lot better at selling shows than I am at cooking meals. As was evidenced by my borderline meltdown while trying to bake a simple chicken dish. But since then, I've kept working on it.

Now, after years of being on the cooking train, instead of going from recipe to recipe like I did when I first started really trying, I decided to take the repetitive approach of trying the same meal a few times to see if I could get better at it. Some recipes are now my favorite because they take a short amount of time and I know they'll be delicious, although nothing new. Other recipes fall off because they take a lot of effort, and end up being just okay. However, boy is it rewarding when a new recipe turns out to be not only edible, but delicious.

I've also started borrowing recipes from my childhood, like my mom's baked chicken, and tweaking them to make them mine. And I've borrowed staples from my dad, too, taking his famous collard greens and adding lemon for my own spin. Like a Pokémon, the greens have evolved, but both are still incredible. Both of these meals help me maintain closeness to the legacy of my family while branching out on my own path.

My current meals might not spark the deep, satisfied, joyful bites that I'm looking for each time, but I know the fact that

I'm trying makes my boyfriend feel loved, and that's the most important part of providing something. I just have to be okay with not being the best at something. It's not that easy for me, but I'm trying.

Regardless of how underwhelming my dish is, or how busy my schedule might be, I still make myself cook once a week. For example, this week I made tandoori-spiced chicken, and it tasted fantastic! And I only had to read the recipe ten times before starting! Cooking has become a good way for me to force myself to look away from my phone for a little bit and come out with something to show for a few hours worth of effort. I've learned that setting small goals, like this one, helps me develop good habits. Who knows? Maybe forcing myself to cook once a week will cause me to eventually bump it up to twice a week and then three times a week, so that by the time I have kids, cooking won't be cause for a potential nervous breakdown, but more of a reflex.

And if not? Shout-out to Postmates.

18

Celebrity

A few summers ago, I went to a Dodgers game with my boyfriend. Our friend, who works for NBC, invited us and some other pals to come hang in the box seats. I don't really care about baseball, but I do enjoy going to the games. They're so fun! I love pretending to know what I'm talking about when yelling "Come on, Puig!" I love how the stadium vibrates with the roar of the crowd and the sound of peanut shells crunching under my sneakers. Above all, I love watching Los Angelenos come together over something, maybe the only thing, they can all passionately agree about. And box seats? Say no more! The height of luxury. I've come to learn that they have charging stations for your phone, cup holders that can actually fit your beer, and carpet that you don't have to clean when you eventually spill that beer! You don't have to touch elbows with someone you don't know while trying to put relish on your Dodger dog or have to say "my fault" when you inevitably swipe your butt across their legs trying to get to the bathroom. Another plus: more space. Because the truth is, I often have anxiety in large crowds, despite loving performing for them.

That's right. Even though I'm very personable, anxiety rears its ugly head when I feel I could be recognized by someone. It's not that I think someone will do something bad to me — most interactions I have with people who like my work are good — it's just sometimes, out of nowhere, I become afraid of someone knowing me. Of being "famous." There's a strange pressure to being known by strangers.

When people approach you with expectations, it can be stressful. You know you're going to look like an asshole for not having the same connection with them that they have with you, but also you have to go to the bathroom and you're tired and can you go now, please? It's exhausting to make sure you're on your game constantly. There's also the fear that someone will try to sneak a photo. I'm used to not having control of how my image is used, thanks to memedom, but I at least usually have control of how it's produced. When people tilt their phones toward me, I feel paranoid. "Are you about to snap a photo, or are you just checking your teeth for shit?"

Two innings into the game, I decided I wanted to get up to get a beer. You can get them delivered to the box, but they cost a lot more and I'm still cheap when it's justified. "Anyone want anything?" I asked my friends as I slipped my wallet into my jeans. They all politely declined.

"I'll come with you," my boyfriend offered. He knows I get anxiety wandering alone through crowds, but he also knew that seeing as I was an independent person, I'd never ask him to come myself. Have I mentioned he's the best?

At this point, you may or may not be saying, "Ay, Quinta,

chill out. Not only did you ask for this, but you're not that famous. You ain't Beyoncé." And . . . you're right. I'm not. But the weird thing is, it doesn't matter. In a world where internet content is in the palm of everyone's hand, people who create content get recognized. We're more relevant to people than the star of a network sitcom. Consider the Paul brothers or Liza Koshy. Today's kids know them more than they do Stephen Colbert or Jon Stewart. Fame in this day and age is all over the place, and, like it or not, I am caught up in the middle of it.

We made our way to the concessions area, which was a floor down from where the boxes are situated. As we walked down the hallway to the stairs, I stayed close to my boyfriend and held my head down, a trick I had learned to avoid awkward interactions. If people can't see my face, they are less likely to stop me and say, "Hey, aren't you that girl from . . . that thing?" By the way, that may seem like a harmless question, but here's how the interaction can go. Place yourself in my shoes, if you can:

THEM: "Hey, aren't you that girl from that thing?"
ME: "Uh, I mean, I've . . . done things, yes! It's probably me.
　　Hi—"
THEM: "But what are you from, though? How do I know
　　you?"
ME: "I don't know exactly how you know me. I've been on,
　　like, the internet and TV."
THEM: "Yeah, but like what exactly were you in?"
ME: "Well, it's kind of hard to name everything."

THEM: "I mean, but can you just name a few of the big things,
   I'm trying to figure out what you're from."
ME: "That's hard to do."
THEM: "Wow, well, you don't have to be rude!"

This conversation has actually happened to me before! And the possibility of it happening again terrifies me. I don't want people to think I'm rude, but also I'm not gonna stand there reciting my IMDb page like I'm on trial for not actually being me. This is the situation that I'm always trying to avoid, for everyone's sake, even though the majority of my interactions with people may not be like that.

We got our beers and a couple of hot dogs, because they make beer taste better, and headed back to the box. As we walked, someone yelled out, "Hey, Quinta, I love your work!" That was great. Sweet, brief, to the point. A warm compliment. I love it. I yelled "thank you so much!" while waving back. Not even a minute later, I heard someone else loudly murmur to their friend, "I know that girl — I think she's from BuzzFeed?"

"Man, it's wild being famous," I thought, quickly cringing at my own corniness. Who the fuck did I think I was? Lol. But part of friendship is me sharing with you how corny I can be as a person sometimes, so you're welcome. Also, don't worry, because I was humbled with the quickness.

My boyfriend and I got on the escalator to go back up to our floor. As we lazily rose higher and higher, I heard someone behind me whispering, "Oh my God . . . oh my God. Is that . . . I think it's . . . oh my God, it is!"

Since we were in a semi-enclosed space, there was no avoiding it. I turned around to say, "Hi, yes, it's me from that thing," when I noticed the people coming down the adjacent escalator, turning their heads with the same "Oh my God, look who it is" energy. But they weren't looking at me—they were looking behind them.

Sure enough, I followed the excited glares to see America's own Rob Lowe coming down the escalator. *Everyone* was talking about him. "Shayna, it's Rob Lowe!" "Dude, look! It's the guy from *Parks and Rec*." They weren't even really whispering at this point. Who gives a shit about baseball?! A real, flesh-and-blood celebrity was here for us to ogle at!

I was quickly taught what immense fame looks like in comparison to my experiences. Rob was wearing nice jeans and a Dodgers shirt, with one of those quintessential LA hats. Nothing special . . . but on him, it a looked like a million bucks. As he came down the escalator, Rob Lowe waved at people, and kept his head held high. He had the energy of "Yes, it's me. Hi. Nice to meet you, and nice for you to meet me." He was used to it. The people around him were delighted; they now had a story to come home with: "You'll never believe who I saw at the Dodgers game . . ." It was wild to consider, and made me feel so embarrassed for even thinking anyone was worried about me.

It's hard to talk about any of this stuff without feeling like I sound like a dick. It's just that I've been thinking a lot about celebs lately: Are they important? What's our connection to them? Do we need them? Most of all, what is my relationship to celebrity? If I am considered famous by some, what's my responsibility to the idea of it?

When it comes down to it, I have a complicated relationship with the concept of celebrity, particularly as the word pertains to me. In some ways, I actively shy away from the idea of being considered a celebrity, because from what I see, celebrities serve as distraction for people's moral work. I don't want to fill a space in a person's heart that should be filled with the makings of their own thoughts and expressions. I definitely don't love that celebrities get away with shit that average people wouldn't. I don't think it's right, and it's not a lifestyle I even want to be part of, so I try not to do anything nonfamous Quinta wouldn't, even in situations where I know someone would give me a pass.

I think there's an assumption that people become actors, and singers and comedians, because they want to be famous. And, sure, there's something to that—maybe some people are just in it for the notoriety. But I think there are a lot of us who do this because we respect the craft, are called toward it, want to elevate it. And if we get famous, so be it. When I made the "He Got Money" video, there was no plan to be famous. The plan was just to make people laugh and innovate within my craft by using the newly formed Instagram video feature. When it took off and led to people recognizing me, I was glad to see my joke resonated with so many people. That made me confident in my skills as a comedian, which was the most rewarding thing. To me, fame is just a by-product of good work, not a necessity.

Being good at my craft has most certainly opened the doors

for me to walk into celebrity land. I've gone to award shows and been invited to be in magazines. I've rubbed shoulders with the other famouses. At first, it was cool. It's fun to step on a red carpet and have your photo taken, or for someone to tremble when asking you for a selfie. But now, after thinking more about how our society is set up and what role I want to play in it, I find the propping up of others to be counterproductive to making sure everyone is healthy, safe, and free.

Right now, the world seems to be having an awakening for the first time in a long time. It feels like everyone is thinking long and hard on whether celebrity culture is even beneficial. Up until this point, celebrities were the rulers of our kingdom. After decades of worshipping at the church of the human idol, the pandemic and social uprisings are causing society to reevaluate our obsession with placing one human's importance over another. People have lost their jobs. People are poor and hungry. People are fighting to live. It's difficult to witness certain celebrities with so much money, power, and privilege not even attempt to put any of it toward helping solve the problems Americans are facing today.

I hope we as a society can grow to a different place in the coming years. I hope we can take this moment of dismantling broken systems and apply it to broken social systems as well. I also hope I never again have to care where I fall on the famous/celebrity scale — because maybe, one day soon, the scale won't exist.

I'm being idealistic, I know. Even saying these things goes against my realist heart. But I just want a world where we all are our own celebrities. Where we cherish ourselves. Where we honor and uplift our own families. Where we cry when a person dies; not because they were famous, because they were here and they were breathing. I want us to treat each other like we are all worthy. Like we're all Rob Lowe.

19

2020: Perfect Vision

··

Greetings from my living room! It felt fitting to end this book where I started it: on the couch. A couch that I've been sitting on for the past seven months, going on eight, as I'm writing this. As you well know—or depending on when you're reading this, as you've learned in history books—I'm stuck on the couch because we're currently experiencing a global pandemic. Times are tough. People are dying. Emails are starting off with a sad "Hope this finds you well" and the sender actually means it because they're worried your lungs might be corroding. And the majority of the population is dealing with all of this trauma from our couches.

When the pandemic arrived, it felt like life for everyone, especially in America, hit a record scratch. At the beginning of the year we all just kind of watched this storm roll in, not knowing what to expect. Then it all, in a sense . . . stopped.

A few weeks before everything shut down, I had lunch with two of my closest friends, Nadia and Kate. I arrived at Taste in West Hollywood armed with anxiety and research about virus transmission, safety precautions, pandemic protocols. As is my brand, I had been glued to Twitter for months, reading about how the disease was spreading overseas. COVID was all I could talk about, and it was driving everyone around me insane.

This was one of our unofficial monthly catch-ups, a tradition that I would deeply miss in the coming year. After ordering and receiving our food, I decided to launch into my pandemic panic, curious to see what Nadia, my Carrie-esque friend, and Kate, my Miranda-esque friend, had to say about it.

"Thousands of people have already died," I said, having trouble controlling my volume. I looked around the restaurant to make sure there weren't any snifflers or coughers nearby.

"I have a trip to Bali soon and my girls aren't gonna cancel. I don't think it's a big deal," Nadia said, digging into her baked mac and cheese.

"It's just like the flu, I've heard," Kate added, while eating her salad.

"It's literally not." I leaned over my plate of huevos rancheros and lowered my voice. "There is no vaccine. I think . . . I think this is going to be really, really bad. Like VERY bad." Kate and Nadia looked at each other and shrugged.

"We'll see, let's just eat together in this crowded restaurant of one hundred people, something we'll be able to do forever and always." No one actually said this. It's just funny.

This was my last lunch before this restaurant (and many others) shut down (some for good). If I would've known that this would be my last chance to catch up with friends at a restaurant for a year, I would've ordered a martini and stopped trying to be "not drunk at 2 p.m."

Reader, I love to say I told you so. It's like one of my favorite things to do. I don't even hesitate the way most people do.

Sometimes I yell "I told you so" before the thing I said would happen even happens. But I have to say, this time . . . I wasn't excited that my predictions were right.

A week before the lockdown, I told my boyfriend I wanted to go to the supermarket and buy a bunch of nonperishables. Sure, I was panicking a little, but I was worried about Americans Americaning and greedily buying up all the food. If there was a chance we were going to be locked in our houses and wouldn't have access to markets, I wanted to make sure we could survive without going to the stores for a while.

"There are rumors floating around that the water department could shut down if no one was able to go to work!" I yelled while pacing back and forth looking for my reusable grocery bags.

My boyfriend looked at me like I was crazy, spouting off my tinfoil rhetoric mixed with cold hard science, but he knew better than to tell me to calm down. So, we went to the store.

. . . And I was right AGAIN! I told you, I love being right. (This one felt a little better.) When we had gone grocery shopping the previous week, the shelves were full and only a few concerned shoppers were packing their carts with canned and dry goods. When we went that day, the shelves were bare and getting barer. People were buying things that weren't even necessary for survival, like pool toys and kumquats. Who panic-buys kumquats?! Scared and greedy Americans, that's who.

Armed with our toilet paper, pastas, and pool toys (maybe the panicked strangers knew something I didn't?!), my boyfriend and I got home, locked the door, and plopped on the couch to silently scroll through our phones looking for news of what was to come next. And that's exactly where we stayed the next day, and the next, and the next, and the next times eighty.

Staying in the house doesn't seem like a bad thing, until you are forced to stay in the house. People on Twitter went from being all, "Introvert's dreammmm. I love being home!" to "Day 2: We are out of food. The entire family is not speaking, and we sectioned off the house to survive." Dramatic, but I get the sentiment. Spending all that time in my apartment was hard for me. I move. I make. I do. Without the ability to be around friends and people, hearing laughter in real life, I started to get tired from the constant doomscrolling.

It didn't help that the only way to keep connected to the world was through the internet. Spending so much time on my various feeds, I began seeing behavior that was super disappointing. The coronavirus has exposed so much about the American public as a people: we truly are as selfish as our TV shows and movies paint us out to be.

People were refusing to wear masks. Others claimed the virus was a hoax. Some were so upset that they couldn't get their hair and nails done that they went to their state capitol buildings with guns demanding to open up stores again so that they can get their hair cut and possibly catch this virus while doing it! INSANITY.

As an avid Twitter user who is constantly inspired yet repulsed by the app, I noticed myself and the rest of my generation spending our newly found free time either expressing our exhaustion at being indoors all day or talking about making fancy breads. There was a collective feeling of boredom rippling through my social and social media circles.

One day, all of this talk of boredom and bread-baking started to bother me deeply. While the coronavirus made everything stop, for my peers and me, the day-to-day could've been a lot worse. Those who were either impoverished or housing insecure, people who already struggled before the pandemic, had to face an even more uncertain future. Others lost their jobs and couldn't get unemployment because the systems were too strained to function. Students were unable to go to school, while their parents were unable to watch their kids *and* work. But yeah . . . let's talk about making bread?

That said, I couldn't be mad at all the people on the internet handling their personal life situations the only way they knew how—by disassociating from the problem, or even joking about it. That's a coping mechanism. Even in my own world, I made jokes about how much I was able to play *Mario Party* from my comfy couch. I made light of the situation to turn away from the pain of losing a friend and a family member to COVID. But in dealing with the sadness and anger that followed those needless deaths, I caught myself wishing that America could be jerked out of its apathy and into a place of caring about others more than ourselves.

Then my wish came true, sadly.

On a Monday morning, three months into shelter-in-place, I walked to the Whole Foods to get some more "stuck in the house" supplies. Bread. Cereal. Pool toys. The usual. I was definitely starting to get tired of being indoors, and daydreaming about a change of scenery. It felt like my mind and eyes were melting from looking at the same thing every day. I called Kate so she could "join" me, because I like to use my walking time to catch up with friends on the phone. It's no replacement for the real thing, but, hey! Adapting to the situation!

"Did you hear the cops killed another Black man?" Kate flatly asked.

"Yeah. It happened like a week ago. That story is old," I told her.

"No, it happened yesterday. In Minneapolis. I'll send you the link."

I let Kate go and headed into Whole Foods. I did my shopping as quickly as possible, dodging all the potential COVID carriers in the store. After loading my milk, deli meats, and yeast infection medicine onto the conveyer belt, I went to check my phone. The link Kate sent me sat in the middle of my screen, so I mindlessly tapped it.

As the first few seconds of the video played out, I shuddered. Suddenly, I became painfully aware of the woman standing behind me, waiting to check out with her pandemic haul. She was too close, the video was too graphic. The cop's knee on a man's neck, both faces contorted. One in anger. One in anguish. I wasn't able to watch the rest. Knowing that what I was seeing would end in death was both enough and too much to take in. The fluorescent lighting of Whole Foods felt like a grotesque spotlight. I grabbed my groceries, thankful for the first time in a long time that my face was mostly covered up in a mask.

George Floyd's death hit the world differently. Perhaps it

was the undeniable inhumane nature of the murder that woke America up; that underneath the bright sky, a person could be killed with a knee, begging for his life, over a possible counterfeit twenty-dollar bill. Or maybe it was because he was murdered in the midst of a pandemic, during a time when many were gasping for air, feeling suffocated by the institutions supposed to protect us. Maybe finally, people understood what it felt like to have your ability to breathe stolen by those in power—to see that our country had a problem caring about its people.

I checked Twitter to see that the video was already being shared rapidly and that people were rightfully expressing their disgust over the killing. I walked back home, upset. This time, I didn't call anyone to keep me company.

My boyfriend, who had not yet seen the news, was in a good mood. I didn't want to bring the death up to him, because I didn't want to ruin his high spirits, something that had been very rare for both of us during our stuck-in-the-house pandemic time. However, I didn't have the option to return to my high spirits. This is often what it feels like for me when another Black person is killed by the police. I am forced to deal with the weight of the situation because I am Black, alive, and concerned with my people living in this world.

I told him what happened, and could tell that he didn't immediately see the gravity in it. Maybe he was desensitized to the killings of Black people, like I was before Kate sent me the link; after all, we had been hearing about the problem since Trayvon Martin. It's easy for the sentiments of Black Lives Matter to become noise in the background when change isn't made. But this time, I didn't give him the chance to not understand the weight of what was unfolding. I told him to look it up. We'd spent too much time cooped up in our tiny apartment together; there was no room for misunderstanding. Nowhere to hide emotions. We had to face them.

I sat on the couch next to my boyfriend and spent the next few hours talking about how this was a huge problem and how everything in this flawed nation needed to change. Even in a pandemic, when half the country was shut down and life became a fleeting privilege, Black people were still being murdered in broad daylight by authorities whose jobs are to protect and serve.

We spent the rest of the evening talking about how this affected me, and how it affected us. The conversations were layered and complicated. What does the world look like for our possible child? Why has this been okay up until now for so many people? What will we do to change this? What will we no longer be silent about? As our conversation wound down, we were both emotionally exhausted.

My boyfriend went for a long drive to think. At first, I was sad that he felt he needed his own space, but I quickly understood that it was his way of processing and decided to take my own space to think as well. Relationships are personal, and I'll reserve the right to privacy when it comes to everything we discussed—but I will say this, the night could've easily led to a breakup with anyone. The fact that it didn't meant we were even stronger than I thought. It was one of the hardest moments in our relationship because we had to give each other the space to come to our own conclusions, while trusting that we were on the same page about how we individually felt. We learned a lot about partnership and support that day. It felt like the rest of the world was learning it as well.

The following night, after I spent the day sitting on the couch, posting on social media about the unjust killings of Black Americans and talking about change, protests broke out in Minneapolis, Minnesota, where George Floyd was killed. Protests were nothing new to me or any other American; not even two weeks before, people were protesting the murder of Ahmaud Arbery, another Black man who was killed by two white men while running in Georgia. However, things felt different this time.

I watched livestreams of people taking over the streets. Entire communities were staying out all night to make sure their message was projected loud and clear: we're hurt, we're angry, we won't allow it anymore. The sight of that officer's knee on George's neck paired with the other officer's nonchalant facial expression showed everyone that this was just another day on the job for them—I think that struck people in the heart.

For me personally, it felt like a metaphor for what our government had done to Black people for a long time and what it was doing to all American citizens currently during the pandemic. The government's knee was on our neck, while we were gasping for air—and now, people were fighting back; we were tired, we were stuck at home, we had time to sit with how much wrong was happening in society. People were done looking the other way. For the first time in my lifetime, Black Lives Matter had become a phrase comfortable on almost everyone's tongues as people of every race and creed took foot to pavement in every major city. Seeing all this unfold via my newsfeeds, I was moved to do the same.

"I'm going to protest," I told my boyfriend, my eyes still glued to my laptop, watching the bodies marching through the streets. "You don't have to go if you don't feel safe. I get it. We're still in a pandemic."

"If you're going, I'm going," he told me and that was that.

It meant a lot to me. We hadn't been out of the house besides a grocery trip here and there for months. We were both still very afraid of getting COVID, and knew that a protest could put us both at risk.

Masks on, we got in the car and headed to West Hollywood to join that day's protest at Pan Pacific Park. When we first arrived, we saw a modest amount of people with signs and chants. There was an exciting, but also somber, energy in the air. People were joining forces to make our voices heard; it didn't matter how small the gathering, we were amped up and ready to be heard.

But as we got closer, my boyfriend and I saw that the small crowd was only the outskirts of a massive group of people gathered at a baseball field getting ready to hit the streets. It was incredible. I was astonished at such an enormous group of people coming together for anything other than a concert.

I had only been to one protest before; one I joined in 2014 as it passed outside the Improv Space near UCLA, where I did stand-up for the first time. I was on stage, talking about Trayvon Martin's death—I was too sad to even try to write jokes that night, so instead I turned the stage into a space to let out my anger—when I saw a small group of protesters pass by with signs.

The stage faced these large windows that perfectly framed the street, so I had a good view of the moment that small group faced off with campus police. As the commotion grew louder, the audience started looking over their shoulders to see what was going on and the energy of the protest grew. I quickly ended my zero-joke set and went outside almost without even realizing that my body was moving. I barely remember that night, but what I do remember is questioning a Black cop about his character. Hope he heard me that day. Happy I wasn't pepper sprayed.

The protest I went to during the pandemic was a whole different experience. There were maybe five thousand people already at the park—and they weren't just Black, they were all races. Even though it took a minute for non-Black individuals to learn their place in a protest for Black lives, it was good to see people of all sorts of backgrounds out in the streets caring about the issue, which is, after all, a human issue.

The large group left the park and walked all the way to the Grove, the same mall where I filmed one of my "He Got Money" videos. The walk there was peaceful. People chanted, some sang, others danced. My anxiety about being around people for the first time in months subsided. Seeing a large group of people risking their health to join together and fight for humanity changed something within me. I'd never seen anything like it. My whole career I'd been chasing the high of using humor to unify the masses, and here they were, the masses, unifying over something much deeper, more critical. I was floored. And as I soaked in the power of the moment, the energy of the crowd shifted. The police had shown up.

The police barrier alone was enough to cause a panic wave to ripple through the crowd. What set me off was their gear. The police were all decked out in authoritative shields and gas masks when protesters didn't have anything. We didn't have guns, we didn't bring violence, no tools or shields aside from (mostly) homemade face masks. It was all so aggravating. We had nothing. What were they scared of? It felt like the shields were there to protect the police from our message. Protesters began to speak up. They didn't want their voices muffled behind the barrier of an over-resourced department. This angered the cops and they began beating away protesters.

"White bodies to the front," a chant erupted. White people from all sides began moving up to where the cops were getting unrulier.

I turned to my boyfriend only to see him disappear into the crowd, heading to offer his body for protection. I understood why he went, I'm glad that he didn't give it a second thought, but my body went numb with fear. Fear that he'd get arrested, trampled, or even worse.

At this point, both sides were pushed to their limits, and that's when the tear gas and rubber bullets started flying. I ran into the heart of the madness to look for my boyfriend, but was greeted with sheer chaos instead. People were running in different directions, coughing, crying, sputtering from the tear gas. Mixed messages of safety and danger collided into nonsensical yelling, making it impossible to figure out which way to turn.

When I couldn't find my boyfriend, I began to grow dizzy. My breathing became unsteady, I grabbed my knees and focused on the ground: I was having a panic attack. My friend Jak, who we ran into at the protest, instantly recognized what was going on, grabbed my phone from my shaky hands, and dialed my boyfriend, who of course didn't answer. Jak continued calling him over and over until he got through.

When we finally found each other, on the street, in the chaos, I hugged my boyfriend. Hard.

Still clutching each other, we left the protest when it felt like all the peace had been thoroughly sucked dry from the streets. On our way back to the car, we heard flash-bangs, saw a cop car on fire and people sprinting as if they were being chased. It was disorienting. But, still, as we headed away from the insanity, we passed people making their way into the storm. It was an inspiring show of resilience that I will never forget.

So much has changed since the day I ventured out to protest. Well, I mean, I'm still on my couch. But instead of simmering in frustration about the tight boundaries put in place by the pandemic, I've been inspired by what I've seen around me. I've watched a shift occur in this country. People are shedding layers of complacency and figuring out ways to make actionable change. Including me. I've learned more about the benefits of mutual aid programs and begun to donate. I've made efforts to communicate with community organizers in Philadelphia, who are figuring out alternative ways to take care of people, outside of just relying on the state. All around me conversations are getting deeper, change is becoming more accessible, and systemic injustices are being loudly protested.

At the beginning of this pandemic, I felt like life had come to a screeching halt—but, as much as it pains me to admit this, I was wrong. Life didn't stop, it exploded into all sorts of different expressions. People pushed through their boundaries to read more, connect more, create more, become more politically active, raise more money, and sure, yes, bake bread.

Even though I felt trapped to a life on the couch, I learned that a lot can happen on the couch! For example, I was sitting on this very couch when I found out that *A Black Lady Sketch Show* was nominated for three Emmys.* I was also here when I found out I sold a show to ABC. I was lying on this couch when my friend texted me to say she just had her first baby, and then a few weeks later when I found out another family member died because of COVID. I was standing next to it when my boyfriend got down on one knee and asked me to marry him, and fell onto the couch with him when I screamed yes. I was also sitting here when, after three years of writing, I finished this book.

When I first put the concept for this book together, my goal was to come up with a series of defining moments from my life that were worth sharing. I've spent the last three years excavating these stories and evaluating which ones are considered definitional. As I started to do this life inventory, I realized that the experiences that pushed me the most were usually the ones that knocked me on my ass and forced me to sit in these moments. Learning to slow down, pause, and soak in experiences is what led me to become who I am today: a semi-famous, expert *Mario Party*–playing, comedy-loving bad cook.

---

* Thanks to the pandemic, the Emmys were hosted online for the first time ever. How fitting.

We are all made up of these defining moments. Some of them are fun, like going viral on Instagram, and some of them are scary, like living through a global-pandemic social-uprising country-altering election year. But all of these moments give you the opportunity to learn, grow, and become a better person. To evolve. So, don't reject the evolution. Be like a meme —always taking on new life.

Acknowledgments

I'd like to thank my entire supportive unit of family and friends. I love you all. There's too many to name, and I don't want to leave a soul out. That would be the worst.

I need to thank Marina Shifrin, a friend, for helping me sort my words out. For helping me turn sentences into paragraphs. I also want to thank Kate Napolitano, my editor, for making sure those paragraphs formed to be chapters.

Huge shout-out to Adam, my friend and manager, who encourages me to keep going when the going gets tough (and reminds me that I signed a contract, so I technically have to).

Lastly, I want to thank my fiancé, who has been by my side throughout this process. Despite writing this whole book and writing things for a living, I still don't have the words for you. I love you.